THE DILLY DONG BELL

A WAKE UP CALL FOR SPORT

THE DILLY DONG BELL

A WAKE UP CALL FOR SPORT

LEE WELLINGS

PROJECTIS PUBLISHING

LONDON

First published in paperback in 2022
by **PROJECTIS PUBLISHING** (UK)
a subdivision of PROJECTIS CONSULTANTS Ltd.

© PROJECTIS PUBLISHING 2022

Typeset in Calibri by PROJECTIS PUBLISHING
Printed in the United Kingdom by SWALLOWTAIL, Swallowtail Print, Drayton Industrial Park, Taverham Road, Drayton, Norwich NR8 6RL (UK). SWALLOWTAIL is FSC certified.

British Cataloguing in Publication Data.
A catalogue record for this book is available
from the British Library.

Lee Wellings, 2022
The Dilly Dong Bell
PROJECTIS PUBLISHING, London.
Projectispublishing.com

ISBN 978-0-913984-04-5

First hardback limited edition (2022): **300 copies**
The text / IP of this book has been put on the blockchain by PROJECTIS CONSULTANTS Ltd

Keywords: Sports, ethics
Disclaimer: The opinions expressed in this book are not necessarily those of the publisher or the consultant editor.

CONTENTS

ACKNOWLEDGEMENTS

This book has been coming since I first watched sport as a six-year-old boy, the red shirts of Liverpool FC glowing from my TV screen. It's been coming since my first football match as a teenage reporter, the first walk along Fleet Street, through the sports news stories and events I reported on across the globe, from London to Las Vegas, from Rio to PyeongChang.

It's in the past few years that the humanity in sport, the emotion within, has fully taken over my work and my approach to it. I've felt a deep connection to many of my subjects and their stories, and the desire to explain my philosophy on sport more deeply. To share the many lessons in life I've learned from meeting them.

May I thank everyone in the communities who helped and befriended me in such places as Bury, Pontypool and Stranraer. To Frank McKeown, a firefighter and footballer who helped me understand what it means to *feel* a story, not just tell it. My trip to meet him and his team in Scotland in 2013 was probably the start of a new way of thinking about sport for me.

I've also taken inspiration from the work of two authors who became friends. Chris Green for *'Matchday'*, in which his beautiful writing on a return home from a match to his young son floored me. And David Conn, primarily for *'The Beautiful Game? Searching for the soul of Football'*. It was an honour to support David's investigative journalism on Hillsborough content for the BBC.

May I express my condolences and dedicate my chapter on Liverpool FC, *The Red Spell*, to the family of Andrew Devine, who became the 97th victim of the tragedy during the time of publication.

Witnessing Leicester's story unfold was a privilege. I only wish it had all been magical and joyous for them. There was tragedy interwoven with success and the creation of history. The greatest sports story ever. They are special people, and at the football club they had a special person as manager in Claudio Ranieri. This is a man who showed us how nice guys do win, and that empathetic, kind leadership inspires us, and can lead to great things.

The support of friends is precious. My inclination is to try and support, and I don't always find it as easy to accept it back. Even if you've forged your own path you can learn to accept others on the journey too. We learn to listen. There are people who understand who I am, and why I needed to write my truth. I'm very grateful.

So many have supported me as a person I don't like to single them out. But for their special words of encouragement and support on the book I must thank and express my love to Matty, Charlie, Rob, Louise, Kelly, Jules, Sonia, Ian, Mark, Stevie, Jonny, Dennis, Irene, Carrie, Chris, Bev & Mark. Special thanks to Sara & Ian for reading an early manuscript and sharing their thoughts.

It has been such a pleasure to be signed and supported by Projectis Publishing. Christian de Vartavan and Kerensa Jennings identified the potential in sports philosophy, to go deeper into sport and its influence and emotion. I am deeply grateful for their faith in me and my work, the space they have given me, and their sage channelling of my passion. Sports analysts often speak to their own circle. I wanted to include everyone with these stories and observations on life.

It's been of great reassurance to me that this book has been edited by David Miles, a friend since we met at *Hayters Sports Agency* 30 years ago.

I've come full circle in writing my first book....

To Mum, who took me to the local library, my first memory, bought me books, read me books, nurtured me and gave me all the love in the world.

To my sister Kay and to Doug, Jonney, Faye, Adrian and Deirdre thank you.

To the Wellings family here in Horsham, my love for you knows no bounds. To Ava, to Imogen, your intelligence, empathy, beauty and grace lift our hearts every day. When you came into the world together, the blessing was indescribable. The joy you've given us every single day, and the independent, unique, individuals you are as young women fills us with pride and happiness. Noah, I could never have imagined a father and son bond so strong. You are amazing, smart and full of laughter. Spending time with you all is a privilege.

To Lorna, you are incredible. My love and admiration for your kindness, patience and selflessness is plain to see, every day. The support you show me, and those around you, and your calming influence on all, is so precious. I am so proud of your achievements, and it is your beauty and grace I see in our children. With all of my heart thank you.

Forever,

Lee x

FOREWORD

What I've tried to do in my work over the last 30 years as a broadcaster, writer and journalist covering sport is to find the *human* stories and share them. To help people understand why sport can matter. The life within.

I've been wanting to get some of this down in one place, to write a book for mums, dads, grandparents and teenagers everywhere. Whether you're new to sport, a lifelong fan, or someone who doesn't know much about it – I want this way of telling stories about sport to be a game changer.

As I wrote, I realised themes were recurring. They must be important to me. Belonging, identity, acceptance, nostalgia, joy, community, grief and mortality.

How I failed to relate to my father, and the impact of his death. The closeness to my own children and wife, never more important than during the pandemic. The power of sport that started as the six-year-old boy on the cover. The routine it provided. Then the opportunity. To leave south London and travel the world to report on sport.

Sport became news, and across the globe I tried to make sense of the biggest stories. Cheating, doping, corruption and greed became my daily brief. Through sport and my working environments, I've explored misogyny, race and class.

Eventually, I found a way to rekindle my love of sport. And threaded through this book is what one commentator described as "The greatest story ever told." For once the hyperbole may be justified.

Leicester City winning the Premier League in 2016 was scarcely believable. A true fairy tale in the city. I was there. Saw it. Told the world about it. The magic that started when the bones of a fallen king were found beneath a car park. Strange times, once-in-a-lifetime euphoria, then suffering. Their tale will live forever.

The man who led the team inspired them with a bell; *Dilly ding, dilly dong, wake up*! Claudio Ranieri's grace, dignity and empowerment of others had a profound effect. Kindness in leadership over toxic masculinity is an important theme of the book.

I question sports journalism for its cliques and clichés, but I will use one here; *I left it all on the pitch*. This book is my heart and soul. I want you to laugh and to cry. To look at sport differently, to look at life differently. Maybe look at me differently, too.

As the pandemic ravaged the globe and life stopped, and sport stopped, did we wake up to see what the game had become? Had we heard the sound of The Dilly Dong Bell?

Love,

Lee x

Chapter 1: THE BLUE KING

In the year 1485 on a battleground in Leicester lay the body of a fallen king. In the year 2015 a new king appeared. Do *you* believe in magic?

The new king was humble, graceful, silver-haired, Italian. Determination and passion beneath his calm. He gesticulated, he empowered, he inspired. He was armed with a tiny bell. *"Dilly Ding, Dilly Dong! Wake up!"* He rose to glory within a year. But he too was slain, on the strange 'battleground' of football.

The scene is Leicester, a diverse city in the East Midlands of England, proud of its sporting heritage and achievements. This includes a renowned rugby team, a trophy-winning basketball team and at the heart of the city, a football club named Leicester City. Leicester City FC was formed in 1884. Or rather Leicester Fosse was, later to become Leicester City. And this football club staged the greatest miracle in sporting history. The greatest? *Really*? Yes.

No matter how hard we look at sport, there hasn't been anything more unlikely, more incredible, more of a *fairy tale,* than Leicester's story. It confounds belief and logic. I was there. I watched it unfold. It still amazes me. It's not as if sport hasn't had its fair share of unlikely stories. When I think back through them all, a fairy tale of a different sort stands out to me above others. Heavyweight boxer James 'Buster' Douglas beating the seemingly indestructible, brutal, undefeated champion Mike Tyson in Tokyo in 1990. I watched open-mouthed in the middle of the night at my friend Mark's house in south-east London. Another friend, Ian was there too. We felt dazed. As did Tyson.

In boxing's ocean, Tyson was a shark. It was never pretty. He was a predator who was relentless, unstoppable. Many boxers entered the ring in sparkling dressing gowns, as if they had 'Vegas residencies' singing showtunes. Tyson entered the ring in the most basic plain black shorts. This wasn't an accident. It was menacing. Less is more. And often the fight lasted only seconds, with his opponents not reaching their stools at the end of the first round.

Tyson had issues. Out of the ring his life was a maelstrom, he was destructive and harmful to others. Once he stepped inside the ring, he had looked at peace.

But the thing about two powerful men fighting, is that if one punches the other one hard enough in the face, he might go down to the canvas. Boxing is sometimes called a *'Noble Art'*, but this is called a *'Puncher's Chance'*.

In football, the equivalent of a Puncher's Chance comes in 'knockout' competitions, where big teams can be paired randomly against opponents from smaller leagues, and potentially eliminated. Premier League football is thirty-eight games per team. That's a lot of games to maintain an unlikely level of brilliance.

So why was Leicester City's story a fairy tale? Simple really. They had to sustain impossibility with a team of unheralded players. There wasn't the remotest chance of them winning the league. An alien landing was, according to bookmakers, far more likely. They really do offer odds on such things. If I walked into my garden right now and an extra-terrestrial was standing with a cup of tea, yes it would be a shock, but there are plenty of people who believe in the other-worldly, it's talked about, explored. Leicester's chances of winning the Premier League trophy? There would be no mission to explore this, it wouldn't have been deemed worth it by NASA, a team of pundits, or anybody else. Leicester don't *win* Premier Leagues. Leicester can't, shouldn't. How could they?

The magic started in the year 2012 and transcends sport. It's a story of belief, of life. This book is about life. Sport just happens to be our portal. And it brings together history, heartache, despair and triumph. August 25, 2012, was an ordinary day for the city, apart from an archaeological team from the University of Leicester digging for the bones of the fallen King Richard III. In a car park. The Grey Friars car park, Leicester.

Years of research had given the team hope that the last medieval king could be found beneath the city. But no guarantee, far from it, even when they were granted permission to start the dig. On day two, beneath a parking space marked with the letter 'R', the team unearthed two leg bones. Eventually a skeleton. The team had followed their conviction and persisted, to make a truly astonishing discovery. Such seismic, historic, unlikely events were to become a theme in the city of Leicester.

Forensic, exhaustive processes were used by the archaeologists for the next few months until the team could confirm 'beyond reasonable doubt' that the skeleton they exhumed was that of the last Plantagenet King. The House of Plantagenet originated in France and is used to identify four royal houses. The family held the English throne from 1154 until 1485, when Richard III was killed on that battleground in Leicester. By February 2013 the archaeologists could proudly reveal their news to the world. There was applause at the press conference, this was a stunning discovery. A King exhumed after half a millennium! That's something an excitable football commentator could work with. Imagine the hyperbole. *"The King is risen! What a goal the team have achieved! A fine, fine dig!"* It was not certain King Richard's remains would remain in Leicester. York Minster contested it; there had been a strong connection between him and the city. But Leicester won. His eternal resting place would be Leicester Cathedral. On March 26, 2015, his final journey took place. A procession from the university to the cathedral, with many thousands of people lining the streets. The city of Leicester was enthralled by this news, and the developments. If you had told any of them what was to come, they would never have believed you. *Do you believe in magic*?

The eyes of the world would stay on Leicester. And I mean the world. The Premier League is a global phenomenon. The most watched, most followed, most popular football league on the planet. I wouldn't be surprised if undiscovered tribes gathered around a laptop to cheer Arsenal kicking a spheroid around thousands of miles away. It was like a spell had been cast. Two years on from that magic moment for the city, the team were struggling, the manager was struggling, and so were the fans. Leicester City was about to lose its place in the Premier League. The only place to be for an English club. And yet the following spring, the streets of Leicester would be scenes of wild celebrations, entangled with disbelief. Like something sent from above, a mysterious force, a blue energy wave. Some can summon magic with a wand. Others use a tiny bell.

Chapter 2: THE RED SPELL

He lays a red scarf on the coffin. Is this his identity?

The colour of your team stays with you for life. Ours was red. Liverpool.

The boy in pyjamas reaches out for the radio dial. And searches. A high-pitched whistling, fading in and out, the dial turns, a French voice, fades. Turn the dial again, and now it's English. A voice of male authority, but with clarity and warmth. The commentator paints pictures in the mind, of men in red shirts, that glow, vibrant. "Wearing red on this freezing night. They have to score, but just ten minutes remain." Please score. Three years later, not a radio, a television. Huge, second-hand, with brown pockmarked side panels, a large silver knob for volume, in his room, in his reality. From the TV, another familiar voice. Comforting. On the screen those glowing, mesmerising kits. Red. The boy's tiny kit is red too. It's a final. An impossibly exotic location to him. Paris. His team against revered opponents. Red v White. Please beat them.

The connection to his father is about blood, not understanding. *Blood flows through our veins, that's where our similarity ends*. His mother gives all the love in the world, what is needed in the formative years. *Give me the boy until he is seven and I will show you the man*. Through the screen he sees his place in the world, his calling, his future. The bell. The first line of TV commentary. Poor audio quality from a land overseas, somehow enhances it, lifts it. Goosebumps. Two doors away, Nan will be watching. She's from there. Born red. Loves her football, though sometimes she can't work out why the players are not wearing red. I've told her before, but it sometimes fools her. "It's the *away* kit Nan."

I think of our conversations, her voice. Her sing-song accent. He can hear it now if he closes his eyes. Red, rosy cheeks. Hair like Shirley Temple. Red trousers and red shirt. Red earrings. And the smile. Illuminates. Glows. There is laughter.

The players' shirts are a deep red on the TV screen. And on their red cotton are giant numbers stitched in white. There's number seven. Whenever number seven scores a goal his smile is wide, just like Nan's. Scotsman. Genius. Teeth shining. Arms outstretched. Like a child told it's fish and chips for dinner. Bum like a tank. Brain like Einstein. Dancing feet of Nureyev. He's our man.

More memories. Me. The boy in the pyjamas growing up. A red pen, writing the score. His special book, his bible. Knows every fact, knows every player, recreates each game. 92 clubs, 92 backstories. The strong, the weak and the near-anonymous. He soaks it all in. This will be his life. He WILL be a sportswriter. He will do this. This is him.

*

Now the boy is a man of 17. Working at football stadiums. Pen, pad, Press Pass, glasses. For over a year working as a 'junior reporter'. Writing about other teams, while his own team was playing elsewhere.

One day, many thousands of fans went to watch 'The Reds'. As they usually did. Men, women, boys, girls. Individually and together. To sing, to win. To reach the promised land. The final.

96 people didn't come home. *Ninety-six* people. Crushed to death. Men, women and children were crushed to death. God love them and their families. They went to a football match. And they never came back. While I was writing this book, another victim lost his life. Andrew Devine had suffered life changing injuries on the fateful crush at a football ground in 1989. Hillsborough.

Then they were besmirched and abandoned for years. We clung to a false hope. *They'll protect them, won't they?* But we were wrong.

For those who fell, there was apathy. Nearly as bad as antipathy. And empathy fatigue from those whose lives *hadn't* been ripped apart.

He wanted the truth. He wanted the listener to *feel* it. *Find* the truth. *Feel* the empathy. But how to do it?

One story. One tragedy. In the media, they call it a 'case study'. But he didn't want to think of it as a case study. These are lives, not cases.

He found what he was looking for, and he told his truth. A father back in Liverpool had been watching at home on TV on that Saturday after-noon, in the spring of 1989. The coverage was interrupted by a news-flash. From that second, the dad's life was never the same. A living hell. When he spoke you felt his pain. Too painful. Almost unbearable. And that was before the blame came. And the lies. And the cover-up.

When some justice eventually came, the correspondent stood in the rain and reported the facts. It rained so hard. It felt apocalyptic. He spoke into the camera, describing what was going on in the building behind him. What it meant. The Prime Minister of the United Kingdom was apologising in Parliament. Finally. It wasn't really his apology to give but it was needed. Exoneration for the fans cruelly blamed for the crush. Relief for the grieving families. But not *proper* justice. Not yet.

The boy who became a reporter was now standing as a man in the driving rain, asking for the viewers to consider the *individual* tragedy. Not only the collective, not just the *number* 96.

What colour are you defined by? What place? Do you belong? Are you a red? Just like Nan?

When he thinks of her, he thinks of the smile first. Then of watching football together. She loved that number seven, they all did. The num-ber seven became manager of the team. Dalglish. He was in charge when it happened. He went to every funeral of the 96 fans. A heavy toll. His smile eventually returned, but it took time.

"It's not a matter of life and death. It's more important than that."

That's what the trailblazer of this football club had famously said, dec-ades earlier. He had understood the people. He had understood what community is. He had told the team they were there to represent the fans. And that they were invincible. He told them it would take a 'team from Mars' to beat them. He believed.

Years later, when Nan died, that young reporter draped the scarf over her coffin. It made him feel close to her, to them. *Red.* Identity. The need for the discipline of routine, the distraction. The need to write down the scores in the book in the bottom drawer. It would make everything alright.

Miracles sometimes happen. I've seen it. Istanbul. 2005. The Reds needed a miracle. But would it happen? It's 0-1. Then 0-2, Then 0-3. No goals scored, THREE conceded. Half a match still to play. What's the score going to end up as? Nil-six? Nil-seven? Has that even happened before? Humiliation. Losers. Don't let them see the pain. Sing. Find it. Hold your nerve. Find it.

Do you believe in magic?

You don't quite understand the noise, the togetherness, until you're amongst it. The red sea of scarves, and noise. A family. A tribe. A community. A shared goal. The energy crackles and fizzes.

In Istanbul, the Reds finally score a goal. Perhaps the mark of the greatest players, the greatest people, is that they carry others on their shoulders. Maybe that's why this furrow-browed captain looks so intense. Maybe that's why this man would struggle to smile if a panda hugged him. What a player, what a warrior. Gerrard. Finding it. One goal back. Only losing 3-1 now! Is there a way out? Do you believe in magic?

Football is not easy to watch. A 'Professor of Football' (there really is such a thing) at the local university describes the experience as a *"Theatre of Disappointment."* He says a scarcity of goals breeds frustration and anxiety within a football stadium.

In Istanbul, the Reds have scored again. It's 2-3 now. What is going on? They are finding it. They can't, can they? Do you believe in magic?

Is anthropology working for this team? Some scientists and statisticians will tell you that teams who wear red have more success. To the eye, physically and psychologically, wearing red can have a *'marginal gain'*. You can't put on some red shorts, red boxing gloves and expect to knock out a champion boxer. But even the slightest gain can help.

They wore red in Istanbul...it's a miracle! Can we believe what's going on? It was 0-3 and now it's 3-3. Bang! Bang! Bang! So quickly. How? How are the Reds now level? Keep going, keep feeding off the energy of those who travelled to support. One of the greatest finals in the history of the UEFA Champions League – it's even known as The Miracle of Istanbul. They never lost belief. Never lose belief.

Do you believe in miracles?

A year later. A miracle in life. The notebook still keeps the scores, but some things are more important. Precious. He is blessed. And blessed again. Thank you. The cottage has a red door. The woman with the long dark hair was always there in that cottage, then he found her. Now she's with him. And standing with them are two small girls in red coats. Identical. Perfect. Not a day passes, not a moment, where the miracle isn't with them. A biological miracle. The blood they shared. The doctors said it was a million to one. Monochorionic monoamniotic. Even the stars shine brighter tonight. Nothing's impossible.

In the hospital, six years on, the blood flows. Red. Traumatic, time stops. It is an emergency, red for danger, while he holds his newly born son. Please. Find it. Hold on, hold on, please. Thank you. Thank you, God. We're okay. I love you.

Life changes. Priorities change, responsibilities change. The boy needed the Reds, does the *man* still need the Reds? Does it still mean anything? Is it still in the blood? For some magic is a Red Spell. For others a maroon scarf and a 'boy wizard'. *Do you believe in magic?*

When 'The Red Spell' stopped working for Liverpool, something special was needed. *Someone* special. From Germany's Black Forest, a man arrived who could see 'the wood from the trees.' His name is Klopp.

He arrived like a rock star crossed with a puppet, in cool spectacles. A leader. The manager. Called himself normal. Humility, humour, empathy. Understanding that leadership should not only be about authority, but also about support. Made people a better version of themselves. Helped them find their confidence. It matters.

In 1978, in 1981, in 2005, and in 2020, the Reds' captains stood expect-antly. One-by-one they lifted a trophy. They believed, they found it. Together.

Today, somewhere, a small child reaches out. Seeking magic, seeking miracles, seeking routine, comfort and joy from red shirts. A new King raises his arms skywards. This time, a red shirt with the number eleven on his back. Salah. The child raises his arms skywards too.

They connect. They *belong*.

Chapter 3: THE LUCKY FEW

Two men make their way along Fleet Street. I say men, but one of them is better described as a boy.

It is the end of the 1980s. Fleet Street is hanging on to one or two of the newspaper offices that made it famous, the heart of that industry. Most papers have moved by then. The office of The Beano comic remains, with editorial values more serious than some tabloids. Tucked away at the end of a cobbled alleyway off Fleet Street, is a sports reporting agency named Hayters. This is where he is headed. To start a new life. And maybe meet the man himself. Reg Hayter. Godfather of sports journalism.

The boy is still a teenager. He alights from the train at Charing Cross, having made the 30-minute ride from the estates of south-east London. Commuters rammed like sardines. The throng is approaching the ticket barriers, like bees in a giant hive, working, working, getting the job done. Through the barriers, and out into one of London's many famous streets, *The Strand*. Black cabs like peppercorns and *Routemaster* red buses, open at the back, so you could jump on and risk your life, grasping onto the pole and watching the tarmac whizz by, like Buster Keaton in a 1920s movie.

The boy is dressed how a boy dresses to look like a man. Wavy hair, organised chaos, the front hanging over his forehead in the shape of a croissant, a scholar's glasses with pear drop lenses, 'Harry Jotter' notepad to hand, and a beige mac coat with big brown buttons. Well of course a mac! This is how a boy dresses to look like a grown-up reporter. As he walks along The Strand, central London is being central London. Hundreds, thousands, with somewhere to get to. It's like a giant computer game, avoiding the traffic. Richard Ashcroft of 'The Verve' would have been knocked to the pavement had his famous *'Bitter Sweet Symphony'* music video been filmed here.

To the right, *The Savoy* hotel, tucked away in a cul-de-sac, its own hive of activity since 1889. Doormen in three-piece suits and top hats as the well-heeled guests arrive. And on walks the boy, on to Fleet Street. To the left are *The Law Courts*, standing majestic and imposing. A tall, bespectacled woman, a lawyer we'd guess, scurries into the building with a pile of folders under her arm. The same sense of urgency we've seen since the train station.

When the boy makes this journey at weekends, it is quiet in central London. There are no people, and it is near to silence. Apart from an occasional rumble of a taxi or bus engine. But there is one exhilarating, spine-tingling sound from behind Fleet Street. The bells of St Brides Church. Chiming, soaring, calling. The sense of history and purpose is overpowering, it is like the sense you have when you peer from a window and see snow. A majesty, a tingle, you feel alive. The boy felt the sense, the need, to be someone.

Into the centre of Fleet Street, compact and bustling. To his right, the entrance to a wine bar, *The Wig and Pen*. Give it four hours and it will be open, packed with lunchtime office workers and journalists, before social media made their jobs '25 hours a day, eight days a week'. By evening, drunken journalists, lawyers, judges. Like a tavern from old London, but one where people wear suit trousers, top buttons undone on shirts, ties loosened. When work time is over.

One of the black cabs, a famous 'Hackney Carriage', pulls up at the entrance to the alleyway in Fleet Street. A taxi door opens and out of the back, slowly, emerges a man. A septuagenarian. Grey hair, slightly wider around the girth than his days as an impressive amateur sportsman – he had been a cricketer of some distinction. Grey trousers, white shirt, a coat over his arm, and a case. A slow firm hand on the black door pushes it closed, he raises a hand to thank the driver and pivots, more gracefully than when he disembarked from the taxi, before disappearing into the alley.

The grey-haired man walks past *Ye Olde Cheshire Cheese* pub, tucked away in the alley. A sign hangs: *'Rebuilt 1667'*. 1666 was an eventful year. Plagues, fires. The man emerges into a space between tightly packed three-storey buildings in the little arteries of central London. One passer-by in a pin-striped suit walks past him and imitates a cricket shot. In response he puts down his case. And motions with a flat arm. The signal for an imaginary four runs scored. He smiles. The 'cricket' man hurries on, smiling too.

He reaches a small square. Gough Square is the name. The buildings are tight and square like part of a *Lego* city. But at one end of the square is Dr Samuel Johnson's house. The man who wrote the first dictionary. History enveloping the tight space, an energy, a step back in time. This tiny square with an archway on the corner could, with only a modicum of imagination, be the 18th century. It *feels* like the 18th century.

The man reaches his office entrance, two wooden doors with giant gold knobs. He pushes the one on the right, and shuffles up the narrow staircase, two floors, the hardest part of the day. Puff, wheeze. Stairs creak like the *London Philharmonic* tuning their instruments. He grips the bannister. Push. Onwards and upwards.

The bespectacled boy has now also entered the alleyway and hurries past *Ye Olde Cheshire Cheese*. When the boy became a man, he would return to this charismatic pub on every last Friday in November. His friends would gather in the same room each year, at the same table beneath a painting of Dr Johnson, with sawdust on the floor and a roaring fire. Holding their flagons of ale, like the 'olden' days. They would laugh, a lot, and talk about what life had thrown at them for the other 364 days. Great triumphs, great loves, some tough times. The relentless demands and joys of life. A safe haven for a day.

The boy darts diagonally between two office workers like a 1950s footballer, a 'winger', dropping a shoulder and finding the gap, flirting with a possibility of bumping shoulders, but finding that gap and accelerating away into the space. Through a second alleyway, towards the big brown doors. He reaches the doors and stands beneath them, pausing for a moment. Daunted, inspired, hungry.

The boy reaches the square and pushes firmly at the right-hand door. He quickly climbs the stairs, more a jog than a walk, like an Olympic runner chosen to light the torch, or a fit rambler on the early foothills when the energy levels are high. The boy only had one floor to climb, the foothills of sports journalism, the engine room, while the writers were on the floor above. All the boys had to start here, and it was just boys in those days, an education in life with the richest array of characters no work of fiction could match.

First, there was Alan the office manager. He was joined by the outwardly, comically grumpy one they called 'Angry'. He got the nickname from an Aussie pop star, and though he favoured a sardonic moan, you still couldn't help liking him. There was no malice. On the lower floor, everybody apart from the boy seemed to smoke, so through the clouds it would have been difficult to pick out who was working.

In one office at the back was Lawrie the small accountant with a distinctive hunched back and infectious laugh. He'd joke that you needed to buy him a scotch if you wanted your wages. At least they hoped he was joking! And in the other small office was Frank. He'd been there, seen it, done it all before. A legendary sports editor. In charge of the best-selling sports tabloid for years. When he climbed the stairs to the first floor, it was always epic, and always the same routine. He'd huff and puff, say his hellos, and reach the kitchen. The unwritten rule was to refill the kettle after use. "Oh, for goodness sake" he'd cry out with exasperation.

For the boy, this was Day One. The phones were ringing, they barely stopped in this agency, serving the sports papers of Fleet Street and well beyond with stories and content. It was an 'internal' ring, one ring not two. The boy answered one of the calls keenly, moments before anyone else. 'Angry' was pleased not to have to deal with another call. A few years later, after the boy left, legend has it he became so angry one day, his nickname changed to 'Livid'!

There was a pause on the phone. It was Reg Hayter, gathering his thoughts. The founder, boss, the 'Godfather' of British sports journalism, the legend, the maker of careers, he hated being a 'breaker' of careers. Couldn't bear to sack anyone. Today, he had a mission for the new boy.

"Hello," he said in deep authoritative tone, searching for a voice on the other end. "Hello Mr Hayter" the boy replied, feeling like a journalistic amoeba and his voice sounding like he'd been sucking helium.

"Is that Wing Commander Wellings?"
"Yes, it is, hello Mr Hayter."
"Slip upstairs please".

It was the grand call, the summons upstairs. This was the boy's first full day, his first meeting with Hayter. Remember the golden rule. FIRM

20

handshake. Hayter likes a firm trustworthy handshake. It was rumoured one employee's file had a small note and nothing else: "Good firm hand-shake!"

The boy's heart was beating like he was taking a penalty to win the World Cup as he entered the top floor. The established writers, most of them in their twenties but seeming like veterans, were crashing away typing on their keyboards, or on 'landline' phones. Some managed a friendly half-wave as the boy had already spent two years around them, learning the trade by helping out at football grounds.

The office was compact and neat in design, but filled with papers, note-books, ledgers, pigeonholes and journalists. At the far end was Hayter's own office. The door was closed but part of the door was glass, meaning you could see inside, and adding to the feeling of nerves and the un-known.

The boy had heard so much about Hayter, so many impressions of him. What was this first 'mission'? A big match to report on? Better than that? Legend had it one young sports journalist of the 1960s got to in-terview Marilyn Monroe after somebody confused Hayters for a straight news agency. Rules at the company included not letting the phone ring more than twice and never saying no. Whether the request was sport or not. As if anyone would be saying no to Marilyn Monroe!

The boy knocked gently on the door. He could hear the clatter of type-writer keys within. "Come in!" boomed Hayter's deep voice, and the boy entered the inner sanctum. On the desk was a prominent sign: *'A cluttered desk is the sign of a genius'*.

Hayter was in the flow, always, and bashed at the keys like a grand pia-nist playing 'Beethoven's fifth'. The 'golf ball' typewriter, named after the little ball that hit the page to print, had been usurped by computers, that would these days look like ancient relics.

In Hayter's office, the typewriter remained king, and 'typos' were scattered liberally. When Hayter left the office each day, usually after a late surge of work, any reporter left in the office and with half a brain would read his notes, hoping for good news amongst the long list of reminders full of typos. *'Mjust promote Wellongs'* was the type of mistyped sentence the boy would search for, like Inspector Poirot let loose on Fleet Street.

Hayter was a sturdy man with a regal face, like a much-loved actor known for playing moguls, the essence of a newspaper man, white crisp shirt, tummy pushing against it, prominent eyebrows and stern eyes, that could easily start to twinkle and soften, and regularly did. You see, Hayter was a kind man with a good heart. Yes, he was absolutely terrifying, the proverbial 'old school' boss, but there was kindness beneath the 'bollockings'. A bit later on in the job, when the boy asked why he'd stopped being allowed out to report on matches he was sternly rebuked:

"There are many of us working hard sonny. We can't all spend our time at matches. That's the privilege of the lucky few."

When reigning in the excesses of those who used flowery writing, Hayter told them: "Never use two words where one will do." He pointed to Churchill's speeches as some of the greatest writing in history. Simple, effective and for all to understand. He emphasised each short sharp word. "We. Will. Fight. Them. On. The. Beaches."

When the boy wrote a note, this time to protest against his endlessly meandering working hours, Hayter warned sagely: *"Never write a note in anger. Always sleep on it."*

When encouraging the boys to improve their vocabulary, to embrace Dr Johnson's work. Hayter would dryly say:

"Do you own a dictionary sonny? No? Congratulations. You clearly know the lot! Well done to you."

He was their 'Mr Miyagi' and the methods worked. *Give me the boy until he is 27, and I will show you the man!*

Boy after boy entered Hayters sports agency. Man after man embarked on a writing career. Or a radio career. And some into television, all using these core skills. Many regional, many national, some international. And they passed on their skills to new generations.

Two of those who left to spread their wings, Gerry Cox and Nick Callow, have forged a modern Hayters. Same name but differently run - embracing the new era of video and social media. New boys, new *girls* learning vital lessons, using the same principles the grand old man had taught.

Back at that first meeting on that first Fleet Street day, Hayter eventually, apologetically, looked up at this boy. He held his glance for a second, stood up and shot out a firm hand. *"Welcome to Hayters."* The boy knew the form, so he stepped forward with purpose and went for a 'bone crusher', the type of grip a wrestler would use. Who knows if it was a career-enhancing handshake?

Hayter didn't invite the boy to sit down, to his quiet relief, saying: "*I'm sure you're very busy. But I have a question.*" The boy dared to dream. Is this the chance to interview a star player? Or write on the big match? Or to investigate a scandal? Is the boy's *Watergate* story going to arrive before his 19th birthday? : *"If you're popping out for some lunch, could you bring me back a sandwich,"* said Hayter. *"Cheese and salad please. The best place is the little sandwich bar in the alleyway".*

Never mind Olympics from summer to winter, from Rio to PyeongChang, football World Cups, Pelé, Ronaldo, big fights in America or any of the global deployments that lay ahead for this boy. This was the big one. The 'cheese sandwich' deployment. There were many such tasks in the early Hayters years. For the boy. For us all.

As the boy left the office, Hayter's impassioned cry could suddenly be heard: *"Leeeeee".* And the boy returned, alarmed. *May I also have a cup of loop-the-loop? Tomato flavour please."* The boy double checked with the experienced lunch-buyers. Hayter did indeed mean soup.

But the boy messed up his important first mission. The soup part went well, but he allowed the sandwich shop owner to recommend granary bread for the cheese sandwich. It was a perfectly valid and healthy path to take, but the *wrong* path. He returned to the office triumphantly, like a warrior returning from victorious battle, 'the great sandwich war of 1990'. He had fought off the other office workers, and fearlessly journeyed to the front of the queue.

The boy climbed the stairs like Rocky shadow boxing in Philadelphia. The music was playing in his head. The boy has NAILED this. Today a cheese sandwich, tomorrow reinventing sports journalism! He handed the sandwich over to a grateful Hayter, fuel for his early afternoon surge before a large glass of red or two beckoned in Fleet Street. Sadly the 'bat phone' on the first floor glowed hot five minutes later.

"Is Lee there?"
"I'm here Mr Hayter."
"I'm so sorry sonny but I can't eat this sandwich. I wanted white bread. This bread has got nuts and bolts in it!"

One day the boy would report on *Usain* Bolt winning a historic gold medal in Rio. Right now, the only bolts, and indeed nuts, were in Hayter's sandwich. Another boy was dispatched on his first day to Billingsgate fish market to buy Mrs Hayter some haddock. He was known as the *'fish correspondent'* for years.

A few months later, after much hard work, the boy had learned to just get on with it. His time would come. Patience was not his virtue, but persistence was. One night, his head was close to dropping. In Gough Square all was quiet. The only offices with lights still on were the first and second floor at Hayters. Two hundred and fifty years ago, Dr Johnson would be in the *'Cheshire Cheese'* on his second brandy.

The boy was on the first floor and the phone rang, it was Hayter working tirelessly, but this was slightly unusual, it was almost worrying for him still to still be beavering away *this* late. "Is that Lee? Slip upstairs please sonny."

Up the boy went. It was foreboding. His hopes had been dashed too many times that he would be given a writing job or sent out to report on football. Or better still cricket. The door was open, and the boy entered. Hayter was annihilating the typewriter keys, as if 'breaking' a world exclusive newspaper story. As if he was writing a movie script needed by dawn. And he didn't look up. And time stood still, leaving the boy on the verge of asking somewhat awkwardly: Did you need to see me?

Suddenly, Hayter looked up and held the boy's gaze. In a deep soft voice he spoke, with no change in expression: *"Two men looked out from prison bars. One saw the mud, the other saw stars"*.

Hayter returned to typing. He knew the boy would still be looking, expecting more. And he knew. He *knew*. With his head down, Hayter raised his hands and pointed skywards. Message received. He could see me. He could actually *see* me. He craved some of my youthful energy, and I craved his gravitas, his wisdom. I craved acceptance. To be seen. To belong. We all need to *belong*.

Chapter 4: BLACK AND WHITE

To understand the magic of sport, the power of sport, the influence of sport we must ask: What *is* sport? I found a quote by Ernest Hemingway, where he considers only three examples acceptable: *"Bullfighting, motorsport and mountaineering; all the rest are merely games."*

A slightly more conventional definition comes from the Oxford English Dictionary and consulting it would surely meet the approval of both Mr Hayter and Dr Johnson. The OED describes sport as: *"An activity involving physical exertion or skill in which an individual or team competes against another or others for entertainment."* It's the use of the word *'physical'* that causes so much debate.

A sport that is dismissed for not being 'physical enough' is darts. To some, the image of darts is of large men with red faces, wearing cheap shirts, drinking beer and not exerting anything apart from their drinking elbows. Others recognise it as a sport, a form of which is recorded historically to have been played in the 16th century by King Henry VIII, and requires skill and precision, not unlike archery.

With a huge fanbase and packed arenas, darts replaced football as the 'working class night out'. Beer and smoking were banned from the stage decades ago, but the beer is certainly flowing in the crowds, and the standard of competition is one of the attractions. There are more than a hundred fiendishly good players, capable of beating the best in the world 'on their day'.

Darts is played and watched around the globe. The best player was a 16-time World Champion, the now-retired Phil Taylor, whose nerve under pressure was almost scary. He was playing for a lot of money yet consistently showed how important *temperament* is in sport. He was the king for two decades, the 1990s and 2000s. Darts was starting to generate substantial amounts of money through television and sponsorship deals, as well as ticket sales. Hundreds of thousands of pounds in some tournaments. This was thanks to the genius of entrepreneur Barry Hearn and his innovative media production team who brought it to the masses.

In the '90s players started to walk on stage in a style that said *'showbiz'*, if that's still a word. Loud signature tunes are pumped into the arenas, songs that are generally crowd-pleasing, and often funny. One of the few players deemed to be 'easy on the eye', the Dutch World Champion Jelle Klaasen, began walking on to *'Sex on Fire'* by Kings of Leon. You haven't lived until you've stood amongst a sweaty darts audience belting this out. Though I'm not sure the potential to 'sex up' darts was in the minds of Kings of Leon when they wrote the song,

More seriously, it's a sport that has enabled women to compete against men, and beat them, without any segregation, or fuss. It's always struck me that Hearn deserves more credit for the way he has developed and delivered events to the public, watched by millions on TV. When someone comes out of Essex with a 'working class' persona, some will sniffily focus on the money alone, and forget the difference the man also made. There is equality and opportunity in his content. He has innovated for decades with tournament formats and techniques to keep some sports in business and thriving, and who else could hook in television sports channel executives by selling them live fishing and calling it *'FishOmania'*?! Hearn pushed the definition of sport to the limits, and what harm has it done?

Darts is not part of the Olympics, but it might be one day, because it's officially recognised by the International Olympic Committee. Other sports recognised by the IOC include orienteering, dancing (unsurprising considering the popularity of the dance competition *Strictly Come Dancing*), and bridge. Yes, bridge. But recognition of status as a sport can be inconsistent outside of the Olympic movement.

I was in the High Court in London in 2015 when there was a bid by the English Bridge Union to have bridge recognized *legally* as a sport and qualify for funding. The bid was rejected, but I learned a lot from exploring the game. One of the most important aspects is bringing people and communities together. I remember being quietly moved by watching dozens of people playing in a bridge hall, many who were elderly and living alone, getting a chance to interact and compete, then socialise afterwards. I've always liked to learn something from my deployments, rather than make the story fit into the box of a pre-conceived idea.

Bridge requires mental agility and concentration, but the word that enabled it to even be considered as a sport, is *competition*. To compete is to take the key step towards being recognized as sport. And in the bridge hall the competition can be fierce. There is a strong desire to win, on top of the social aspect. Sometimes a battle of mental agility comes in teams, in a room full of people. In other games, in other sports, it's one on one.

Late in 2018 in London, I entered a soundproof giant glass cube with a cameraman and filmed the world's best two chess players locked in concentration and combat. I don't profess to understand chess, I wish I did, but my lack of expertise did give me an advantage over the 'chess media'. They were operating inside a metaphorical bubble, communicating to chess followers and each other. My job was to try and spread the net wider.

The duel I covered, spread out over several weeks, was gripping. On one side of the board was world champion Magnus Carlsen, for whom formidable is an understatement. Carlsen is the *Bond* of chess. Ruthlessly going in for the kill on the board. Unconventionally handsome and ice cool in a smart grey suit, like a blue-eyed college quarterback attending an awards dinner. Almost aloof, but with a dry suspicious sense of humour and a reticence that became intriguing.

His opponent was a geeky Italian-American by the name of Fabiano Caruana, so good that he was given a chance to beat Carlsen. He looked like the school nerd who wears a smart jacket to an event and suddenly attracts attention because he 'scrubs up' so well. And then you notice his other qualities. Measured and quietly charismatic. A dark horse. Someone with a quiet charm behind a little mop of wavy hair and glasses. A cross between a character on *The Big Bang Theory* and Buddy Holly. When he spoke, he had the aura of a young smart executive. He was measured in his delivery. I really liked the pair of them, their similarities, their differences.

These two were genuinely making chess cool. They had started to appear in glossy magazines for reasons of fashion. Not only *'Chess Monthly'*. The venue was *The College, Holborn* in Central London, the one famously namechecked by Jarvis Cocker in Pulp's epic song *'Common People'*:

"She studied sculpture at St Martin's College, that's where I, caught her eye".

In the pre-event press conference, tightly packed into the room, were the chess media, and me. Could I take chess away from the intricacies of the board battle, and explore a populist route? I was aware viewers would know the board was black and white, and be aware of some of the pieces, but some would have no idea what the queen is capable of. Or the king. Don't even start on the pawns.

This wasn't time for a question in the style of a chess move, something clever that confounds the recipient. I was straight to the point: *"You guys have started appearing on the front of magazines. Are you conscious you are making chess cool?"*

They both reacted like teenagers asked to perform a dance routine in front of their parents. Like Princess Diana on *The Crown* on 'Netflix', faces down and blushing. Naturally, both these intelligent and polite players gave great answers, humbly acknowledging it's good for chess to gain mainstream attention. Which happened significantly soon after through another Netflix hit, *The Queen's Gambit*. Both Carlsen and Caruana didn't want to talk too much, that's not what they were in London for. They were here to *win*.

"How do you feel about attracting attention from women?" Carlsen was suddenly asked by a female Russian reporter, making me feel slightly awkward about starting that line of questioning. *"Women hate me. I repulse them"* he shot back, deadpan, to a shocked pause then roars of laughter.

There was huge respect between them, but a steely determination to bring the other one down. It's often said that 'second is nowhere', in chess, in sport. Winning is a huge part of what sport is, whether or not some refer to the sport as a 'game'. And yet it's so much more. It's not just black and white. It takes the special ones to see beyond that.

Bobby Robson, who was a much-loved manager of football clubs and the England national football team, could see the deeper meaning. He was often consumed by football, and he was defined by it. But he also understood what sport means to some of us.

He heard the warning bells:

"What is a club in any case? Not the buildings or the directors or the people who are paid to represent it. It's not the television contracts, get-out clauses, marketing departments or executive boxes. It's the noise, the passion, the feeling of belonging, the pride in your city. It's a small boy clambering up stadium steps for the very first time, gripping his father's hand, gawping at that hallowed stretch of turf beneath him and, without being able to do a thing about it, falling in love".

I never miss an opportunity to use that quote. I may not have gone to football with my father, chance would have been a fine thing, but if it happens to you it's a beautiful thing. Maybe you are thinking of that first moment now.

In 30 years of reporting on sport, the access 'behind the curtain' *can* be hard - it can wear you down sometimes. Even though you are one of 'the lucky few' – as my old boss Reg Hayter would say - getting to report on it. The superstars who turn out to be cheats, dopers or just arseholes. The corporate nonsense. The hype. The joylessness in the work of some people. The egos and ambition taking over. But none of us should forget what we came here for. Find the joy in sport. Look beyond the black and white. Find the colour. I'm trying to do exactly that right now. With this book. And with my production company, Kalleyedo Films. See the kaleidoscope.

I've been lucky to see some historic sport live. To cover World Cups and Olympics, finals and glorious events. A montage, or a mixtape as we used to call them, could be compiled from the unforgettable sport on television. Things to be stirred and moved by. Moments you will never forget, pieced together like a tapestry.

When I think of my childhood, and my love of sport. I think of a snooker player named Alex 'Hurricane' Higgins. An unpredictable tearaway. A handful. And the night in 1982 that can still make me want to cry.

Snooker was huge in the 1980s. How huge? The famous final of the 1985 championship had a UK television audience of over 18 million people watching. On BBC Two. At midnight! That's almost a third of the population at that time. Dennis Taylor beat Steve Davis on the final black, a huge upset by a man wearing upturned glasses to help him see the balls clearly while he was leaning over the table.

The game's popularity largely came from trailblazing BBC bosses and one in particular. He commissioned a programme named *'Pot Black'*. Incredibly people used to watch this on black and white televisions. And when colour TV boomed, so did Pot Black. The name of the clever commissioner? David Attenborough. Yes, that David Attenborough. He was a decision-maker at BBC Two in the 1960s.

This was theatre to reflect the made-for-TV dramas of the time. The characters had real depth, proper dimensions. These weren't pasty robots from a production line. They'd been policemen, miners, sometimes rogues. Their faces were lived in, though they wore smart shoes and bow ties with their 1970s glam shirts.

There was no doubt who the star was. Higgins, the tempestuous Northern Irishman. I have no idea why men who hit balls with a stick were given names of natural weather phenomena just because they walk around the table quickly. There's also Jimmy 'Whirlwind' White, and James 'Typhoon' Wattana. Several other stiff breezes. There was nothing calm about Higgins, the only man who has made me sweat with nerves while watching him. He was always on the edge, and so were his fans watching.

He was my father's favourite, and he was my favourite. We watched him. It was the thing we did together.

Higgins was extraordinary. He was dashing, mesmeric, fun, suave, stylish, loutish, scruffy, ill-disciplined, distracted and rude. Often the catalyst for the change from gentleman to tearaway was how much he drank while playing. Snooker players used to 'put it away'. The roly-poly Canadian Bill Werbeniuk needed a few pints *and* some tablets to steady his cueing arm.

I recognised the swagger and danger in Higgins. Because it was there under my roof too. My father. Under the influence of alcohol, the eyes became harsher, the warmth disappeared. The feeling of unease was expertly managed by the rest of us in the house. But Higgins was beyond control, banned for headbutting a snooker referee in one incident. What you crave are the good times. When the unease evaporates. When the smile was there. And the good times were in 1982.

Higgins was losing his semi-final to Jimmy White, who needed one more 'frame' to win. The scene was the Crucible Theatre in Sheffield, shrewdly converted to the 'theatre of snooker', and now synonymous with the event.

White had potted enough balls to be almost sure of completing the win. But not quite. Higgins came to the table chalking his cue, all jerky mannerisms and nervous energy, wearing a brilliant blue shirt that only John Travolta would risk – and only in that era – and having entered the arena in a *Fedora* hat. Not the obvious choice for a game of snooker.

You were drawn to him, enthralled by him, before he even leaned over the table. On this night, Higgins showed how sport, from elite athleticism to snooker, ultimately starts and ends with talent. Every shot was challenging and 'missable'. Potting the balls was tense and improbable. And yet one by one, down into the pockets they went. Snooker players think ahead to be in the right position, but he was in a strange mesmeric zone where he would 'sink' a ball from what looked like an impossible position. Repeatedly.

Higgins brandished his cue like 'Zorro' while he struck the white ball, known as the cue ball. There were seemingly insurmountable issues of distance and angle. He sent the blue ball fizzing into a right-hand pocket in a shot we never even considered. That was mad enough. But then the cue ball, somehow, spun *back* towards us, completely unconventionally. A famous shot that defied logic, even science. I've never seen anything like it before or since.

Snooker is often gentle. This was an explosion. The crowd erupted into appreciation. He really was going to do this. Every single ball was sunk and so was poor Jimmy White. Higgins won the frame and then won the deciding frame too. Followed by a handshake, a wink, and a baby's dummy planted in his mouth, belonging to his young daughter Lauren.

The final was billed, as can happen unreasonably in sport, as 'good versus evil'. The 'Evil' opponent came in the form of Ray Reardon, a

Welshman nicknamed 'Dracula' for his hairline. In comparison with Higgins, he was a plodder. But he won the world title six times, four more than Higgins. Maybe winning isn't everything? His shoulder-shifting ponderous chuckle was a saving grace with the audience, so he wasn't universally disliked. He was a 'pantomime villain'.

It wasn't that people were desperate for Reardon to lose. He is by all accounts, a good man, generous with his time to younger players even into his eighties. But they were desperate for Higgins to win, and Reardon threatened that. The final takes place over two days, and it was difficult to say for sure who would win, until that final evening.

Higgins, in another memorably bold choice of shirt, green with red cuffs, pulled away to become world champion. I don't remember a single shot. Because what never leaves me is what happened next.

The crowd was still bubbling in The Crucible, the handshake and some celebrations had happened, and the trophy was awarded. Higgins was the victor, the showman, larger than life. But vulnerable, even in victory. At the age of 10 came a big lesson for me, about the man behind the mask. Suddenly the showman crumbled. It hit him, and he broke down. This was a celebration of Higgins, yet the scenes still break my heart.

Higgins beckons and pleads towards the audience, and now he's weeping, sobbing desperately. "*My baby, my baby*". His wife Lynn, the clouds of turbulence parting, enters the theatre floor to greet him, with baby Lauren in her arms. She hands Lauren to Higgins. In that moment a family had stability and hope. Higgins clutches his daughter while holding the trophy, still weeping. Remember, he was meant to be the *winner*. These weren't tears of joy, they were tears of turmoil and release. The fragility of life.

A documentary decades later recreated the scene. Lauren, a woman still clearly besotted with her father, recalled the impact of this unforgettable night on her life. She talked fondly with Steve Davis, the player her father had such a difficult time accepting, the opposite in character to Alex Higgins in practically every way.

Davis was a majestic snooker player whose defeat by Taylor, with the upturned glasses, was an anomaly. He was world champion six times throughout the 1980s, managed by Barry Hearn. He was polite and respectful but dismissed as 'boring' and one of the most hated sports-men in Britain in that era. His success often came at the expense of fans' favourites.

Davis turned out to be a wise, funny, self-deprecating broadcaster, and is now much-loved by millions for his wit and wisdom. There is a kind-ness in his eyes, an empathy. He feels safe. Boring? He is a part-time DJ, not a novelty act but techno. Something he takes very seriously with a deep knowledge and passion for the subject. The way he spoke to Lauren, the forgiveness of her dad's rage towards him, the clear wish that Higgins had *liked* him. It enveloped me. I was back in 1982. The tears came again.

Who's the hero? Who's the villain? Is it a sport or not? In snooker, in sport, in life, it is best not to see the person in black and white.

Chapter 5: THE NEED TO WIN

Winning is everything, second is nowhere?

On the Yorkshire moors as day breaks, it is calm, silent and a graceful athlete glides over the hills, like a Rolls Royce, purring, glossy black mane, heart pounding but on the surface serene. Striving, pushing, accumulating, legitimate gains. Maybe his father would approve. To all the world he looked like athletics royalty, like a 'silver spooner', he talked 'properly' in interviews.

On Brighton beach as day breaks, it is calm, silent and a warrior pounds across the sand and glistening pebbles, like a Land Rover, a bearded animal, heart pounding and we can see the effort. Striving, pushing, accumulating, legitimate gains. Maybe his critics would approve. To all the world he looked like one of us, like a kid done good, he didn't care much for interviews.

Two very different men, with a lot in common. Sebastian Coe and Steve Ovett. Their rivalry on the athletics track in the 1980s brought their names together. Coe v Ovett was a big deal. Two British runners dominating the glamorous 'middle-distance' events in a glorious era for athletics.

So intense was their rivalry, so fierce was their need to beat each other – it wasn't a desire - it was a *need* – that sports fans tended to feed from it and pick one or the other. I can't remember anybody at the time expressing indifference. You either wanted Coe to win, or you wanted Ovett. And their demeanours become caricatures. One seen as graceful, the other a warrior. Fairness and subtlety didn't come into it.

Race one. Moscow, 1980, Olympics. 800 metres final. They wait a few metres apart. The best two in the world. Representing the same flag. They had raced each other only twice before. Beat him, just *beat* him, the rest will fall into place. Only gold will do. Two laps. Slow first lap. Bumpy ride. Work to do. *The bell.* The bell is the warning, the alarm, the motivation. When do you make your move?

The graceful one. Coe. He's the favourite. This is his distance, his race, look how composed he is. Wait for that moment when he'll start to glide, start to drift past the others seemingly effortlessly.

Ahead of him, poised at the shoulder of the Russian leader, is the enforcer, the grinder, the powerhouse. Ovett. Not expected to win this one. Not the two-lap race. His event is three-and-three-quarter laps, later in the Olympics.

Is there really going to be a surprise in this shorter race? Surely 'the warrior' won't win *this* one? But it is starting to look that way, as the man from the south coast can look unstoppable when he hits the front. Where's Coe? Here he comes, but it's too late.

The finish line approaches, those sunken cheeks, tombstone teeth, glistening balding pate, what a warrior. What an ATHLETE! What a triumph. What an achievement. GOLD for Ovett! For his country. And just as importantly, beating *him*. Coe had drifted past the rest of the runners, naturally, but had to settle for *second* place - he looked haunted, devastated, beaten, shocked. But was he broken? What would the media say? The public? What would his father say? And he had lost to *him*. Empty. Find it. He has to.

There's another chance, the 1500 metres. Coe now *has* to win the second race. *The graceful one must find redemption.* Six days later. A long six days. Torture. Three-and-three-quarter laps. Ovett's distance. But so much pressure. Find it. This has to be his moment.

Race Two. Moscow, 1980, Olympics, 1500 metres final. Slow, cagey and unbearably tense. Only a stride between them. The bell. The alarm. The motivation. When do you make your move?

The warrior? One gold medal in his bag, and he's the favourite this time. This is his distance, his race, look how composed he is. Wait for that moment when he'll start to motor, and surge past the others. Unstoppable?

The final straight. All that work. All those dawns. This is history. It has to be now. Need to beat him. It has to be gold. Find it. The finishing line approaches, but still the race is in the balance. The graceful one has found that special gear, but he hasn't broken the warrior. Until. A second kick. Where did that come from? Another, almost impossible gear, and enough drip-drops of energy to just about *win* this time. Gold. For Coe.

The photo is taken. One moment in time. An extraordinary moment. The finishing line had brought victory, gold, redemption. His raises his arms and looks to the sky and it's like an exorcism. Begone demons. "Ecstasy, elation, euphoria, revenge, vindication." That's how Coe described this. Redemption.

This is what it means to win. This is the difference between gold and silver. To be validated. To be top of the podium. To not understand why athletes are desperate to win is not to have seen the exorcism of this man.

Later, Coe become a leader of his sport, the boss. He's been many things to me as a journalist. Wary, grateful, friendly, angry, defiant. Always respectful. Once, he really, really didn't want to speak to me. It's not that I offended him, or that he doesn't have any respect. It was the subject matter. Just too sore. World Athletics Championships. A controversial winner of the 100 metres. Understatement. Everyone had expected their hero to win, but it wasn't to be. And the crowd weren't happy. I ripped my television wires off (literally) and ran after him. He outpaced me of course.

It reminded me how a 'jobsworth' official at Lord's cricket ground had apparently refused to give him entry once, telling him to go to the far side of the ground instead. Eventually, exasperated, he pointed out to the gatekeeper who he is. *"Really? Well, it won't take you long to run around to the other gate then Mr Coe!"*

Time softens rivalries and gives perspective. Coe v Ovett. These two extraordinary runners eventually opened up about their respect for each other. The had their own characteristics. But a shared goal. At the time, to win appeared to mean everything to them.

The pursuit of winning is often made more acute by beating a rival. For some, true satisfaction comes from meeting their own standards. But others need to measure themselves against challengers and prevail.

There are athletes who can only produce their very best when needing to beat a certain individual or team. There's almost an animalistic need to be one-up on the rival. To beat or even humiliate them. Sometimes it reaches hatred.

*

This area is never more fascinating than in boxing. Because boxers usually need to feel some antipathy or aggression to their rival. Imagine repeatedly punching someone you like in the head. Do you also feel that sense of empathy when boxers hug and grip each other post-fight? It's almost unbearable to watch. Commentators will talk about respect. It's more than that. It's a shared struggle, humility, vulnerability and basic human instinct.

You can tell when it's real. Like it was for another man from Brighton, a boxer named Chris Eubank, and his equally fearsome rival from London by the name of Nigel Benn. In their early-90s prime, as part of a gripping soap opera at middleweight-level, these two English boxers were centre stage and full of bile. Behind the gloves, there was more to see. For Benn, a brutal, bruising destroyer, later a philosophical man of faith, there was despisal of Eubank.

His opponent was a complex character, ridiculed for his eccentricity and lisp. Defensive in and out of the ring. And yet brave, *so* brave, and statuesque. These two men are amongst my favourite sportsmen. Their intrigue never dims. Benn used to try and intimidate me when I interviewed him, and sometimes succeeded. *"Two questions and that's it."* I didn't risk a third. He was menacing, no matter how tough you think you are. In retirement, Benn developed a strong Christian faith. Listening to him look back at the man he was, and had to be, talking to the subtly brilliant Fern Britton in a BBC interview, was deeply moving. There's always more to a boxer.

Eubank brought a lot of negative attention on himself and was vilified by some, but I wanted to see beyond the caricature. A brilliant craftsman in the ring. A proud man fighting for survival. Someone who wanted to be accepted as not just smart, but fiercely so. It's not a crime to want to better yourself, he just went about it in an eccentric manner.

When a documentary maker refused to get in the boxing ring with him, it said far more to me than the script did. Did he think Eubank was going to kill him? No, he refused to enter Eubank's environment to try and understand him. Outside of the ring it was easy to patronise him. Eubank wore a monocle, strutted like a cartoon cat and wound people up with attention-seeking stunts. Such as driving through his hometown in a giant truck, clogging up the streets. Somehow this didn't interest me. Because in the ring his bravery was something to *really* notice.

The two Benn v Eubank fights were seismic events. At a time when the British people had only four television channels to choose from, prime time on Saturday nights, it gave ITV an audience of 17 million viewers.

You may feel slightly ashamed watching such brutality - I've hardly watched boxing for years. Yet it was electric, raw and real. For a teenage boy it energised you, it fizzed. Benn's relentless brutality, countered by the brave Eubank, who beat Benn in the first fight and drew in the other.

Did Eubank recover from the terrible brain injuries inflicted on an opponent in one of his fights? I doubt it. Maybe it stopped him from the necessary flurry of blows needed against the brilliant Irish boxer Steve Collins, whose victory was greeted with glee by Eubank's many detractors.

Eubank's son Chris Junior followed him into boxing, also at a height level. Watching him verbally spar with him on the TV programme 'Celebrity Gogglebox', still seeking acceptance for his verbal dexterity and insight, quietly moves me. Look behind that caricature and see the man. We can be one-dimensional when we look at sport. These people are not cartoon characters, this is not the movies. These humans are a punch away from losing their reputation, and one punch from losing their lives.

Boxers as well matched as Benn and Eubank couldn't be separated by some judges. But sometimes who wins, and who loses, has an inevitability.

The biggest character in British boxing at the time was literally a heavyweight. Frank Bruno. So popular he could walk onto any TV variety programme and the crowd would clap and coo. Everyone's favourite gentle giant. Though that's not always great for a boxer, the gentle bit. And he had a reputation as a loveable *loser*. In 1989 when he nearly beat Mike Tyson in Vegas by catching him out suddenly, the way Buster Douglas successfully did, the excitement was off the scale. The world was a very different place when Tyson and Bruno had a rematch in Vegas, 1996. I was there.

Bruno's chances were talked up by most of us. Tyson had been in jail and was reckoned to have lost his edge. He was jailed for rape. A rapist, centre stage. Horribly, notoriety and heinous crimes add to hype and ticket sales. The promoter Don King was in his element at the MGM Grand venue. The hype was off the scale as King waxed lyrical about how pigeons would fly from London and circle Frank Bruno sat beside King looking embarrassed, while Tyson was surrounded by an entourage, including a prominent cheerleader named *Crocodile*. I interviewed Tyson after the fight in a car park and he brought this entourage. I couldn't get my head around his thinking. As if he needed a gang to answer a few questions from me.

Tyson beat Bruno in the third round. I knew this would happen, not because of my boxing analysis, but because sometimes the identity of a winner reveals itself before the contest. This was no Coe v Ovett or Benn v Eubank, rivalries that are too close to call. On a giant screen we saw Bruno repeatedly cross himself as he made his way to the ring. Bruno had lost his nerve, remembered the fear, remembered what Tyson was capable of. It happens in this unforgiving sport. There was a wad of money to cushion the fall. But for a boxer, winning isn't usually a luxury. It's a necessity. And even a winner can end up battered. Bruno, lest we forget, won far more fights than he lost, was a world champion, and remains loved by generations of the British public.

*

In other sports, there are times when the most aesthetically pleasing of competitors have to fight with every drop of energy they have. Think of Roger Federer v Rafael Nadal. Tennis is lucky to have had two such titanic figures. The contrasting styles adding to the spectacle and excitement.

Federer universally seen as a man with a cool, elegant demeanour. You couldn't imagine him swearing at somebody jumping a queue. Wielding his racquet like Shakespeare, producing a final flourish with his quill. All's well that ends well for him, usually. Nadal all rippling muscles and beach volleyball vibe, addressing the ball as if ready to dispatch it into another galaxy, and yet usually landing with laser precision on the opposite side of the net.

'Peak' Federer v Nadal felt like it came in 2008 with an unforgettable five-set final at Wimbledon, won by Nadal despite clay being his preferred surface, and Federer oozing quality on grass. I was giddy with relief. If the final had not been completed before darkness set in that day, I would have been in charge of providing a location for covering the match for an international news channel the next day. You may be aware that around Wimbledon, this can be an extremely challenging task.

Despite his dignity in defeat, there was no way Federer could accept this as 'Nadal's turn'. In defeat he was polite, articulate, but hurting. When you've spent two weeks playing imperiously on the manicured lawns, then battled for hours against your closest rival, you don't take kindly to a narrow defeat. Champions are all about the win. They don't shrug their shoulders when their rival is holding up the trophy.

Contrasting characters and styles, coupled with a desire to be the number one produces sport that is so good it demands your attention. Both Steffi Graf and Monica Seles were outstanding champions. But against each other, it felt unmissable. How I loved their rivalry in the 90s. There was a point where they both appeared to be lifting each other to new peaks, infinitely more entertaining than what was being served up by the big-serving tennis machines of that era.

This compelling rivalry led to a horrific intervention. Seles was stabbed between the shoulder blades at an event in Hamburg by a deranged 'fan' of Graf, who couldn't bear the German player losing. She recovered from her injury, but was out of tennis for two years, and was never quite the same on the court afterwards. So desperately cruel. The young woman who'd been taught to play in a distinctively kooky manner had illuminated the sport, and now had to deal with the physical and psychological impact of this crime.

Pushy 'tennis dads' can be a big problem in the sport, but the story of Seles appears to be different. Her father was a cartoonist, who drew pictures to make tennis more fun. It helped develop a style where she played two-handed on two sides. I can still see it now. That effort into each shot, punched with both hands. She was so, so good to watch. She felt larger than life. I wish I heard her name mentioned more when we talk about the great players.

Sports fans often pick a player to cheer. We sometimes turn it into good versus bad, hero against villain, and ultimately there is a winner and a loser. But with Seles versus Graf it was win-win. Or lose-lose! Because I really liked Steffi Graf too. Graf was a forerunner to Federer, always keeping her cool under intense pressure. There was so much grace about her movement, suddenly producing a devastating shot, ponytail bouncing up and down. Another point won, another match won.

The clash of styles when Graf played Seles was mesmerising, absorbing. Publicly there was respect. But in the heat of competition, they would not have given each other the fluff from an old tennis ball. You see it in Serena Williams now, the look of absolute focus. Champion's focus. Win, win, win. Like Tiger Woods, or Lewis Hamilton, or Michael Schumacher in their day. Serial winners.

The 'serial winner's serial winner' can only be Michael Jordan. This was already known by basketball fans. And most sports fans. And now millions of people who only watched a documentary on hoops because they were in a lockdown. The Netflix documentary series *The Last Dance* was about the almost pathological need to win. To be King of the Hill. Top of the Heap.

How many times in did we see Jordan sit, holding a tablet, being shown quotes from other contributors that challenged his authority, that somehow didn't sit right in his kingdom. How many times did a glacial, disapproving, combative look take over his face?

His recollection of his incredible six titles with Chicago Bulls in the 90s, was of a good team, that he pushed to greatness. Relentlessly finding a way to win and prove he is the greatest basketball player of all time.

What's intriguing is his suspicion of opponents, bordering on affront, who are perceived to have matched or bettered him. But never completely. Always *temporarily*.

'King Jordan' gave his royal seal of approval to several of his adversaries, and some of his team-mates. But they were exceptions. This was a tale of impeccable standards. To some it's tough love, to some it's borderline bullying. This was a tale of a winner. The indefatigability of Jordan was coursing through the veins of Coe and Ovett, morning after morning, on the moors, on the pebbles.

Winning is everything, second is nowhere? That's not the whole story. Some of the most celebrated and loved teams in sports history are technically, *losers*...

Chapter 6: HOW YOU LOSE

What can a *moral victory* ever be worth? Depends what memories you create.

There are few greater honours than lighting an Olympic flame. In Rio in 2016, the man with the torch in his hand and the eyes of the world upon him was a Brazilian named Vanderlei de Lima.

Brazil is celebrated for having the most success in the world's favourite sport, football. Despite much speculation, the torch in the famous *Maracanã* stadium wasn't lit by a famous *footballer*. The torch ended up in de Lima's grasp.

De Lima deserved to win gold in the historic marathon in Athens in 2004. He *should* have, but he didn't. The statistical record of the race shows de Lima finished third and won a bronze medal. The statistical record of the race doesn't explain the extraordinary reason de Lima didn't cross the line first.

Put yourself in his running shoes. He starts as a cross-country runner, representing his country at two World Championships, eventually winning his national championship. He makes a transition to marathon running that wasn't planned, but it suits him, and he wins a prestigious event in Tokyo before competing in his first Olympics, Atlanta 1996. He finishes in 47th place.

De Lima doesn't actually get to compete in another Olympics for eight years. By which time he is 35-years old. This might be his last chance. And of all places the Games are in Athens, hosts of the first modern Olympics in 1896. The 2004 is an event of huge significance and prestige.

After 22 of the 26 miles de Lima is leading. And looking strong. He is leading by 25 seconds, quite a gap when there's no sign of tiring. He can dream of entering the stadium and receiving his ovation from the crowd.

Suddenly out of nowhere, a saboteur. He grabs de Lima so forcefully that he is pushed a few metres to the roadside and into a line of spectators. The assailant holds on to him. De Lima is shocked and cannot free himself immediately. A spectator helps him free. He is safe, unharmed, but the momentum, the rhythm has gone. Crucial time has elapsed. And he cannot recover. The saboteur is notorious, a former priest from Ireland, who has form for such intrusion into major events. He seeks attention. He is not worthy of any more attention than to state what he actually did on that day.

Not one, but two runners pass de Lima. Sport is unpredictable, it's not an exact science, so it's possible they would have caught him anyway. But there had been no sign of this before the incident. Could de Lima still win? Miracles happen. But it didn't look like one would happen here. The men ahead of him now are Stefano Baldini of Italy and Meb Keflezighi of the USA.

What would you do? Keep going? Keep fighting? Finish strongly? Would you be bitter, haunted, angry?

De Lima's response came naturally, just like his running ability. He battled and pushed and did not drop his head when his opponents passed him. Baldini took the gold medal, and de Lima was the *third* man to enter the stadium. The crowd's response was louder and warmer than if he had entered the arena first, as he should have done. This was special, unique. He did not look distressed, quite the opposite. He even blew some kisses to the crowd, zig-zagging playfully along the track before crossing the line. On the podium, on the *third* highest level, his kissed his bronze medal and waved some more to the crowd.

Brazil have a formidable volleyball team, the sport is hugely popular in the country, and a player named Emanuel Rego offered de Lima his gold medal: *"I can't accept Emanuel's medal,"* said de Lima. *"I'm happy with mine. It's bronze but it means gold."*

Acceptance. De Lima taught us a lesson.

I was in Rio 12 years later when he made his way up to light the Olympic flame, still with the purposeful strides of a marathon runner, the crowd and a worldwide audience showing their appreciation for his grace and his dignity. De Lima is as celebrated as any marathon *winner* in history, in fact more so. He was awarded the *Pierre de Coubertin* medal to reward the noble spirit he had shown, a rare and special award named after the founder of the *International Olympic Committee,* the man responsible for the oft-used idiom: "The important thing is not to win, but to take part."

The Brazilian public voted him as athlete of the year. It is not always the colour of the medal that counts, it's not always about winning. Sometimes the story means more.

I also reported on the 2014 Football World Cup, as Brazil tried to finally win the trophy in front of their own people. They felt it was their destiny, hope hung in the air. It was tangible. The game really does mean so much to them. But it was not to be. They have *still* never done it in front of the Brazilian public. To make it worse, that night, they were humiliated in a 7-1 semi-final defeat against Germany. And the rain lashed down, as if washing away the hopes, and even dousing the anger.

The pain of defeat is not to be underestimated, and I'm taken by the account of Alcides Ghiggia, the Uruguayan whose two goals stopped Brazil winning the other World Cup they hosted, in 1950 in Rio. It deprived a nation, including an extraordinary crowd of an estimated 200,000 crammed into the Maracanã Stadium, of a desperate need to finally win something, to show they were *worth* something. So disturbing was the sobbing of Brazilians when they lost, that Ghiggia said he didn't actually *enjoy* the achievement of winning the World Cup, with his unexpected and historic pair of goals.

Outside of their own country, Brazil's footballers have won the World Cup an unequalled five times. But they are not judged merely as winners or losers. They are renowned, revered, celebrated, for flair. I would argue it means more. Reputation over silverware.

There have been times when there is no greater sight in football than a Brazilian national team in full flow, caressing the ball, liquid movement in the famous yellow shirts. And not necessarily winning. I'm pleased that when I asked Brazilians to name their favourite-ever team, most of them mentioned the 1982 team that *failed* to triumph. Even younger generations attach a 'heart eyes emoji' when they mention that team.

Technically, you could call the 1982 team 'losers', because they failed to reach the semi-finals, beaten 3-2 in Seville by Italy. Paolo Rossi scored all three goals for Italy, like a ruthless hitman, in one of the finest games of football ever played. Until that point, the Brazil team had been magical *and* successful.

In that resplendent Spanish summer, in packed stadiums, on pitches with 'ticker tape' attractively scattered on pitches and colourful crowds, the Brazil team sparkled. Effervescence, vibrancy, charisma. Think of a wonderful, precious childhood memory. To many of us, this Brazil team were that. I don't even think of it as sport. It was life-enhancing, it was magic. I get goosebumps, shivers. I punch the air when I see the footage. I smile when I think of it. I want to run in my garden, smash a ball against a tree and scream the name of one of the players. Then celebrate. There is life in these memories. We cherish them.

The great Pelé had retired, but the character of the team is encapsulated by the four players in their 'midfield', all known by the Brazilian custom of one-word nicknames.

The best of the four was Zico, who looked like a cool lead guitarist, and had it all. Fast, powerful, creating and scoring beautiful goals. Dark hair, yellow shirt, blue shorts, white socks, he looked amazing. They all did.

Alongside him, and similar in look to Zico was Eder. Sometimes you distinguished them by gait. Eder's best goal came against Russia, flicking the ball in the air and lashing it high into the net from long distance with his left foot.

The third man was Falcao, who looked more like Simon Garfunkel than a lead guitarist in a rock band. Tightly curled hair and earnest expression – until his moment of euphoria. A famous goal in that match against Italy with a gloriously spontaneous eruption of hand waving joy.

The quartet was completed by my favourite, Socrates, the captain. If anybody knew winning isn't everything, football isn't everything, it is this unique character. Tall, wiry and statuesque, a chain smoker, wearing his white socks high making his legs seem even longer, with a beard and a headband. Another man who could front a rock band. Maybe the four of them should have formed one.

Politically active with a medical degree, he was a deeply philosophical man – no irony intended. Socrates challenged the way his country was run and challenged the clubs he played for. Such as Sport Club Corinthians Paulista, better known simply as Corinthians, founded in Brazil by an Englishman in the early 20th century. The famous *'Corinthian Spirit',* the sense of fair play, was not quite evident enough for the strong will of Socrates. He wasn't a man to be pushed around by anybody, and to him, the collective was what was important. "There's more to life than football," he once said. "My political victories are far more important than my victories as a professional player."

Like Eder, Socrates also scored with an exquisite long-range shot in that early match against Russia. If footage could fade from YouTube clicks, this would no longer exist. But it is his goal against Italy, that match in Seville again, that is most celebrated. His intelligence and teamwork forging a path and then a clever angled low shot past the goalkeeper.

If you think of the most colourful, visually stimulating movie from a by-gone era, then this is football's equivalent. It is *'La La Land',* it is glorious sunshine, a vibrant shimmering kaleidoscope, and a lead character of star quality triumphing in a glorious scene.

This Brazil team and its vast array of admirers were denied their perfect movie ending. But if they *had* won, would Socrates have settled for 'living off the memories' in a backstreet café, in the type of functional plain blue jumper a fisherman would wear at work, smoking and drinking? I doubt it. Instead, he imparted philosophy, showing as many have how sport is allegory for life.

Asked who is the best player in history was Socrates would scoff. "Grow up!" he would scold. "*I'm* the best, no *I'm* the best" he would sarcastically mimic before asserting: "Football is a *team* game".

Socrates died at the age of 57. I wish we could have had him airlifted into a Premier league television pundit panel in the UK, with a translator, putting pins into the inflated egos around him. If asked if a jar is 'half empty or half full', Socrates would ask what the jar is made of.

Unlike Vanderlei de Lima, Socrates and Brazil's 'Class of 82' didn't even win a medal. But they do have a place in the hearts of their people, and far beyond Brazil. As do the specialists in losing big games. The Netherlands.

So good were the Dutch team of the 1970s, that they re-imagined football. I'm not sure it was even football. It was art. A vision in orange. Glowing, enchanting us. The black numbers on their shirts so stylish, so chic, they add to the legend. And my theory is that they are particularly celebrated because they *didn't* win. In Britain particularly, there is a lot of love for a dashing loser. But the Netherlands team of the 70s are on a level of their own. Creatives, not pragmatists.

It's 1974. And Netherlands are illuminating a World Cup in what was then *West* Germany, with an intriguing mix of teams. The tournament included a match between West and East Germany, with all the security and political issues that brought. There was also a famously bizarre moment when Zaire player Mwepu Ilunga 'misunderstood the rules' and smashed the ball into the crowd. It was Brazil's 'free-kick'. But he didn't care. He was having it. I've seen it replayed dozens of times and it's still funny. Zaire lost all three games. So did Haiti. Yes, Haiti. For the first and only time they have played in a World Cup. They scored the first goal in their match against Italy, before eventually losing by three goals to one. There was nothing straightforward about this World Cup or the teams involved.

The match ball, like the Dutch shirts, was a visual treat, with distinctive black panels, a masterpiece. And an orange tide swept the Netherlands to the final. Their coach Rinus Michels was profoundly influential with his deployment of a style in which an any outfield player can theoretically take over the role of any other player in the team. He had developed it at Ajax Amsterdam, the newsreader's nightmare team. Pronounced *'Eye-ax'* but looking like it should be *'Eh-Jax'*.

The best player and captain for Ajax and Netherlands was Johan Cruyff, quirkily adorned with the number 14 at a time when teams were numbered 1-11. He liked to be different. Cruyff could pop up anywhere, gliding across the pitch, unlocking doors with his passing movement, seemingly shape-shifting, and so innovative he came up with his own move, *'The Cruyff Turn'*, feigning to move one way backwards before turning the other way while dragging the ball back through his own legs.

Millions tried this and fell over in school playgrounds. Sweden's Jan Olsson has the infamy of the man being humiliated by this in the World Cup, left searching for Cruyff and the ball like a drunk seeking his bearings at closing time of *'Oktoberfest'*.

The final was played at the Olympic Stadium in Munich. The hosts West Germany had broadly adhered to their reputation for efficiency, solid and unspectacular. Defeat against East Germany in Hamburg had been a nasty shock for them, as a team and a nation, but in the context of the tournament it was an isolated setback, and they were able to recover.

By contrast the Netherlands had been imperious in their progress, delightful to watch, the neutral's sweethearts. Brazil, Argentina and East Germany amongst their victims, only Sweden had held them to a draw despite Cruyff torturing their players with his swivelling hips.

The referee was an Englishman, Jack Taylor, a butcher by trade and sporting impressive lamp chop sideburns. And he found himself centre stage by awarding a penalty after less than a minute of play. West Germany hadn't touched the ball and couldn't get near it. Were they about to be ripped apart, humiliated in front of their own people and the watching world?

Another man named Johan, Neeskens, scored the penalty, and for 20 minutes *'The Oranje',* as they were often referred to, toyed with the hosts. But they forgot to score again. West Germany equalised, and in the second half they scored the winning goal. It is what West German national football teams used to do, it's who they were. Winners.

I'm sure many Germans old enough to remember the tournament remember it fondly. But outside of the country, there was grudging acceptance. 'The crowd went mild'. Whereas *'The Oranje'* and Cruyff are still celebrated.

The Netherlands provided more great memories in the next World Cup four years later, in Argentina in 1978. This time without Cruyff, who at the time was said to feel unsafe to travel in an unstable country ruled by a military junta. He subsequently said a kidnap attempt involving his family in Barcelona was the reason. Whatever caused his absence, the Cruyff shaped hole was noticed all the way through the tournament.

The Dutch reached the final without him but were beaten by the hosts again. On a pitch almost completely white with the 'ticker tape' that decorated football of that era, the Dutch scored first again. But Argentina equalised and scored twice more in extra time to win their first World Cup. The future always looked bright for 'The Oranje' but the trophy never came.

Cruyff went on to deploy his football philosophy at the prestigious Spanish club FC Barcelona, as a player then manager. It evolved to what is called *Tiki-taka*. Players constantly passing and moving. Pass, pass, pass. Pass them 'to death'. And then Barcelona became the most successful club team in the world. Managers including the highly successful Pep Guardiola, took the style forward. The evolution of football. History matters.

The Netherlands are still waiting to win a World Cup, beaten in the 2010 final by the Spanish national team who were still playing a version of Cruyff's football. But there's always more to a story than winners and losers. Can failure ever be glorious? Is second nowhere, or can it be somewhere? How about third place or worse? Do we forget the losers?

Cruyff, Socrates, de Lima. On the biggest stage, they didn't win. They are celebrated, not for their victories, but for their ideals, their integrity and the class they showed.

Chapter 7: A QUIET CORONATION

When 63-year-old Claudio Ranieri arrived in Leicester in July 2015 there was no fanfare. Nobody was doubting he was an experienced, likeable manager who could win football matches. But had he won *enough* football matches?

A man who landed job after job, but still with much to prove. Naples, Florence, Valencia, Madrid, London, Parma, Turin, Rome, Milan, Monaco. Over a dozen clubs, a few domestic cup victories, but prestigious league titles were missing from his CV. *Will you still hire me, will you still fire me, when I'm 64?*

Ranieri's last job before Leicester had ended nine months earlier, 'sacked' as the manager of the national team of Greece. Not one of football's superpowers, though they surprisingly became champions of Europe in 2004, something not achieved by many higher ranked nations, including England. The defeat that ended his short time in charge of Greece came against the Faroe Islands, whose population is barely more than 50,000.

The Hellenic Football Association President Giorgos Sarris took full responsibility for an "unfortunate choice of coach". Claudio himself said he "had no words to explain what happened." It was a result to be ridiculed, and Claudio's stock could not have been lower. And yet.

Leicester had spun the proverbial *'managerial merry-go-round'*. Nobody in financial management, or human resources, or even fairgrounds, is described as being on a managerial merry-go-round. But in football the term is ubiquitous. Football reporters use the term like it's *not* daft, often accompanied by a knowing nod. And when the roundabout stopped, Claudio jumped off in Leicester.

In the Premier League, English football club ownership had reached Thailand. Leicester City FC's owner was Vichai Srivaddhanaprabha, better known as 'Khun Vichai', a billionaire businessman who owned '*King Power,*' a powerful business dealing in 'duty-free' shopping. In 1997, Khun

Vichai watched the English League Cup Final between Leicester City and Middlesbrough at Wembley Stadium. I was there and reported on Leicester winning. They won the trophy again three years later. These felt like good times for them. But they still weren't regarded as one of England's *elite* teams.

In August 2010 Khun Vichai bought Leicester City FC and installed himself as chairman the following year. In a familiar scenario in English football, Leicester themselves moved from their home, a ground named Filbert Street, to a new sponsored stadium in 2002. When Khun Vichai arrived, he renamed the stadium after his business empire, duly calling it *The King Power Stadium*. Do you believe in coincidences? At that time, King Richard III's bones still lay undiscovered beneath Leicester.

In 131 years, the club that started as *Leicester Fosse* had won a few trophies, but they weren't 'big hitters'. There are clubs that can win major trophies, and clubs who 'make up the numbers'. For Leicester City FC, like so many clubs, the priority was staying in the Premier League. They had slipped down to the third tier of the English league, without the prestige and money. The merest threat of what they call 'the dreaded R word', *relegation*, strikes fear in to club executives, managers and fans at the best of times.

A manager named Nigel, respected for his organisation of teams but sometimes questioned over a spiky relationship with the media, had kept Leicester in the Premier League, the golden tip of the league pyramid. But the football club's survival at the highest levels was highly unlikely when King Richard's body was taken through the streets of the city in March 2015.
Leicester were stuck at the bottom of the Premier League table, 20th position out of 20, for 140 days. Nigel's coat was 'on the shaky peg'.

Suddenly, the football aspect of Leicester's strange magic started to work. With a lot of determination, and a change of luck, the wins started to come, and kept coming. Somehow, to the disbelief of the experts and indeed their own fans, they stayed up in the Premier League. This was treated as a 'minor miracle'. The people of Leicester *'Ain't seen nothing yet'*!

Despite overseeing an act of unlikely escapology, Nigel was sacked.

Football works like that. Back on the managerial merry-go-round for him. But dig beneath, like the archaeologists of Leicester University, and there were foundations that had been built by Nigel and his coaching staff. From journeymen, he had started to build a very decent team.

In goal was their most obvious asset. You couldn't miss Kasper. Tall, blond and statuesque, he has the presence and look of a Viking, with the temperament of a gentle giant. Early in his career, he was always compared to his father Peter, one of the greatest goalkeepers in history for Manchester United and Denmark. But he was to create his own history, while showing admirable human qualities on and off the pitch.

In defence Danny, a reject from Manchester United who eventually showed them what they had let go. Christian, the Austrian joker. His surname Fuchs got its share of laughs. Then it became clear just how good he actually was. Robert, looking like he'd been carved from granite. Reliable and effective. The line of four was led by the captain Wes, statuesque but rarely heralded, the 'wrong side of thirty' as they sometimes say about experienced footballers. These weren't stars. These weren't players whose names were written across the back of football shirts bought by fans. But unmistakably, these defenders 'had *each other's* backs'.

In front of the defence in 'midfield', another Danny who had failed to make it at United. Another one who then found his feet and then felt he could walk on water. Alongside him, a small man who made a big impact on world football over a decade, very few footballers achieved more for clubs and country. A French worker bee named N'Golo. Tiny and unflashy, 168 centimetres tall, 'humble' as well as bumble. Busy, busy, busy.

On the 'wings', providing ammunition for the goal scorers, was Marc, tirelessly up and down-like a steam train and in the best form of his career. And Riyad from Algeria, an extraordinary talent playing for the 'ordinary boys'.

In attack - often Shinji, a Japanese player who wasn't a headline-maker, but a hidden story. A 'handful' for the opposition. As was Leonardo from Argentina when he made the team. Andy would come in occasionally. Jeffrey, Ritchie, Nathan, Demarai. They were all contributing. Every one of them contributing something positive to the team when called upon.

The focal point, the developing sensation, was the striker Jamie. He arrived at Leicester City after playing for Stocksbridge Park Steels, Halifax Town and Fleetwood Town. Respectfully, these three clubs aren't quite to football what *The Three Tenors* are to singing, they are the equivalent of 'end of the pier warblers'. But they are precious clubs. For the community and the English football pyramid.

It was refreshing to see a Premier League club using a player who hadn't come through the youth teams of the big establishments. A 'non-league player', a 'boy from nowhere'. Jamie had been with Leicester City for a few years and not made a significant impact. He, and the club, raised modest expectations at the time. When the season started in August, Leicester City were 5,000-1 outsiders to win the Premier League with bookmakers.

Claudio's fall from grace in Greece meant he wasn't given the respect and attention his appointment merited. So why did Khun Vichai and the Leicester City board hire him? Did they really have any idea it would be one of the most inspired appointments in the history of sport?! Khun Vichai clearly believed in magic. He insisted that in Claudio, they had one of the world's elite managers.

The Italian, ever polite, gracious and warm, offered thanks to "The owner, his son and the executives of the club for the opportunity they are giving me.". It felt typical of the weird world of football that somebody could fail so emphatically and walk into the next job within days. But this was a chance Claudio was ready to take, and make the world take notice.

On August 8, 2015, the Premier League season began, to be played through to the following May, with television rights sold in over a hundred countries. 20 teams, playing 38 games, 19 in their home stadiums, 19 away. You could split the teams into two unofficial categories. Those perceived to have any chance of winning the title - Chelsea, Liverpool, Arsenal, Tottenham and the two from Manchester. And those perceived to have no chance at all, including Leicester City, with their 5,000-1 odds.

Hindsight will show there were tiny clues to the credulity-stretching events of the next nine months. But they were so tiny that nobody spotted them or bothered looking. The intrepid Leicester University archaeologists would not have wasted their time investigating Leicester's chances. A professional football pundit would have risked ridicule to even dare suggest Leicester might be eventual challengers. But on that opening day of the new season, Saturday, August 8, 2015, Claudio Ranieri's team beat Sunderland 4-2 in their King Power Stadium in front of 32,242 fans.

Of quiet significance were goals scored by Riyad and Jamie, the two most eye-catching players. Jamie was to become a talismanic figure. With a chin like Bruce Forsyth and the sudden burst of speed you might expect from a greyhound. He was ruthless with a chance to score.

Jamie scored again in the fourth game at Bournemouth, to give his team a 1-1 draw. And it was not until the seventh game that Leicester were defeated, getting their backsides kicked. Losing by five goals to two against Arsenal. In their own stadium. So that was that then? Normality resumed in the Premier League? The more money, the more power and the more chance of success, so it felt like only 'The Lucky Few' know what it feels like to be at the pinnacle, the summit.

The aim for a club like Leicester is survival. To simply be part of the league. To safeguard what they have. An apparently joyless scenario, but despite their outward moaning, football fans can be surprisingly forgiving of the reality. And return for more. Some even perversely enjoy the bad times. I know Manchester City fans who preferred their mediocrity before success came from the oil money. Because the little victories tasted sweeter.

But win the league? No way. In that respect Leicester were *Charlie Buckets.* The also-rans expected to stay with the faces pressed at the window of the sweet shop. Only in fiction does the outsider get a golden ticket to the chocolate factory.

The magical place, the forbidden place, is at the very *tip* of the football pyramid.

Chapter 8: THE TIP OF THE PYRAMID

Once upon a time there was a pyramid.

Every stone of the pyramid contained hope. Every stone mattered.

The stones at the bottom mattered less to the masses.

The stones at the top of the pyramid were seen as the special ones. These stones were illuminated, they were celebrated. The people loved them.

At the top of the pyramid there were once 22 stones. These stones had a name for many decades: 'The First Division'.

For many decades the pyramid had stood proud and dignified. Simple and understated. But late in the 20th century, there was growing malcontent.

Why wasn't the pyramid making more money? Why weren't the shiny expensive stones at the top getting more exposure?

So, in the year 1992 Anno Domini, a group of agitators came together to push for a 'rebrand' of the pyramid. And succeeded.

No longer would there be an unsightly 22 stones. Instead, there would be a more palatable 20. There would be MORE exposure, MORE money, MORE hype and Sundays could now be called 'Super Sundays'.

The tip of the pyramid would now be called *The Premier League*, and football fans around the globe would be enthralled. They would collectively pay billions to watch the action.

The English football pyramid, a wonderful thing with many hundreds of football clubs large and small, now had a jewel at the top. The Premier League was not just a league, it was now a slick, successful business.

Nations, continents, devoured it on television. Teams became brands. Manchester United, Arsenal, Liverpool, Chelsea were celebrated far and wide. Stars were signed, managers became soap opera characters, and the money flowed in from the television rights, sponsorship and substantial ticket prices.

Success sure did feel as sweet as sugar, more successful than the executives dared hope. Over three decades the growth never stopped, the bubble never burst. The money continued to flow.

Where once English football clubs were owned by local businessmen 'made good', now the mega-wealthy from foreign lands wanted one of the shiny stones of the pyramid.

In came the oligarchs. In came unthinkable riches from the Middle East, consortiums, bringing credibility and soft power.

Players' wallets were being inflated as if pumped by foot. Agents had never had it so good, there were vast fortunes to be made from moving players around.

And the hyperbole was reaching new heights, or depths, depending on how much football you were prepared to consume: *"Monday Night Football comes to a Thursday. Live and exclusive."*

"The Football never stops" gasped comedian David Mitchell in a television parody sketch so painfully funny and accurate you'd almost expect TV executives to notice they were being ridiculed.

The hype continued, and new studio toys and gimmicks appeared, with 'on-message' presenters to tell us how fantastic the action was. Slick or glamorous 'pitchside' reporters, depending on which gender stereotype was needed, ingratiated themselves with the managers and talked up every game.

People barely noticed a shift in status, with managers replacing players as the main stars. *José, Alex, Arsene, Harry* and co. Managers who were famous yet still needed initial letters stitched into their sports jackets to remind us!

The world's superstar players usually ended up heading to Spain, some of them to Madrid to be referred to as *'Galacticos'*, others to Barcelona, but it didn't spoil the insatiable appetite for the Premier League.

By now it was commonplace for football fans to pay subscriptions that could involve tolerating a dull game on a Monday night, because a better match was coming along on Saturday lunchtime, or a 'Super Sunday'. There were also matches on 'Terrific Tuesday' and 'Wow Wednesday'.

And still the contracts were signed, and still the money came. There was no dispute that this was the most popular league in the world. Worth hundreds of billions of dollars. An extraordinary piece of business.

The wonderful thing about a pyramid with moving stones is that everyone can dream. Who knows how far up a stone could reach?

What was becoming a problem in this 'land of milk and honey', was the very tip of the pyramid. There was only room for one club at the pinnacle. The Champions of England. There needed to be some mystery and unpredictability. Didn't there?

If you climb Everest, don't you want to get the summit? The actual peak? Only the mega-rich could sustain a challenge to become the top stone, the champions.

There wasn't enough disruption. Not enough jeopardy and surprise. The word fairy-tale was sometimes used about an unlikely rise, but did the little guy actually get to the *top* of the beanstalk?

In a league billed as the world's most competitive, only *five* separate clubs won the title in the first 24 years. Manchester United repeatedly, Manchester City when the oil money came in, Chelsea when an oligarch splashed the cash, Arsenal and Blackburn Rovers.

Blackburn's 1995 triumph was bankrolled by a local man who built a fortune in steel. But football was changing. A lot. And this was the last time an English businessman could build a formidable, successful team.

There was no hint at what Leicester City could do. Yet. Before the 'miracle of Leicester', it felt pre-determined who was *special*.

Chapter 9: SPECIAL

When you proclaim yourself "*special*" you are going to be noticed. Managers were becoming the stars in English football, but when José Mourinho held his first press conference at Chelsea Football Club, he took the concept of a celebrity manager to another level. He told the world: "Please don't call me arrogant, but I'm European champion and I think I'm a special one." The media loved it, and 'The Special One' stuck.

Charismatic, handsome, ambitious and successful, few characters in sport have broken out into the wider public consciousness than this Portuguese football manager. He has demanded attention, and got it, for two decades. Laughing, sulking, shouting, beseeching, persuading, inspiring. He created an aura, and has lived off it, perhaps too much later in his career. Jobs where the attention sometimes outweighed the success.

I'm fascinated by the interest in Mourinho. I have always tried to reach out beyond sports fans with my work, and characters who make front page headlines take on an extra significance because of their recognisability with non-sports fans.

Mourinho has enjoyed success that has been impossible to ignore, winning trophies at some of Europe's biggest clubs, including Real Madrid and Manchester United, but is talked about for much more than his tactics.

He had a modest career as a player in Portugal, getting nowhere near the top of the game. While in his early thirties, he developed his coaching at one of the major Portuguese clubs, Sporting Lisbon, under the management of Bobby Robson. Much of his work for Robson was as a translator, and this image stuck for some of his detractors, who wanted to use the humble start in the football 'hierarchy' against him.

When Mourinho got to be the main man late in the 1990s he made a strong start, and then got noticed beyond Portugal. His FC Porto team produced a big surprise, knocking Manchester United out of the Champions League in 2004. It wasn't just the achievements of his teams it was his own *performance*. When he celebrated the vital goal by running exuberantly along the side of the pitch, it became a memorable piece of sporting theatre.

His subsequent move to Chelsea could be defined by trophies and success, but asked to name one moment, most of us remember *that* press conference and *that* 'Special One' line. Perhaps only Brian Clough had exuded such star quality from the manager's dugout before him. Plenty is still written and said about Clough, who called himself '*Old big 'ead*', and most notably took unheralded Nottingham Forest to become Champions of Europe in 1979 and 1980. The film '*The Damned United*' is excellent, with Michael Sheen capturing Clough's idiosyncrasies, quick wit and charm.

'Peak José came during his successful first spell as manager of Chelsea FC in 2007, but not via a football match. He was arrested and cautioned while protecting his dog from quarantine rules. By the time he was released without charge, he had emerged heroically, playing into the English reputation as a nation of dog lovers. The story became headline news, and now he was showing a caring character to add to his appeal. There was swooning. I don't say this lightly or salaciously, there *was* swooning. It was close to '*Josémania*'.

We'd seen this unfold over the decade before when a *player* became a superstar and transcended sport. A certain David Beckham. Everything he did was noticed, talked about. And this was before the social media tsunami. I remember reporting on the 'Intercontinental Cup' in Japan in 1999 when he was still playing for Manchester United. Beckham, hair in an Alice band, made his way to take a 'corner kick', and that part of the stadium in Tokyo went crazy. There were thousands of flashes and screaming. A year earlier he had been a national hate figure in England for a petulant kick that meant he was sent off in a World Cup match against Argentina. Then he married a *Spice Girl*. The fickle nature of fame and popularity.

Now we had a forty-something manager in the spotlight. I was at the sharp end of his newsworthiness, as 'Sports Editor' for a major television news network in the UK. When Jose was sacked by Chelsea for the first time it was pandemonium. I had to dictate the coverage needs to the management for once, including deploying the channel's helicopter over

Chelsea's training ground. Though being woken by an urgent sounding producer at 3am wasn't one of my most enjoyable working experiences. I was in the office within an hour and the story took over our lives for the next couple of days.

One of things that struck me from the start is how José played the public and media like a puppeteer. The black and white interpretations of him show the pitfalls of analysing someone we don't actually *know*. Intelligent analysis of a complex man can be elusive. The ongoing claim is that he's 'great entertainment', but that distorts the reality. The public and media have always wanted José to be a little more compelling than he actually is. He's a smart football coach, but not a razor-like wit like his most charismatic forerunner Brian Clough. What we're seeing with José is the performance, sometimes to deflect attention when things don't go right on the pitch, where his style of football often places pragmatism over expression. It's his modus operandi. The theatre. The 'sizzle around the sausage' to distract us.

Mourinho has been football's chess 'Grandmaster' seeing each piece having its own job to do. But the cool demeanour could be quickly replaced by a sharp tongue. He publicly 'calls out' players who refuse to do their jobs, always a tightrope to walk when needing their trust.

Conversely, he has been adored by many players and staff. There is clearly the need to please him and seek validation of his approval. His private kindness is regularly mentioned, and clearly authentic. He showed genuine support for a journalist that attended weekly Chelsea media conferences and was absent while fighting cancer. José was clearly moved and relieved on the day the journalist returned, and accounts of his human qualities away from the spotlight are common.

As Mourinho's hair has turned from jet black to salt and pepper, to distinguished grey, our relationship with the man in the spotlight – I repeat that we do not *know* the real man - has been like the relationship with a character in a soap opera. When he entered the Premier League show the storylines were mainly positive, and he was a ratings-winner.

Back in 2004, Chelsea Football Club had been bought by a Russian oligarch, Roman Abramovich. The oligarch's arrival changed world football and was part of an emerging trend, where football clubs helped reputations. In recent years many billionaire businessmen have attained soft power, influence and acceptance through football clubs. Football clubs being bought up like toys. The global power of the Premier League, still increasing, made it a perfect status symbol.

When Abramovich bought Chelsea FC the manager he inherited was Claudio Ranieri. A man who hadn't yet revealed his *Dilly Dong Bell*. Most football fans liked him. Though there were reservations. He seemed a good manager, but a *great* one? The right man to spend Roman's considerable 'transfer money' on the right players? For that you would need the very best. Ranieri's nickname back then was *'The Tinkerman'*, and it wasn't a compliment.

He had excellent players to choose from, but his team was not settled, and he liked to make changes to the team for each match. Even his mother was, according to the man himself, questioning selections. On his use of Irish Chelsea player Damien Duff, Ranieri said to the media in his distinctive English: *"She says, why you not play Damon Doof?!"* His mother had a point. But the way Claudio carried himself made you want him to succeed. The accent, the eccentricities and foibles, they drew you in.

This is football though. It's a strange world. Those who love and comment on it become accustomed to the limited patience given to managers. Some have the lifespans of dragonflies. Claudio's days were numbered.

The pundits were savaging him and using a curiously unsubstantiated cliché liberally: *"He's lost the dressing room."* It's terminology that pundits and fans still use without a moment's thought, as if it's a final verdict, an absolute truth. But there is not much disputing Abramovich made the right move replacing him. The proof came in the success Chelsea had under the replacement manager, Mourinho. The club won five major English trophies in José's three years in charge.

The modus operandi for Abramovich, which has worked for him and filled trophy cabinets, is to rapidly fire and replace a manager who is not getting results. So Mourinho himself was sacked in 2007, and I left my bed at an ungodly hour to 'cover the story'.

Eight separate managers took charge of Chelsea before José was rehired six years later. He won the Premier League in his first year back. But the success didn't last second time around. Some of José's 'special' powers seemed to be absent and his critics started to suggest the game had moved on, and that his tactics and methods were no longer working as well.

The end of his second spell at Chelsea in 2015 finished under a cloud. There was controversy over his public criticism of medical staff, then an allegation of discrimination which ended up in court. A settlement was reached but his behaviour towards staff had come under close scrutiny. We don't know the full story behind the scenes. We do know his departure came after a run of poor football results, which we have learned is seen as unforgiveable in this 'business' of football, if not always among the fans.

When José was sacked by Manchester United in 2018, a fall softened by millions of bank notes, I described his reign as memorable for his "sullen, defensive and argumentative approach." I didn't intend to be harsh, as this was a carefully considered assessment that I standby. These weren't words thrown about under pressure in a broadcasting 'edit suite', they remain the words I would use. It was a bizarrely melancholic reign.

His achievements and aura over time protected his reputation, so the big jobs kept coming. He walked into Tottenham Hotspur in 2019 and declared himself 'The Happy One', so the media fawned over José like he was a newly-born puppy. But his modern record was questionable, and I tend to take issue with powerful male figures who dictate the tone and mood of a room.

Or the mood of a house. I like to make my *own* mind up on someone's mood, and this felt manipulative. Honestly it did. But overall, it was a relief that José's early days at Tottenham were less tense, whether or not the presence of documentary cameras played a part.

I get the sense he would take back some of the jibes he used when surrounded by microphones. Mourinho once said of Ranieri: "*He is too old to change his mentality. He's old and he hasn't won anything*". At the time, in 2008, they were rival managers at two big Italian clubs, Inter Milan and Juventus respectively. They didn't get on.

But José eventually softened and many years later publicly supported Claudio Ranieri's management. A day is a long time in football. Opinions can change in one game. Stories gain new chapters.

Sports journalists and the wider world of social media can try to make a person's actions fit their reputation and billing. One-dimensional takes. People are heroes or villains. Good or bad. But José Mourinho, like most of us, is a complex character. And when I've seen him try to manipulate a room, set the tone, or publicly criticise a player whose confidence is low, it's never been my job to accept that and be obsequious. It's surely sensible to put a public demeanour through a careful 'filter' – I consider that my responsibility as a journalist reporting the story.

It feels important to make a distinction between what I or anyone else feels about José Mourinho 'the man', and the *José Mourinho Show*. He clearly has qualities that people privately appreciate. But when he speaks publicly, I listen, and then I put it through that filter. I use my brain. He'd respect that wouldn't he?

Who is *special*, and who gets to decide it? It should not be predetermined, or stated, or constant, or the preserve of the lucky few. We all have special qualities. And if we don't have sustained success, we can still have our time, our day. What's truly special is seeing someone in authority making people feel better about themselves.

In their own ways and with their own methods, José and Claudio have helped others to improve themselves. José has achieved success through his methods, but Claudio had the power of *The Dilly Dong Bell*.

Chapter 10: LEADER

In football, in sport, in offices, in life, there are some leaders who manoeuvre themselves into power but don't know how to lead. Their ambition far outstrips their leadership qualities, which can be non-existent in some cases.

For every Reg Hayter, an undisputed boss, there are many agitators below, scrambling to assert themselves. In football clubs, in offices, it has never been surprising when bosses, predominantly male bosses, try to show how tough they are. I fear many of you will have experienced and recognised this.

Some footballers conduct themselves as 'hardmen' in the safety of the 'football bubble'. Showing aggression that would be unlawful on the streets. And some use intimidation amongst office desks. From outright hostility to subtle passive-aggression We are getting closer to a time such explicit bullying behaviour in office environments will look so strange, so outdated, that the perpetrators may be more exposed. I've seen a lot of it, most of us have, and like 'playground bullying' it never worked on me.

Speaking loudly over the top of colleagues in a baritone voice, making the weaker feel uneasy to reinforce status, this is commonplace behaviour, but is it acceptable? A counter-intimidating aura can act as an antidote, but you shouldn't need to have to use it. Nobody needs trouble, nobody needs drama, and when you have to 'take people down' it's rarely pretty. A calm dismantling of the invariably thin sheen of swagger has sometimes been the only option.

I saw new generations of young men in newsrooms, whose self-assured demeanour was used as a weapon. There is nothing wrong with being middle class and well educated, quite the opposite. But confidence should never usurp *competence*. I've seen them copy the bravado and the language of the newsroom and the meeting room. One familiar line was *"It's kicked off,"* when referring not to football, but to violence. Nothing wrong with that. But It was too often accompanied by a flippant smile. Some of these young guys had clearly never been exposed to real violence, or spent much time covering football hooliganism, which sadly became a speciality of mine. The insouciance over the reality, reminding me of smug politicians, could be unsettling.

Many would go on to be leaders. In name only. The johnny-on-the-spot who drifts into a managerial role. I saw it, heard it, challenged it. I hope and trust the poisonous office environment, which so many millions experience, will evolve because of pandemic working changes. It crossed my mind that it's not my place to call it out. But after 30 years of it, why *not* me?

Real leadership is about empowering people. Having the empathy and self-assurance to enable others to trust you and flourish. *Actually* having their backs, not suggesting you have. And not being cagey. The sudden email silence, or silence across the desk and withholding of information. The lack of reassurance. It says everything about them and nothing about you.

Throughout the history of football, of sport, much success has come from hard-line leadership. The perpetrators wouldn't have it any other way. And those who played for these uncompromising bosses usually say it brought the best from them. But it feels 'old hat'. It feels like the tradition of a football team getting their suits from Burtons for the FA Cup Final, or smoking in pubs. Some things need to be left in the past. There's a time and a place for 'tough love'.

Where does tough love end and bullying begin? Was there an essence of bully about the uncompromising Brian Clough? Would anyone want to change him though? Would he have been successful without it? Do such leaders have 'the best interests of their players at heart'. Usually. And the best interests of society too? Often yes. Clough had a wonderful social conscience. But his methods probably belong to another era.

The man who has redefined how to lead in sport is Jürgen Klopp, the man from *The Black Forest* who rejuvenated Liverpool. To think for a moment he's a soft touch because of his effervescent smile would be ludicrous. Look at the steel behind the smile? Imagine letting the man down? Imagine playing for him, how that would feel. That energy, that encouragement, that belief in you. And someone who understands the need to let people thrive individually and collectively, for the greater good. He has a shrewd tactical brain, but so much of the success he's had is to stand back and let others do their thing. Building a formidable team around them. Then if a decision needs to be made, if he needs to get tough, he will, he does.

*

Football is not the sport in which the captain, the leader on the field, needs to have the biggest influence. That would be cricket. Cricket is more like life than anything I've experienced except life itself. The bell rings and the day starts, events unfold. Can you see the life within? Can you hear the bell? 'Proper' cricket, Test cricket embodies the processes and the psychology, the shifting fortunes, the fortitude required. And lends itself to deeper exploration.

The captain in cricket is all things to all men or women. He or she can be instrumental in picking the team, analysing the weather, the pitch, being a confidante, a union official, a diplomat, friend, boss, colleague, batting partner, decision-maker, tactician, strategist. And then take the blame for defeat. It is often said that a captain in football is a token gesture, a ceremonial armband, but in cricket the leadership role on the field is pivotal.

Mike Brearley is renowned in England by many as the greatest cricket captain. Not a great talent, a great leader. Some argue that this captain of the Middlesex county team and England national team of the 1970s and 80s was not worth a place on the strength of his batting. He was a decent enough batsman, but not of sufficient quality to hold a place against international bowlers. He was appointed England captain for his brain and demeanour. He was picked for his ability to lead.

Brearley famously motivated the best player, Ian Botham, to achieve a celebrated victory against arch-rivals Australia in 1981. Cajoling and inspiring him into extraordinary feats with his bat and with the ball. Matches between the countries are played for 'The Ashes', a term which originated in a satirical obituary for English cricket after its first defeat to Australia, in 1882. The 'trophy' remains a tiny urn. Sport at its glorious quirkiest.

Brearley used gentle psychology and a deep understanding of what makes an individual respond positively. Strong-willed Botham was not exactly known for his love of those with plummy tones, such as Brearley, but there's no denying he had the utmost respect and admiration for him. In 1981, after only two of the six Test matches in 'The Ashes', Botham who was originally captain found himself sacked from the job, humiliated. Brearley stepped in and delicately managed a tricky situation, restoring Botham's gusto, and leading to one of sport's most enduring redemption stories.

If I close my eyes, I can still see bearded stocky Botham in his 'whites', open necked shirt and cable knit sweater, swatting the ball up into the crowd with his bat repeatedly like he was dealing with flies. Then charging in, bowling the ball, smashing the stumps down and grabbing one from the ground, brandishing it in victory like a hunter with his kill. Smiling, exhilarated, flushed with adrenaline, youth, success, pride. And redemption.

Unsurprisingly Brearley has spent many years as a practising psychiatrist. He's compelling, with measured delivery, on the barracking he received as England captain on one tour in Australia. When his beard became the focus of the crowd's jokes, he simply kept on growing it. Until he looked like he'd been found on the other side of that desert island in the film 'Castaway', living off coconuts. He really didn't care. There's a touch of the army general about him, keeping a cool head when others are throwing shade.

There have been many excellent players in cricket who have been exceptional captains. Bringing two great assets to the team. But for pure leadership, Brearley is lauded as exceptional. As you can probably tell, I'm an admirer of his, but he's not my favourite cricket captain. My favourite cricket captain is my favourite sportsman.

A man a lot of sports fans have not even heard of, or long forgotten. His name is Adam Hollioake. And he peels bananas like a monkey.

Adam Hollioake was born in Australia in the early 1970s but spent some of his childhood living in England and Hong Kong. Talented and confident, he developed into an exciting cricket prospect, and signed to play for one of the best county teams in England, Surrey. As did his younger brother Ben.

In 1997 Adam and Ben played in the England international team together. Part of a team that won three consecutive matches against a very strong Australian international team. The memory can play tricks when nostalgia kicks in, but in my recollection the pair of them are smashing the startled Australian bowlers all over the sunlit grounds. Both with fresh-faced good looks, playing with a freedom and an exuberance that was unrecognisable from England teams of the time. England's style was more like 'frightened rabbits'.

Adam became captain of Surrey, a county cricket team with a rich tradition and high status, one of the 'haves' rather than 'have nots', run as a shrewd business while bringing through many players of international quality.

Surrey's ground, 'The Oval', is the most ugly-beautiful of places. It was like a cathedral to me. I actually prefer quiet games of limited consequence in stands dotted with a few people, rather than the hubbub of a big international game, of which many are played here. As a BBC campaign at the time cleverly said about favoured quiet spots: '*Everybody needs a place to think'*.

Adam being captain didn't mean glitz, glamour and guaranteed success. Surrey had endured a decade of limited success, and in the sport of cricket talented players, which they undoubtedly had, need to blend together. The team needed leadership. In Adam, they had a man leading in a way I'd never seen before. A natural gift for it.

When you watched Surrey play, you could see him, hear him, but only if you were looking for it, because he was unshowy. He was supporting, enabling, motivating – all of it tirelessly. Selflessly. Adam was an 'all-rounder', as Botham was. Batting, bowling, fielding. Adam's main talent was with the bat, but as the team grew in stature, his individual contribution receded. Always slipping into the support role. With the bat, and with his bowling. Then suddenly he was needed and 'bam', there he was. Hitting the ball for six or bowling out the other team's key player.

Even when he was in the spotlight there seemed to be the minimum of fuss. He would barely get a mention. Even when he oversaw the England team winning a trophy in 1997, not a major trophy but an elusive piece of silverware, nobody seemed to be talking about Adam Hollioake.

What, or *who*, was Adam Hollioake himself spending time talking about at this time? Not himself, but his brother Ben. Adam would never tire of supporting Ben and explaining how much more talent his brother had. Adam could be a destructive batsman (that's a good thing) but yes Ben was more graceful. Adam could be a very effective bowler, but Ben was taller, faster, more fluid. Adam was an excellent fielder, but there was Ben with a better catch. All the while with his brother behind him, energising, reassuring.

Adam's Surrey were now winning trophies at the turn of the century and Ben was making an important contribution, but he still hadn't fulfilled all of his potential. There was more to come. For his county team and his country.

One Surrey game turned out to be the perfect day, frozen in time. With my favourite people around me, including my wife on her only ever visit to cricket, Surrey played Sussex, the county that later became our home. On the coast in Hove. Deep blue skies, a perfect late May day, the sound of seagulls, salt in the air, sun like a yellow ball, a gentle hum around a ground with deckchairs, an ice cream van and a beer tent. An England that almost feels fictional. The simple pleasures. Surrey won. The Sussex fans were grumbling. They disliked Surrey. A lot. But that's sport. And the day was perfect.

And a moment crystallised for all time. Ben was batting. He leant on the ball. His bat like a magic wand. A gentle caress, and the ball could not be stopped. In cricket it is called timing. It's important, as in life. The ball reached the rope. This meant four runs to Surrey. It landed at my feet in the queue for the beer tent, a more civilised queue than you could imagine. A man with a grey beard and a sun hat knew I was a Surrey fan. They could just tell. He turned to me and avoided being partisan: "*That,*" he enthused, "*was beautiful.*" I smiled. This is sport. This shared experience. I wonder if the man remembers that shot. I wonder if he's still alive.

On March 23, 2002, Ben died in a car crash in Perth, near his childhood school. Aged 24. So cruel. So horribly, devastatingly cruel. I think of Ben and it breaks my heart. I think of Adam and I want to cry for him. His devastation and dignity. I don't know Adam Hollioake. But that's the thing about sport, it brings you closer to people you don't even know. I don't have many heroes. He is one. Adam was never the same on a cricket ground. I doubt he's ever been the same as a man. What happened must have been so impactful, so devastating.

An excellent sportswriter named Paul Kimmage interviewed Adam years later. Kimmage was a former cyclist who knew what it was like to battle through a *Tour de France* and developed a style that was enthralling. It was a rare interview with a man now living back in Australia, with his family. So many ex-players are defined by cricket. Not Adam.

During the interview Adam demonstrated how he peels a banana. He peeled it from the bottom. Kimmage asked why. Adam asked why *wouldn't* he peel it that way? It's what "a monkey does" after all. Have you ever peeled a banana from the bottom? It's easier. Really it is. The 'handle part' is for trees. Once you slightly dig into the bottom it peels smoothly and you don't want to revert to the 'normal' way. Who knew? Adam did.

The banana is a clue that Adam didn't lead cricket teams conventionally or via a handbook. He listened, he learned, but he knew his own mind. Ultimately, he was able to quietly influence. His team played like they had a forcefield of energy around them. They were individually brilliant players, but also with an aura, an energy, a glow like the kids in the TV advert with after eating their '*Ready Brek*' porridge. They were a special Surrey team. And he was a special leader.

Mention the banana to some people and they give you a 'look'. The look that says: "Yeah well some people just try to be different don't they. I'll stick to my way thank you." The alternative or deeper thinker can be treated like a maverick, a show-off. Treated with suspicion.

No matter how single-minded, how talented, how selfless, how confident, everybody needs support sometimes. Everybody needs to be understood. Can you offer that support, encouragement and empathy? If you can't, you're no leader, no matter what the little title says under your name on the email.

Chapter 11: KILL HIM!

Claudio Ranieri's Leicester City Football club were still, curiously, under the radar. The team had made a surprisingly good start to his reign, but were meant to get back in their box, wind their necks in, return to the position of also-rans, no-hopers, after a brief flirtation with the upper reaches of the Premier League. Like a late summer holiday romance, it was time for a reality check. Now for another winter of hard-fought survival, like their nickname, *The Foxes.*

Leicester's defeat against Arsenal hadn't deflated the players or manager though. They achieved three wins, one draw and no defeats in the following four games. And by the time they were due to play Watford at their King Power Stadium in early November 2015, they were within striking reach of Manchester City, hundreds of millions of dollars richer than them. City's *'Aristocats'* to Leicester's foxes.

Despite Leicester's unusually high position, there wasn't much excitement or attention about the game against Watford. If there was a quiet stirring, not even a hubbub, it was about Jamie Vardy, the striker who had scored in eight consecutive Premier League games. An assassin to rival that Italian hero of the 1982 World Cup, Paolo Rossi.

Leicester's tactics were still confounding their opponents. Ranieri's team would use a primarily defensive formation, then suddenly 'break out' towards the opposition goal at high speed. The furthest forward, Vardy would lurk on the shoulder of an opposition defender and then suddenly break free. Within a few seconds the ball would be in the net. And Leicester would take three more points. It was simple, effective and bigger clubs couldn't cope.

At Premier League clubs the manager will usually conduct a media conference a day or two before the game. For a club like Leicester City FC, this means a mixture of national media (TV, radio, newspapers, online) and local media. Many of the same faces would be there in the media room at the King Power Stadium every week. Occasionally, a story at a club like Leicester will become a bigger deal, such as when a manager clashed verbally in this room with the media and it got personal. But mainly, there was a perfunctory, routine feel about this type of conference.

Most of the reporters and camera operators here will be good people simply earning a living from a profession they quietly like. But the sports media are in a bubble, and in that bubble there is a language, a narrative style. Nobody tends to be the person to stand out, be different. Well, I say nobody but there are one or two. And there is Claudio Ranieri.

When you've been there, done it and seen enough as Claudio had, there is room to be philosophical. Yes of course you can be angry, or defiant, or rousing, or combative if you choose to be. But there is mainly calm. A quiet, satisfying calm.

He showed perspective, he could see the madness around football. Not everyone can. He could see that ultimately, beneath the hype and cliché, there is just a game of football taking place. Watched, played and managed by human beings, with all their strengths and frailties. It cannot, should not, be taken *too* seriously.

*

The new Watford manager, Quique Sanchez Flores, had arrived from Spain. Watford had once flourished with the chemistry between chairman Elton John, yes Elton John - and the manager he appointed. His name was Graham Taylor, a genial and successful club manager who was then ridiculed for failure when he managed the England national team. Taylor's head was infamously depicted as a turnip on a tabloid back page after a defeat against Sweden. '*Swedes 2, Turnips 1*' was the headline. But at Watford Football Club, the two men supported and understood each other and thrived for years.

Modern Watford FC have a new method, debatably a successful one, of changing managers every year or two. The proverbial mythical magical managerial merry-go-round spinning so fast it was close to taking off (proverbially of course, we'll explore the strange world of sports clichés in the next chapter).

Flores had replaced Ranieri as manager of Valencia Football Club in 2005. Claudio had more clubs than Ibiza. But here's the important thing. Flores hadn't agitated, or badmouthed, or snuck in. Claudio had been dismissed from the job, then they appointed a new manager, who happened to be Quique. There was no drama, there was nothing to stir up here.

In a football media conference, for some reporters and networks, such coincidences can offer an opportunity to work up a supposed rivalry, a bit of tension, to liven up the conference and the coverage. Over the years, I couldn't help but wish some reporters would take that hype down a peg or two. I've seen many journalists in TV studios talk about a football transfer a like it's a geopolitical crisis, overly dramatising the situation and not showing enough light and shade, *enough* perspective. The way an inconsequential matter can be salivated over and talked up can make my toes curl a bit. I'm surprised I didn't have to attend conferences in jester's shoes. I've never wanted to feel like this, I tend to get on with the reporters around me. But it's the truth. I've always felt a step outside of this aspect of reporting. Not above it, *outside* it.

*

Ahead of the Watford match, one of the reporters made a move on the subject of '*Valenciagate*'. Turning the 'confrontation' between them when Leicester played Watford into a Shakespearean plot: "Is this your chance for *revenge* Claudio?" was the question posed to the Italian.

The question landed. The room silent. Claudio sat behind the microphones in his smart blue pullover and white shirt, grey hair, spectacles and a poppy on his lapel. His face turned to quiet thunder, and he snarled, he had been stirred, he had been poked with a stick, the television cameras would get their piece of action, the newspapers would get their headline. Not on the back page though, this is Leicester, not one of the big teams. Claudio inflated his body, and pumping up his right fist, face contorted: *"Yeah, big revenge. I want to KILL him!"*

For a moment, it was startling. But just a moment. Because Claudio was, of course, joking. And chuckling. "He's a nice man. It's football," he said with his shoulders shaking in mirth, and laughter lines across his face, the laughter infectious and engaging. Why revenge for Quique or another? I was sacked."

Claudio continued, animated and gesticulating with his hands, his voice still quivering with mirth. He could see the question for what it was. A bit daft but harmless. I appreciate there may be some sports reporters reading this who don't regard the question as 'daft' at all. Different strokes for different pens.

What Claudio was doing was gentle and endearing, not humiliating the reporter and his peers. It was a very quiet reality check, a quiet peal of the bell. The reporters had a new little story: *'Ranieri jokes at Quique revenge talk'*,

The progress of Leicester City Football Club had been noticed by many football fans, but this was the moment I noticed *Claudio Ranieri's* influence on the rise. He was in a good place. For him, for them.

The match? Leicester beat Watford. Jamie Vardy scored. Quique survived.

Chapter 12: POTENTIAL BANANA SKIN

To understand sport and the people who love it, you need to understand the language. It's a strange code, and often impenetrable to 'non-believers'. In my work, I've always tried to include casual sports fans, or non-sports fans, and I told a good friend Sara the book would try and offer some explanation of why some lives revolve around sport. *"Good,"* she said with her trademark deadpan humour. *"I can't bear sport, yet it always seems to be on. It's ruined my life. I want to know what the obsession is."* It's partly I think because of the way we do the storytelling.

There are of course some fine sports journalists and there's some great journalism out there. Immediately I think of two Davids, and how they have challenged wrongdoing. David Conn's work on Hillsborough and football finance is laudable, forensic and inspirational. The tenacity David Walsh showed in exposing corruption in cycling ended up making a significant impact on the sport and helped the credibility of sports journalism overall.

Sports journalism is a subject I am passionate about because it's been my working life. But ultimately, it's also worth seeing the funny side of the world of sports coverage and sports clichés. To not be frustrated by the world around you, to delete the emoji eye roll and try and accept it for what it is.

Let's use the phrase *"potential banana skin"* as our example of 'sports speak'. You may never have heard this phrase, but It's incredible how often this line is used within football. I have no idea why, but the absurdity of the cliché makes it one I use as an example.

Firstly, let us approach the act of slipping on a banana skin, whether or not it's been peeled from the bottom. Have you ever actually seen someone slip on one? I don't think I have, but in cartoons it used to be commonplace. Barely could a character move without flying through the air on a darkened, slippery skin, with crazy arms and a *whoooaah* exclamation. The simple concept is that a banana skin ahead presents a dangerous obstacle, on which you could slip.

So how and why is this phrase used so regularly in *football*? Well, the scenario involves a big team and a little team. Imagine Rochdale FC are the first team pulled out of a random draw for a knockout competition. The second team that is pulled from a bingo-style ball machine is Manchester United. And they will play each other at Rochdale's small stadium.

Rochdale is a town not far from Manchester in the north-west of England, and its football club can be found in the lower tiers of the football league, with crowds of a few thousand at most. United are one of the 'giants' of English and world football and can usually be found somewhere near the top of the Premier League.

While Rochdale wouldn't be expected to beat United, they *might*. And what would give Rochdale a much better chance is the game being played at their own ground, which can often be uncomfortable for a visiting big team. They have that 'puncher's chance'.

When the draw was made, what was the broadcaster almost certain to say? You know what is coming, you can set your watch by it and put your proverbial mortgage on it: *"This is a potential banana skin for Manchester United."*

The phrase comes out so easily, it is so ingrained, that it is never questioned. The broadcasters will forget they've said it, rather like me and my 'body of work!' which I shall come to later in this chapter. The pundit will go along with it and nod in agreement, and the viewer will be too busy eating crisps to notice or care. I cannot remember hearing any sports reporter use the banana skin metaphor without adding the prefix *'potential'* to make *"Potential banana skin."*

In the phrase, the potential has become welded to the banana skin, metaphorically of course. Pundits are not using the word 'potential' as a descriptive word, but as a lazy prefix. The words potential and banana are butted together before the genuine potential of a surprising result is even considered!

The banana skin alone is the metaphor! 'Potential' should be treated separately. Metaphorically this is not a *potential* banana skin - it's an *actual* banana skin!

When I raised this subject while reporting on a football World Cup, my colleague ended up in tears (thankfully of laughter) over the concept. Partly because of the absurdity of the phrase and partly because I'd bothered to analyse it so forensically. He refuted my suggestion the word *potential* is superfluous, saying it was needed to underline how Rochdale *could* be difficult opponents. But I had anticipated this and countered: If Rochdale present any danger to United, they should be described simply as a **banana skin.**

My friend and colleague won the dispute. He said the matter had reached a philosophical level over whether the banana skin alone can be the metaphor, or always needs the word *potentially*.

He said he would seek adjudication on the banana skin metaphor from a leading philosopher upon returning from the World Cup.
"And you know a leading philosopher, do you?" I said mischievously.
"Yes, my father-in-law is a renowned philosopher in France." This turned out to be true. I look forward to a definitive verdict.

The best-known parody of sports journalism is Steve Coogan's character *Alan Partridge*, famous in the UK and beyond for the self-importance and lack of perspective. Wearing 'sports casual' and haplessly, hilariously messing up interviews and commentaries, littered with clichés. *"That was liquid football. Did you see that? He must have a foot like a traction engine!"* But sport was just the starting point for Partridge on the caustically funny television news channel parody *The Day Today*. The character has long departed from sport to become almost indistinguishable from real daytime magazine-show and radio hosts.

The *spirit* of Partridge inadvertently lives on in sports coverage. All sports journalists walk the 'Partridge tightrope', but some are at least aware of the need to try and create some distance and try to avoid clichés where possible. Nobody can fully escape it. My own most '*Partridge*-like' moment came in France in 2016, reporting on an international football tournament.

I like to think it's a rare slip, as it was past midnight in Lyon and I was tired after a long day of broadcasts. But it's best just to *own* it! Trying to meet social media requirements, and wanting to refer to a relevant tweet, I was grasping for the term 'social media platforms.' Instead, like an out of body experience, I referred viewers to my *"body of work"*. Like I'm Steven Spielberg or Michelangelo!

Self-awareness of cliché overkill is not often top of the list of attributes across sports broadcasting. There is an endless stream of hyperbole. We could all, sports lovers *and* doubters, use sports coverage like a giant bingo card, looking for phrases to tick off and chuckle as we approach a full house.

Perhaps it's hypocritical, as someone who is weary of 'sports journalese', to take such delight in daft old phrases and memorable one-liners that don't make sense. But certain lines from commentators never leave the mind, they become almost as precious as achievements on the field of play. I remember an ice-skating commentator once saying: *"The crowd are literally electrified and glued to their seats."* Messy business!

Or the legendary David Coleman, most famous for athletics, when he commentated on football. During the 1974 FA Cup Final between Liverpool and Newcastle, watched by many millions live on TV, Liverpool's Kevin Keegan scored the opening goal, a vital one. Coleman would usually have captured the moment with precision and gravitas. In this instance, his line is unusual to the point of unintentionally amusing: *"Keegan! Goals pay the rent…Keegan does his share."* Well thank goodness for that. Back off landlord!

My favourite belongs to the marvellous motorsport institution, Murray Walker, whose death at the age of 97 brought such widespread tributes, memories and appreciation. Pleasingly, his voice sounded like cars zooming around a track, but didn't grate, a perfect synergy and always enhancing the action. He was going strong at the microphone well past retirement age, and never needed to park his occasionally madcap asides. Commentary isn't easy, I couldn't do it, and the gaffes were part of his personality.

In one Formula One race, he suddenly exclaimed, elongating syllables like a well-tuned machine racing along a home straight: *"And un-less I'm ve-ry much mis-taken, and I AM ve-ry much mis-taken."* We never found out what he was mistaken about, but there was no mistaking the affection in which he was held by the public.

Old school commentators had eccentricities, but it's part of what made them legends, and gave us wonderful soundtracks over years of watching and loving sport. They happened to be a certain type of man, not young, very English, clear, deep voice. But each had a personality in there. Walker, Coleman and a 'holy trinity' of commentators on football across the main UK television channels: John Motson, Barry Davies and Brian Moore.

As a boy I'd dream of one of them commentating on me scoring the winning goal in the FA Cup Final. Each was discerning and consummately professional. Each had their own distinctive style and seeming to find the right moment to raise their excitement level. Fans had their preferences, but all were of the highest quality,

Motson was known beyond football for his distinctive sheepskin coat when he stepped in front of the camera, and he loved to hit us with statistics. We perhaps started to look at the caricature and take his quality for granted. Davies is an extraordinary talent, broadcasting not only on football, but on a range of sports into his seventies. From gymnastics to hockey to rowing. Versatile, intelligent and knowing exactly when it was appropriate to show excitement. Moore is the one that brings a lump to the throat. When I hear his voice and the theme tune to *'The Big Match'*, I smell Sunday roast lunch. So warm, so clear. Their voices still bring great joy and comfort when they are brought out of the archives.

The true maverick in commentary was Sid Waddell, a complete one-off, son of a minor and educated at Cambridge through his own hard work, champion of 'working class sports' and with a turn of phrase that took his appeal way beyond sports fans, particularly in the 1980s when darts was on the BBC, not behind a 'paywall'. His best line is still celebrated and referenced by many sports fans, deliberately and convincingly overplaying the importance of the cocky number one player Eric Bristow: *"When Alexander the Great was 33 he cried salt tears because there were no worlds left to conquer. Bristow's TWENTY-SEVEN!"*

The broadcaster held up as the standard bearer, was Australian. Former cricketer Richie Benaud. He looked about 63-years-old for about the last 50 years of his life, debonair and calm. Like an enigmatic guest on a cruise in a panama hat, who, when you express deep concern on a weather pattern would turn deliberately and reassuringly, narrowing his eyes gently and say after a pause: *"Better weather is forecast. It's going to be ab-so-lute-ly splendid by noon."*

Richie was never in a hurry. A master of pauses and letting the action breathe. How we could do with him in the modern world of relentless pace and urgency. When I was young, I'd switch on the television excitedly to watch a day's cricket on the BBC. It might be a big Ashes match between England and Australia. But even better, a county match from somewhere like Worcester. There would be near silence as the camera pulled away from the church spire and clock showing 11am, until we see the cricket ground and the landscape beyond. Still Richie would be quiet, leaving a gentle hum. I can still hear it now. And then, finally, two words: "*Morning everyone.*" In sport this was our first two notes of Wagner. Our waves lapping against the golden beach. Our birdsong.

Nostalgia of course plays a part in this. But this isn't a bad thing. Nostalgia is what it used to be. And when I see and hear high quality in the modern age, I lap it up. In cricket it's Michael Holding, the greatest modern sports voice. A Jamaican voice like warm treacle, and a forensic intelligence, integrity and insight. He spoke to me with huge grace and gratitude when a microphone mentor, Benaud, passed away. And I also love listening to Alison Mitchell, whom I had the pleasure of briefly working with at the BBC, and who has the unbeatable combination of warmth and knowledge, with a voice that calms and engages.

In America one problem they don't have is the way they do their sports broadcasting. They have realised, or perhaps stumbled upon the formula, that '*If it ain't broke, don't fix it.*' Commentary is still treated as describing the action with information, rather than 'zoo radio'. My favourite is the coverage on ESPN of college basketball, a sport I've only come to love recently, mixing sharp insight, knowledge, information, with and creativity. Never patronising. In former college basketball player Jay Bilas they have a gem of an analyst. He's bald, and I don't say that out of bias as I myself am part of what comedian Larry David refers to as '*the bald community*'!

Too often in UK sports coverage, there is a magazine-style stream of consciousness, debate and toe-curling 'blokey' banter, making you feel like you're listing to know-alls holding court in a gastropub. Minutiae is debated incessantly. No wonder so many sports fans say they want to switch off. No wonder my friend Sara can't bear have to overhear this meaningless nonsense.

There isn't enough weight, enough depth, enough honesty, enough searching for the soul. There are too many middle-aged, self-important men swapping platitudes and tributes. Too many people who have risen without trace, clinging on to microphones and laptops and showing themselves at work. Being seen to be doing their job. We can all be guilty of this, myself included. Projecting ourselves, promoting ourselves rather than projecting the *story*. Nobody needs to care that the manager knows your name. They *do* care that you ask questions with spirit, with insight, with verve and intelligence. With perspective.

There is too much 'snark', too much groping for a sassy angle. Much of the self-regard I see from social media from sports journalists, subtly positioning their opinion as so much weightier than the opinion of fans, bothers me. A lot. We need to get over ourselves. Show some humility.

Getting fired up about sports journalism and broadcasting is something that doesn't seem terribly important after what the world has been through. But I also recognise these limitations in some *political* reporters. In the epicentre of a crisis showed themselves to be blinkered, using robotic techniques and career-climbing contact protection to let vital questions go unanswered. Lacking the discipline to ask the right question, the right *one* question in the right manner, and not diluting it with a meandering second question. It became a big problem and I'm sure you've seen it yourself. It's a trait I was familiar with in the less important surroundings of sports coverage.

'Sports journalese' is a language, a code, a nonsense. It can make me laugh and it can make me wince. But working inside sport in recent years I needed all the humour I could muster. When I started reporting, I described footballers kicking a ball around a field. What started out as fun became serious news.

*

Over three decades, the boy from the south London housing estate became a writer, a reporter, a video journalist, correspondent, producer, programme editor, presenter and boss at the main news organisations in the UK, and global organisations too. So why should he still feel like an outsider? Is it *him* or them? Do *you* feel like an outsider?

There's a poignant start to a wonderful song named *'Bubblegum'* by the Mystery Jets: *'I'm always on the outside looking in, its where I've always been,*
But the outside is where the sparks fly when the wheel spins.'

The intelligent rapper 'Professor Green' struck a chord with me on a radio programme when he said he suffered from 'working class anxiety'. The inability to fully appreciate or enjoy success because you work so hard, and feel somebody could take it away, leaving you *"back on your arse."*
He poignantly said he wishes he could go back and take more enjoyment from some of the good times he enjoyed in his work.

I'd like to have spent a day, but only a day, in the sports journalists' 'pack', to see if I preferred to be in that clique. To feel settled as one of them, to feel accepted and to belong. I realise that I've forged my own path, and I don't want to give the impression I'm disliked. One-on-one there is respect and friendship. But proper recognition can remove some of what Professor Green is feeling – that you have to keep fighting for your place and keep proving your style and skills have a place. Show a bit of personality, a bit of alternative thinking, a bit of fire, or try to introduce new ways of thinking about sports coverage in media, and you can stick out. You can be marginalised without malice, misunderstood, able to help others but not so easily helped yourself.

When I have been a boss, a leader, my main focus has been to empathise and support. Not like Mike Brearley. Because, rather like an airline pilot, there's something about a man with the right accent and flecks of grey in the hair that gives them a good starting point. Brearley turned out to be so much more. But I might have a touch of Adam Hollioake. I hope so. Under the radar. I deeply care about the team around me, always.

Sport reflects society and is susceptible to ill-gotten gains, unscrupulous and corrupt behaviour. Eventually my work revolved around allegations of misconduct from those who run football. The epicentre of the investigations was Switzerland, and a spotlight was on the governing body of world football; FIFA.

Chapter 13: "BAD APPLES"

If you ever need a travel guide for Zurich, I'm your man. For a few years I spent so much time in the Swiss capital it felt like a second home. It is the home of FIFA, governing body of world football. And the reason I was there so much? *'Bad Apples'*.

I was always taken by how calm the FIFA headquarters looked on the surface, a resplendent multi-million-dollar HQ. But within there was turbulence, and often drama and chaos, with journalists swarming all over the complex in the midst of controversy and scandal. It was a familiar routine, the flight from London to Zurich, sometimes for a scheduled event, but often an impromptu dash from my home to the airport because a big story was breaking.

Zurich is pretty compact, so it's not a long journey to FIFA HQ, up and down aesthetically pleasing little hills and towards the familiar crossroads. Before you hit the junction, there is a zoo. Once, in the height of a 'breaking' FIFA story, I saw two unaccompanied llamas charging down a nearby hill. Which sounds like I have made it up. Trust me, it's not the most bizarre thing I saw covering FIFA.

Turn left at the crossroads, and within a few metres there is the FIFA sign and front gates. An inconspicuous little entrance, where a pack of journalists would sometimes gather, locked out on this occasion, long periods of inactivity then suddenly a frenzy as a black car with shaded windows pulled into the adjoining entrance, through the gate and down a tunnel to the back entrance of the building. Cameras flashing. Who was in the car? Did you get a shot of them? Once it rained so apocalyptically, a sensible producer possibly saved lives by pre-booking a gazebo for shelter. It wasn't much fun outside. Particularly not at midnight after a long day of world football shenanigans.

More often than not, the media *were* allowed into the complex, which had undulating hills and slopes not unlike the set of the BBC children's programme *Teletubbies*, with a smattering of statues and sculptures. It takes a few minutes to walk across the grounds of FIFA and in true Swiss-style, the grounds would always leave you in no doubt of the season. Vibrant and colourful flower and fauna in spring, while in winter there was often a substantial covering of snow, and an icy approach down to the main building, leaving television crews slipping and skating towards the entrance, their own little 'Winter Olympics'.

The FIFA building, opened in 2007 and of which I felt I knew every brick, is a distinctive and impressive building. I use the word impressive in the sense of its pleasing architecture, it was very smartly designed. But tens of millions of dollars being spent on it might not be considered so impressive, depending on how you see money, football and football governance.

It is a neat square, with one side of the building visible on arrival. And when you look to the right of the entrance there is a full-size football pitch, with artificial turf. Along the far side of the pitch are the flags of FIFA members, over two hundred of them. On the pitch, at lunchtimes, the staff would often have a kickaround on that pitch. For the media officers it was their perk after a morning fielding awkward questions from journalists. Sometimes the pitch would stage a charity game where FIFA officials would get to play with ex-players, superstars, I remember seeing Diego Maradona play in such a game.

For the big political happenings at FIFA the media would gather outside the front entrance, often with a rope to keep us back, like a film premiere. And there was indeed a red carpet. But nobody was stopping to pose in ball gowns and high heels when the 'VIP' cars pulled up and the drivers helped the executives out on to the carpet. It was usually tense, often chaotic. We would push forward with our large fluffy microphones thrust over the rope. "*Will there be a decision today? Will anyone be resigning? Is FIFA in crisis sir?*" Sometimes they stopped. Sometimes they recognised you and smiled. But often hurried through with a wry '*I'm sorry, I can't speak*' smile.

We were not allowed into the building for most of the day, only for the official media conferences at the end of a big scheduled meeting. But it's not what you know, it's who you know. And sometimes, you were in. And when you were in, it was quite an experience, quite a place. There is a huge imposing reception that smells of disinfectant, but the building is mainly underground, with several subterranean levels, exposed brickwork, glass bricks. Even if you try not to be uncharitable, there is a touch of the Bond villain's lair. The first time you are inside, it is undoubtedly intimidating. Hold your nerve. Maybe I like neat squares, the clean, sanitized feel. But if you were designing an important building from scratch, I'm not sure how much better you could do than this.

The most grand, secretive, protected of rooms was the boardroom. I once filmed a documentary sequence in there. Nobody outside of FIFA's invited guests had been allowed in there before, or since, to my knowledge. The large table, the low lighting, the dark fringes of the room, again it was impossible not to imagine anything other than world domination being plotted around the table.

A key reason it is underground, was because of a FIFA President. He said: *"Places where people make decisions should not contain direct light. Because the light should come from the people assembled there"*. The name of this man was Joseph 'Sepp' Blatter.

Has anybody in the history of sport been more written about, discussed, questioned, criticised and ubiquitous than Sepp Blatter? The Swiss lawyer turned football governor, small in height but far-reaching in influence and notoriety. And somebody I jousted with three times in his office, one-on-one. Every time it bordered on surreal. Every time I entered his office grateful for the invite and with an open mind.

I had had my first skirmish with Blatter in 2008, a few years ahead of my own two interviews. It was my first time in the FIFA building, and after this first encounter with him I'm surprised I was ever allowed back. As a well-connected Sports Editor I had set up the interview for my correspondent and was asked by my contacts to be there as a condition of the interview. Blatter had been President since 1998, with a first decade of occasional controversy, but on a tiny scale compared to the meltdown that was on the way in the second decade. One of the issues with Blatter, to be entirely fair, is with his English. While fluent in several languages including English, his Swiss-Germanic version interpretation of the language could cause problems, along with his open, sometimes eccentric trains of thought. When he was asked whether Cristiano Ronaldo should be allowed to leave Manchester United to sign for Real Madrid, Blatter clumsily described him as a "slave".

My own television network 'led' on this line, making it the main aspect of our coverage, but we also covered more important questions, and showed restraint. The UK newspapers 'went to town', to church, they went all the way to the town of 'Frenzyville'. Our interview was across the front pages, and one newspaper mocked up Ronaldo behind prison cell bars. It wasn't particularly comfortable. We weren't given any credit for having done the interview, or any thanks, but I didn't need to care. Because what was more important was maintaining relationships, with Blatter, with contacts, and being allowed *back in* to ask more tough questions.

The restraint we showed gave us another chance, and after that another. It's a tightrope negotiating opportunities like that, with all your nous needed. Ronaldo did sign for Real Madrid soon after, and when I think of the word 'slave' being used, I still wince. But the clumsiness of the phrase should not be ignored. Because the issue of Blatter's clumsy wording resurfaced.

Three years later, on day one of a new job as a correspondent, I was back in his office. I want you to know what it's actually like being in this notorious man's company. We were reintroduced by contacts. He smiled warmly, leaving me to try and unscramble whether he was still quietly fuming about the Ronaldo slip, and my part in the coverage. Apparently not. He had an aura of course, one of the two most powerful figures in world sport, along with the Olympic President, who I'd also jousted with in his office.

When Blatter walked me along the grand corridors of FIFA, filmed by our cameraman, we talked openly about family and life away from football, it wasn't forced or strained. It was good I'm average height and not Peter Crouch, the ex-footballer who was known for his height before scoring lots of goals, doing a robot dance and becoming a celebrity. Blatter is not a tall man, and 'Little and Large' isn't ideal footage of a FIFA President.

Around us was an entourage, the smoothers and fixers, movers and shakers, which don't help with the public perception of Blatter as a 'Godfather'. But it did have that feel, even when you got to know these people around him well. I remain grateful to the people who had my back and got me into his office again. We were at the sharpest of sharp ends, in the kind of building and mixing with the kind of people you would see in the movies when cops complain about 'City Hall' calling the shots and never getting their hands dirty on the streets!

Blatter cordially displayed no impatience during the slightly tiresome choreography of officially filming his entry, into his own office, to shake my hand and take a seat. As if I was inviting him into *my* office. Behind Blatter, as we spoke, was the World Cup trophy. The bulbous, golden, glorious trophy, the thing that football is really about, not politics. The very thing that reminded me of the six-year-old boy inside, being allowed to stay up late and watch number seven play for Scotland. It was a surreal feeling to have Blatter and the trophy in my eyeline.

There was a knot in my stomach. This was serious. On the surface it was calm. Like FIFA. Inside, churning. Concentration. Hold your nerve. Find it. After 15 minutes it had been cordial, to the point of bland. Blatter had gently answered some of my questions, and sort of answered others, meandering like the Limmat River that flows through the centre of Zurich, not really getting to a point, sometimes deliberately. It was just too flat. This was a man with tough questions to answer about FIFA's finances and his own standing, and I needed to push harder. You see, there was no polite way of avoiding his lack of popularity amongst fans in *some* parts of the world, outside of what he called 'FIFA House' and the 'FIFA Family'; the national associations who rely on money coming in. I never forget what 'enablers' these associations become, as they regularly vote for the President who will make them the most money.

I decided to use an approach I'd seen two decades before from a broadcaster and writer named Darcus Howe, that I'd seen him employ to devastating effect. Firstly, I gently praised Blatter using the truth as a weapon: "*Mr Blatter, your rival has pulled out of the Presidential election. From my inside knowledge of FIFA, may I say that if the election had taken place you would have won easily*".

While I was speaking to Blatter, I could see him puffing out his chest. "*But this is only relevant to FIFA Mr Blatter. People on the inside like you, and you make them money. But football is not their game, it's ours, and trust me I know the vast majority of football fans do not approve of you in office. What are you going to do about your lack of popularity outside of FIFA?*"

I had taken a calculated risk. The most important people to me were not my employers, or Mr Blatter. They were my contacts. And I had risked compromising them to 'keep it real'. A flash of indignant fury crossed Blatter's face. He gathered himself, and gave his answer, of course refuting my assertions over the course of the next few minutes.

When the interview ended, I was braced for trouble. He took his lapel microphone off and leapt to his feet. He looked me in the eye. *"Tribute!"* he cried. *"Tribute!"* he repeated. *"Tough questions!"* This is what happened, make of it what you will. Likeable? Dislikeable? It can be both can't it?

I suspect Blatter had a word with my contacts afterwards, asking if they really must keep bringing this bald troublemaker into his office. But he still let me back in. On another occasion – not one of the Blatter interviews - one of FIFA's 'Vice-Presidents' (later to plead guilty to corruption offences and kicked out of FIFA) allowed me three questions only. I stuck to three. He was clearly ready for me to try a fourth question and when I *didn't*, he was clearly more relaxed and trusting. Proving this by jumping out of his seat and starting to box me. A former boxer, huge. He literally started pounding me in the ribs. It was his way of showing approval. Really it was. Expect the unexpected in that building.

The third Blatter interview was the most eventful. In fact, it made headlines around the world. The subject was unsavoury, uncomfortable and extremely sensitive. I asked Blatter about a big story that had erupted the previous weekend, an incident of alleged racism in English football, with a prominent player accused. The case ended up in court, where the footballer was cleared. But the Football Association found him guilty and banned him. Blatter told me that players should leave problems on the pitch and shake hands. *Shake hands?* After alleged racist abuse?

When I returned to London shortly after interview, and stepped off the plane, my phone felt radioactive there were so many messages. It had, as they say, all 'kicked off'. In this situation, in nearly all situations, keep it straight, keep it true, and hold your nerve.

On my own channel I explained why these comments were so unacceptable, the trouble Blatter was in, the impact the interview had had, the deeper issues with racism, and what happened next. What I *didn't* do, was accept the invitation to go on other channels and give him a kicking. I'd immediately challenged him, wouldn't drop the subject and didn't need to over-egg this pudding. This was about him, not the interviewer.

By now, it's safe to say, Blatter had had enough of my interviews and I never saw inside his office again. I once stood arguing outside the door with one of his senior media advisors, after he pulled out of an agreement to answer a couple of questions at an event hosted at FIFA House. *"Mr Blatter has left the building and is attending a lunch elsewhere in Zurich",* said his media officer unconvincingly. *"I know he's in that office behind you, you know he's in the office behind you, and you know that I know."* I replied impatiently. *Let's please stop this charade and get him out. Please!"*

By now, FIFA was becoming pure theatre, an epic sequence of acts. Often with Blatter and his executives on the stage in the large auditorium while journalists, many of the same faces returning for more, took on the 'FIFA family', led by Blatter. The 'C' word was being repeatedly used to accuse executives who were part of FIFA. Corruption. And largely focused on the controversial awarding of the 2018 and 2022 World Cups, to Russia and Qatar respectively. Something that still raises eyebrows and temperatures a decade later. How and why were these countries chosen was the subject of intense scrutiny and suspicion. Hosting processes for sports events have been questioned over decades, and not just at FIFA, not just in football. They involve a mixture of sports governance, politics, business and big money. It can be a potent mix.

The antipathy between Blatter, his entourage and the journalists was like a play within a play. And the barely-contained tension boiled over after one media conference, when Blatter lectured the ensemble before trying to leave the stage. One English newspaper writer's patience snapped: "Come back to the stage and answer our questions properly" he said loudly in exasperation, prompting Blatter to turn on his heel and return to the podium spotlight: "This is the house of FIFA, not a backstreet bazaar." Blatter retorted fierily. *"Show some respect".*

Many of the hacks were open-mouthed with agitation and frustration. By now I'd spent so much time covering FIFA stories I felt battle-fatigued, or like Alec Guinness in the famous film *Bridge on the River Kwai,* disorientated and defeated, before the bridge explodes. The difference being

Alec Guinness's character blew up the bridge. The damage in this building was self-inflicted.

It would be easier to say what *didn't* happen in that auditorium, that building, that city, in the unfolding months. Some members of the Executive Committee responsible for the World Cup hosting decisions were found guilty of corruption for their worldwide football practices, while also holding roles at FIFA. Some were suspended, some tried, some jailed. There were 22 of them. All men. Blatter hung on. At one conference an English comedian, in character, infiltrated the security and famously threw dollars over Blatter. The pictures providing the perfect snapshot of how his Presidency rose and fell. Money.

In one *'FIFA Congress'* the English Football Association, an organisation with its own issues, challenged the integrity of the organisation's executives. A succession of Blatter's allies lined up to throw shade at the FA from the stage, including an Argentinian called Julio Grondona, who raised the *Falklands Conflict* and made it the centre of his attack on the English. As a journalist it was like having ten lead stories, and then someone would throw in an 11th then a 12th, often bizarre, sometimes bazaar, and your head was spinning like that managerial merry-go-round.

Some executives were facing the questionable *internal* justice of FIFA, with the organisation asking the outside world to leave it to deal with its own disciplinary matter, via its 'Independent Ethics Committee'. While this was happening, executives were being pursued for answers around Zurich. Chased through hotel lobbies by the pack, usually including the redoubtable Associated Press journalist Rob Harris, so busy breaking stories he sometimes felt like half man half laptop and one of the scourges of misbehaving sports executives. Rob, to use a phrase from comedy duo Reeves & Mortimer, *'wouldn't let it lie'*.

And on one occasion, dozens of journalists jumped into taxis to cross Zurich and get to an executive 'whistle blower', who was about to say his piece on FIFA at a hotel on the other side of town. Turned out to be a false alarm. And apparently, the hoax was instigated by a taxi company owner who fancied making a quick profit. It was that kind of time. And mercifully I was wired up to a camera, broadcasting in the grounds of FIFA, otherwise I'd have probably been in one of those taxis making an arse of myself too.

In 2015, the drama reached a peak, taking the mafia analogy from the family table to the streets. The prestigious and quaint *Baur au Lac* hotel was where most of the FIFA executives stayed for Congress, displaying all the excesses of sports administrators of the time. Journalists would 'clear' with their own bosses that they were allowed to go in for an exorbitantly priced coffee, maybe even a croissant, and try to grab a word with a FIFA contact. The VIPs were often hidden behind papers while eating salmon and poached eggs. Occasionally a contact would step outside and say: "*You didn't hear this from me but....*"

On this momentous May morning, police swooped at dawn and it was game over for some of world football's corrupt executives. I say "world football" advisedly for it should be pointed out that governing body FIFA was only part of this story, in that executives were being investigated for activity in their own regions while also holding roles at the governing body. In fact, most of the proven corruption happened within football confederations that operate with *and* separately to FIFA. South America was one particular hotbed of corrupt football activity. Central America another. Africa too. And the leaders of these organisations would come together at FIFA. Therein lies the responsibility to "*shake these bad apples from the tree*", a quote from Sepp Blatter.

On this fateful day, breakfast tables were abandoned before the eggs were brought out, as execs were led out in unmarked police cars. For many, it was last time they would be able to 'take a drink' through the umbrella of football governance. And some would spend many months in custody.

This was 'peak FIFA'. Never again will football's governing body be under this much spotlight, the depths of shame can never be repeated. And let us take a reality check. This only got so much publicity because of the world's love of football, and the world's fascination with Blatter, a *perceived* Godfather of a perceived mafia. Because as we now know, football, sport, reflects wider society. Corruption happens where there is big business. Football became a huge business, with FIFA having a surfeit of over a billion dollars at that time. From a game. Of which they were – and are - custodians. That's the business football became.

Blatter was not arrested in that dawn raid. But he didn't last as FIFA President much longer. A couple of weeks later we were back in the auditorium. Still there was denial from him, until a new allegation was unstoppable in removing him from office. The allegation that he made an unauthorised payment to Michel Platini, a Vice-President of FIFA, the head of European football and former superstar of the game from France. Neither man recovered from this or worked in football again, despite an exhaustive, exhausting, series of challenges at 'CAS', the Court of Arbitration for Sport, at the top of a hill in Lausanne. Another place I was too familiar with.

Was Blatter corrupt? The proven corruption from some executives with important roles at the organisation was clear, but those close to him tell me he personally wasn't corrupt. Was Blatter a racist? His words in that interview were unacceptable, but those close to him say he isn't. We need to listen to both sides. What I am comfortable to accuse Mr Blatter of being, is *accountable*. That was his job as President, as leader. When Blatter 'held court' to us journalists, he would often use nautical references, repeatedly calling himself the 'Captain of the ship' and suggesting he was still the man to sail FIFA to "calmer waters". But that ship hit an iceberg, and there was a different analogy that I preferred to pick up on. We would constantly ask Blatter how he could still be President amidst so much corruption, much of it now proven, at his organisation. As I referenced a moment ago, he would say there are often 'bad apples" at organisations, and they must be removed. It is a classic way of thinking from the leaders of world sport that puts space between the organisation and the problem. Rather than being held accountable or taking responsibility, leaders excuse themselves and their organisations from wrongdoing by using that carefully chosen word, which is legally sound, *individuals.* This is a bit like a football club manager saying their defeat is because of individuals, and not taking responsibility for the club's results, essentially removing the club from the result. But it's the club's name in the score line. And with FIFA it was a culture of wrongdoing. A culture.

Individual after individual has been identified and pushed under the bus. That is not to say the individuals are innocent, but it means bigger questions, like the removal of a tournament or the removal of a President, can be sidestepped. The media, and public, become fixated on easy fixes such as such as 'will THEY take away the tournament from the hosts?' or 'will the President be resigning?' The laws and politics are far more complicated.

The Swiss Attorney General's office had been a constant source of enquiries over investigations on FIFA, but the action speeded up when the US Attorney General got involved. A disgraced American FIFA Vice-President was a key reason they decided to step in, though missing out being awarded hosting rights to a World Cup was a significant part of it. I spent hours, days, on the phone to contacts on the legal side. Knowing that all the moral outcry and public dissatisfaction in the world doesn't mean convictions, doesn't mean regime change, doesn't mean tournaments removed from hosts. And the word that was repeatedly used to me about the charges and cases, was individuals. Many were brought to justice. Sporting governing bodies carry on, with new regimes, which they insist are sanitised, cleaner.

I challenged Blatter in the auditorium on his 'bad apples' analogy. And said it was his responsibility to have dealt with football's 'bad apples' as the *'boss of the orchard'*. He got the better of me, with long answers that didn't actually answer the accusation. I was after accountability, not to make accusations. And frustration built. It felt to some journalists like we were losing our grip, or sanity even. Alec Guinness style. Finally, I lost my patience. Others had snapped earlier than me. With Blatter suspended, a media conference was called, and a temporary President installed, Issa Hayatou. He had been poorly, and I felt he should not have conducted the conference for his own sake. At one stage he looked close to being asleep. Without referencing its crisis, A FIFA spokesman started to proudly announce their new idea, an expanded World Cup. And started to go into great detail.

I raised my hand for the last question of the session, and the microphone was handed to me by a familiar press officer. I tried to stay composed, but I had had enough. Where I come from, we don't like being treated like we've just crawled out of a (bad) apple. They were taking us for fools and had no right to: *"Mr Hayatou firstly may I say I am slightly worried about your health. You don't look like you are in the right condition to take this conference, and in fact looked asleep a moment ago. I hope and trust you are ok. Secondly, I need to challenge FIFA daring to raise the prospect of an expanded World Cup at today's conference. It is wholly inappropriate. For the record, I believe 32 teams is a perfect format, and an expansion to 48 is a bad idea based typically on the prospect of more money and more votes from Associations who want a place at the World Cup party. It is unethical. But more importantly, around HALF of the exec-*

utives who decide such matters are absent, accused of corruption, or jailed, or awaiting trial. Your President is suspended. Other Vice Presidents are suspended, and you sir are not well today. I am here to represent my viewers and the wider public. And I can tell, you, TELL YOU (I said, while raising my voice) what they will say about this idea, this diversionary tactic, is TYPICAL FIFA."

Mr Hayatou, roused and wide awake now, answered me carefully, with quiet anger and in French, making me scramble for headphones and interpretation. My question was the worst of my career. It wasn't even a question, it was a protest speech, but I'd had years of this charade, and I wanted to channel the disgrace of this pretence that all was well. It went down well my fellow journalists, one or two even slapped me on the back, but I was a bit embarrassed by my outburst by this stage. It wasn't my finest moment.

The orchard is still there, with bad apples removed and a new President, Gianni Infantino. New FIFA? The drama has largely subsided, and we are asked to trust that there is a different culture now. Specifically referring to Infantino's interview technique and speech patterns, I'm sometimes reminded of the old FIFA and the tendency to meander in delivery when dealing with the media. But Infantino and the many good people who work for the organisation knew it would take years of hard work to regain our trust.

FIFA may be a new, clean FIFA, but we must keep a close eye on the organisation, and all those who run world sport. National associations are still inclined to vote for who and what brings them the most money. This isn't a crime, but it's far from ideal. The associations will still try to shake the apple tree and hold out their baskets. But due to the pandemic, the world has changed. The business football became is having to change too.

Chapter 14: THE MAGIC CUP

Don't be scared when given an opportunity. Something to really be scared of is a *lack* of opportunity.

When I was a boss, and even when I wasn't a boss, this is what I used to quietly say to people about to go into a 'screen test', or an interview, terrified of it going wrong, a familiar feeling most people have when they enter such a scenario. The advice is partly to keep them calm and believe in themselves. Opportunity is precious, and so often it's denied, whether subtly or brazenly. You need a chance to show what you can do when you do get the opportunity.

Sport needs competition that gives everyone a chance. One way of doing this is the 'American model', using a system designed to make teams equal. The worst team gets first pick of the best young talent from the college system for the following season, which evens up the competition. It works for them, but it's not perfect. Teams are franchises first and foremost, and that means some of them suddenly move cities. It is mind blowing that a fan can give thirty years of their life to a team only to see it uprooted and taken to a different city . Meaning the days of watching their team are effectively over.

In football, a way of giving all comers the chance to win doesn't claim to offer equality but does offer *opportunity* for all. Do you believe in the magic of '*The Cup*'?

On a global scale, the World Cup does this. So often is football mired in politics and so powerful has *club* football become, that we can sometimes forget how wonderful the World Cup actually is. The peak of international football. You don't have to be a geek about it like me, poring over the feats of Frenchman Just Fontaine in the 1930s or the unexpected quality of the unknown North Korea team in the tournament in England in 1966, including beating Italy. The World Cup has a genuinely rousing effect on nations. A feelgood factor that isn't mythical or exaggerated.

During the 1990 tournament in Italy, the English public was stirred by the effect of Paul Gascoigne's surging runs, the soundtrack of Pavarotti's *Nessun Dorma* and New Order's *World in Motion*, and 'Gazza' in tears in the brutal semi-final defeat to Germany. Football took off. *This* was the tournament that is largely responsible for taking football from a 'blokey' pursuit overshadowed by the threat of hooliganism, to a family day out.

The world's best football format emerged in England a century and a half ago, and it still feels like the most inclusive and meritorious competitions in all of sport. The FA Cup. A competition which has lost some of its power, influence and allure, yet mercifully clings on to some relevance, despite all of the issues it has faced. It is like a family business in the heart of a High Street that older generations are reassured to see, despite the large supermarket next door taking most of its business.

The main reason the FA Cup is so special, can be explained by the opportunity it gives to dream, to better yourself. Something that probably won't happen, but it could. And that's the point. It *could*.

If you live in England, you may live in a small town, or part of town, that has a small club. Let's call them Small Town Park FC. This club could be watched by less than a hundred people each week and cling on to survival. In August, on a hot summer's day, Small Town might play in a preliminary round of the FA Cup, against another small club, both run by volunteers, both fiercely proud and competitive, both *meaning* something. Both at the bottom of that glorious pyramid, ten levels down, while the glamorous rich clubs enter the competition at a later stage. Over 700 teams compete in the FA Cup, including some of the best in world football. Clubs of all sizes. The final arriving nine months later in May. Sporting democracy.

Small Town FC might score a goal in the final minute to win an FA Cup match, to the unrestrained joy of their small band of supporters, friends and family. Maybe the scorer is a talented footballer who failed to make it at a high level, or someone who has worked hard all week in a local supermarket. Maybe he has problems in his life, maybe he has low confidence, maybe he just happens to be a nice guy. And into the next round Small Town go. If they keep winning, four, five, six matches, against bigger amateur teams, eventually they could be in the 'first round proper', three months later in November.

By now, Small Town FC might have attracted the interest of the national media, or beyond. It might be the adventure of a lifetime for them. Maybe, just maybe, Small Town might beat a small professional football league team, then another. And reach the last 64 teams left in the competition. When that draw is made, they could play Manchester United, or Liverpool, or Arsenal, or a big team from the city a few miles away. It's the possibilities, the stories, the dreams. And these dreams *do* come true. Small teams do occasionally go deep into the competition. They do cause shocks, punch above their weight, create memories, glory. And perhaps – a once in a lifetime achievement.

My local team Horsham FC were still in the competition in December one year. They were in one of the random 'draws' with the balls pulled out of a velvet bag, or a bingo-style contraption. Horsham were paired with Swansea City, one of the two best teams in Wales, whose best teams play in the English league and the FA Cup. The match was shown live on television. I hadn't moved to Horsham yet, and wasn't at the old ground, Queen Street, but my friend Mark was, and he still cherishes the occasion. It's still talked about in the town here. When you are not used to success, the one-off achievement is magical, a fairy tale. There is an electricity that connects people in a shared experience, that they never forget.

When the bigger town nearby, Crawley Town, were still a semi-professional team, they somehow reached the round where only *16* teams remain. Around 9,000 people from the town headed to Manchester, to take on Alex Ferguson's United. With a huge worldwide audience. Many tens of millions, watching Crawley Town live! United won the match, but only by a single goal. Opportunity in action. 'The Cup', as the saying goes, is the 'great leveller'.

So why is the FA Cup no longer so popular? Why does it now rank *third* in the list of trophies a top English club wants to win, a long way behind the Premier league and Champions league?

Until 1991, the FA Cup final was often the biggest event of the year, sport or otherwise. It took a coronation or moon landing to challenge it in the ratings. It was like the *Super Bowl* is to America, most of the nation gripped. The television build-up in the 1970s and 80s would last from breakfast time, with much-loved features. The '*Road to Wembley*' would be relived, the story of the competition and exploits of small clubs. Players making names for themselves.

A few weeks after I was born, early in 1972, a player named Ronnie Radford scored a goal for small club Hereford United against a top division club - Newcastle United - that became part of national culture. A balding bull of a man, surging through the mud and taking a chance, the ball flying through the air as if launched by a cannon, into the net. Delirious Hereford fans, most of them seeming to be schoolboys in 'parka' coats, running wildly on to join the celebrations. BBC commentator John Motson's reputation soared with his spine-tingling excitement: *"Radford again, what a goal! What a goal!"* How is it that something so exhilarating, that made you try and recreate it in the street, that has made you smile so many times, can now bring tears to the eyes? It's only a goal, isn't it? But to me it's beautiful. It's art. It's the best pudding you ever ate as a child, you can still taste it. There is life in that goal.

If your team did reach Wembley, even if you support a big team and it became a habit, it was like visiting a 'Magic Kingdom'. The Twin Towers of the stadium in north-west London are like beacons, as if you are on the fictional 'Yellow Brick Road'. There was no feeling quite like walking up Wembley Way, the slope that takes you to the stadium from the subway. As a child it was overwhelming. If it felt like a one-off for a club's fans, people would be in tears as they walked. Inside the stadium the colour and the noise took your breath. Flags and fans split equally in a crowd of over 70,000, and the traditional singing of *Abide with Me*. Elton John wept in the Wembley stands when the hymn was sung before the 1984 FA Cup final, featuring his club Watford, in the era of Graham Taylor's management.

There was a time when we could name every FA Cup Final result for years. The man who scored the winning goal was a hero for life. Without the slightest exaggeration. What did Sunderland do in 1979 and Villa in 1981? Score the winning goal. Alan Sunderland overflowed with joy in the May sunshine in a sweaty yellow shirt after his decisive late goal for Arsenal against Manchester United in 1979, arms pumping as he celebrated, his perm glistening like a 'prog rocker' who'd just been told his song had entered the charts at number one. In 1981, Ricky Villa, Tottenham's bearded Argentine, scoring a famous goal in a replay under the floodlights to beat Manchester city, slaloming through tackles and squeezing the ball under the goalkeeper. As the ball was about to cross the line, a nation was in collective disbelief at this virtuoso intervention. *He hasn't just done that, has he?*

Unfashionable, unfathomable Wimbledon Football Club beat Liverpool in 1988: The Crazy Gang have beaten the Culture Club" said John Motson. Though the commentator's finest Cup *final* moment was his first in 1977. Martin Buchan's Manchester United team beat Liverpool. *"How fitting that a man called Buchan should be the first to climb 'The 39 Steps'"* said Motson, referencing to the novel by John Buchan. Motson knew it was literally 39 steps at Wembley Stadium for captains and their team to ascend from the pitch to the Royal Box and lift the trophy.

These shared experiences, watched by over 20 million of us combined on BBC *and* ITV on Saturday afternoons, have become sepia-tinged nostalgia in England, like an old family photo on the shelf featuring long-departed grandparents. The reasons the FA Cup's magic disappeared were part-tragedy, part-circumstantial, and largely because football became a business, saturated by games that make money. The Hillsborough Disaster in 1989 was an FA Cup semi-final. It was a miracle tragedy hadn't struck years before. Fans were being crammed into grounds that weren't fit for purpose at football grounds all over the UK. It was Liverpool fans who suffered, and many families are still suffering.

Semi-finals subsequently started to be played at Wembley as well as finals. It was the right decision, and part of a bigger picture. Stadiums became all-seaters. Fans would no longer be treated like herded, caged animals, the game was finally safer. In that context, the collateral damage to the FA Cup is of small significance. But it changed the perfect narrative, that your team, any team, could reach those Twin Towers in May. Semi-finals at Wembley diluted the power of reaching the glorious Kingdom of the final. When football was made safer it *could* have been revisited. Semi-finals should be played at the new, large stadiums in London or Manchester. The semi-finals don't *have* to be at Wembley. The magic has weakened. Even more damaging to the FA Cup has been the rise and rise of the Premier League and Champions League. It became incredibly lucrative to finish high in the Premier League, specifically the top four league places in England. This meant qualifying for Europe's big trophy, helping attract the world's best players. The FA Cup became marginalised.

As always tends to happen with football, owners and their managers took things too far. Teams in the middle of the top division and even lower divisions of England, started picking reserve players to play in the FA Cup matches, so as not to spoil their chances of winning *league* matches, and to keep their 'best' players fresh. They were effectively saying fourth places and more money is better than winning trophies, of daring to dream, of going for glory, of giving supporters something tangible to really cherish.

The upshot is an FA Cup of 'two halves'. From the early rounds to the entry of the big clubs, it has retained its special qualities. But the later rounds are hollow, and the final is the palest shadow of what it was in my childhood, with all the atmosphere of a game of FIFA on a console. If my first final, in 1978, was a cool vinyl record that you remember the journey to buy, the last few finals have been like a samey track offered by a streaming service you never asked for. What the FA Cup still provides is *opportunity*, even if big clubs aren't fussed about trying to take it.

The danger elsewhere in football, in sport, comes from those trying to remove opportunity. Ringfencing assets and closing the door on entry. Many sports administrators seem to love the American football model, the NFL, a closed shop of 32 franchises. But they covet The NFL's model *without* the draft system that makes American sport fair, where the worst performing teams get to pick the best players the following season.

In European football there is continuous, greedy agitation from clubs who want to protect their position and make as much money as possible, such as a famous one in Italy which must remain unnamed here, but whose annual corporate Christmas card to me is unwelcome. I'd prefer them and their peers to stop pushing to restructure European club football, in order to play more games against big teams from England and Spain, largely because their own Serie A league in Italy was usurped for its position of power in the 1980s and 90s.

The European Cup used to be a thing of great purity, played between the *Champions* of Europe's leagues. Every game meant something. Brian Clough's Nottingham Forest winning it twice was incredible. Opportunity seized. Miraculous and inspirational. But doable. Nothing's impossible — unless football bosses find a way to close the opportunity.

There is no doubting the Champions League has been a great success and yes it probably needed to evolve. I accept my own club wouldn't have had its finest hour if only *Champions* had been allowed to play, rather than *four* teams from England (ironically the Champions League allows *non-Champions* to play too).

And yes, the revered Champions League music, adapted from Handel's *Zadok the Priest*, is an enduring stroke of genius. But the people who run football across the world collectively never know when to stop milking it. Trying to seize power, ringfence the money, exclude the masses, remove opportunity.

There *has* to be the ultimate chance for Nottingham Forest, or a historically 'big club' like Ajax of the Netherlands, or the champions of Slovakia and Slovenia, to do well. Football has become a business for the rich. There is nothing wrong with making money and running clubs smartly. But it *has* to be done fairly. Too many of the major clubs are now run by businesses who don't care about the history, the community, the fans. Just the potential to make money going forward. There is room for both. There is a *duty* for both. If the richest clubs could get away with playing the other rich clubs only, they would do it in a heartbeat. It's disheartening and disgraceful. It isn't sport, it's a cartel.

It's not just football where commercial gain has led to questionable treatment of smaller nations and teams. In cricket, England, India and Australia formed a tripod of power where they use their status to take as much of the pie as possible. Never mind that the West Indies used to thrash all three of these nations at cricket for many years. 'Growing the game' is compromised when a few major nations retain too much of the financial muscle. It's short-sighted thinking.

The shortest forms of the game have become the most lucrative. 'T20' is the king of these big-hitting, fast-paced spectacles. It lasts three hours, each team has 120 balls and it's the format of the rich, prestigious Indian Premier League. The world's cricket stars are part of an auction - a huge money-spinner with a bombardment of sponsorship.

Think of this form of cricket as confectionery. The main meal is Test cricket. There must be room for both. A balanced diet. But cricket is gorging on T20 because it is where the money is. Restraint, discernment is wise. The game still needs young players to be able to develop the skills for Test cricket. They are transferable. Short term thinking will kill Test cricket.

Sport, including individual sport, needs access and opportunity. Tennis players who hardly ever win suddenly having a good run at Wimbledon. Olympians who could barely swim finding themselves in the Olympic pool. Boxers who land that punch that changes their lives. Football teams who suddenly lift the spirits of the people.

The bell in sport can sound as an awakening, or a warning. Does anybody want to hear, does anybody want to see, what sport has become?

In Leicester, in 2015 and 2016, there was a different sound. What was developing in the city, at the football club, wasn't normal. Something very, very strange was happening. The power of *The Dilly Dong Bell* was about to be revealed.

Chapter 15: THE DILLY DONG BELL

Battlefields in Leicester belong in the 15th century, not the year 2015, so it was good to see continued proof that Claudio Ranieri was joking about wanting to kill the Watford Football Club manager. But Ranieri's Leicester team were proving to be lethal and beat Newcastle by three goals to nil in their next match to position themselves close to the top of the Premier League table. In the position Sebastian Coe liked to be, poised 'on the shoulder' of the leaders.

Leicester were not expected to remain this high. They still weren't being talked about as serious contenders to win the league, remarkable considering they had lost just *one* match in the first third of the season. There was, however, a lot of attention on the next match at their King Power Stadium in late November, and not just because the visiting team was Manchester United, serial winners of the Premier League until Alex Ferguson retired in 2013.

The reason was Jamie Vardy. When he scored against Newcastle, well of course he scored, it equalled a record in the Premier League for goals in consecutive games; 11 games in succession. It was a big deal. The Premier League is seen as starting in 'Year Zero', with previous heroic feats being ignored to concentrate on what happened from 1992 onwards. Vardy could now break a Premier League record by scoring against Manchester United, having equalled their former player Ruud Van Nistelrooy's scoring record.

Midway through the first half, Christian Fuchs cleverly threaded a perfect pass behind United's defence, knowing that Vardy would always be available, always trying to breach the barrier. Having slipped away from his marker like 'Hamburglar' evading Ronald McDonald, Vardy touched the ball instinctively, just once to set up the shot, and then struck the ball low and expertly past the goalkeeper before setting off in celebration. The commentator Peter Drury, another of Hayters' alumni, nailed it: "*History!*" he cried emphatically. The crowd noise was quite something. There was actually squealing from the fans, such was the level of hysteria under the floodlights in Leicester.

These fans may not have yet believed Leicester could win the Premier League, but they certainly believed in the team and Vardy. Every week was like a party, with the noise level becoming a trademark despite the capacity being less than half the size of some English stadiums. 'Cardboard clappers' were being used by some fans, which revived the traditions of the rattle, once a mainstay of English football and *Pathé* newsreels.

New songs emerged, a mystical feature of football, in that it's difficult to know where they come from, and or who the lyrical geniuses were that started them. In Leicester's case, the main chant was basic, and wouldn't be winning a prestigious '*Ivor Novello Award*' for lyrical composition.

Jamie Vardy wanted the ball,
Jamie Vardy got it,
All the Kings horses and all the Kings men
Couldn't stop Vardy from scoring again

Maybe the influence of King Richard III was still being felt across the city.

Another chant was becoming the most popular and getting attention beyond Leicester: "*Jamie Vardy's 'avin a party. Jamie Vardy's 'avin a party.*"

He had some notoriety for bad behaviour, having had to apologise for a comment to a Japanese man in a casino in Thailand, home of the club's owners. Then the new football season started, and he started scoring goals. His previous indiscipline was pushed into the background. Football works like that. This was a party that was starting to annoy some of the neighbours. They just wanted Leicester to go away and stop bothering them.

Leicester were not keen to turn the noise down. Two games later they beat champions Chelsea 2-1. Claudio was on the touchline as always, orchestrating, organising. His team reached the top of the Premier League standings. Chelsea's manager, José Mourinho, was sacked.

In the space of four days at the start of February, it became clear, startingly, to most football fans, that Leicester City might actually *win* the league. Millions of doubters were suddenly convinced.
But what had happened? How? What blue spell had been conjured?

At the King Power Stadium, under lights and increasingly formidable, Leicester were playing Liverpool. An hour had been played and no goals scored. Liverpool were one of only two teams to have beaten Leicester so far, and most neutral observers suspected they would get the better of Leicester again. Riyad Mahrez received the ball in a tight space in his own half of the pitch but produced a piece of escapology that would have had Houdini throwing his hands up and seeking alternative work.

Once free, Mahrez launched the ball long range into space ahead of Vardy, the sole Leicester player in an advanced, attacking area. Vardy allowed the ball to bounce on this occasion, then suddenly, outrageously, from over 30 metres and at a difficult angle, shot for goal. The ball flew over the goalkeeper into the net in a perfect arc, of course it did! Then Vardy scored again. A two-nil win for Leicester. What was going on?

Four days later, an even bigger 'sight test' on what was coming in to focus from Leicester. They played an 'away' match at Manchester City, without the inspirational noise of their own fans. The unusual was becoming routine for Leicester. The German defender Robert Huth, not a man expected to be contributing goals, scored twice. But the memory of the match came from Mahrez, who was becoming impossible for opposition defenders to cope with.

Mahrez pounced on the ball, burst towards goal, dropped a shoulder, left City defenders dazed like cartoon characters being hypnotised, and shot high into the net with his right foot. At what point do such sights cease to shock? This was not normal, no matter how much talent Mahrez possesses.

Later he was bought by Manchester City and their oil-rich backers for a fee of £60 million. For now, wearing Leicester's black away kit, Mahrez and his Leicester gang had ridden into town and got what they needed. Top of the Premier League. This was not the movies though. It was real.

How was Ranieri's team doing this? What was their secret? These weren't meant to be exceptional players. Mahrez, was now clearly a special talent, but had been signed from French club Le Havre two years earlier, for a fee of just £320,000.

Vardy had emerged from the lower leagues, where the signs he was a miracle worker were well-hidden. Who knew he would turn the biggest league in football upside down? Leicester were top of the table and refusing to budge, so now Ranieri was finally starting to attract attention himself. Why, how were Leicester still on top? What was going on. A little peep behind the magician's curtain was called for.

The media conferences at Leicester remained low key. Maybe if the coffee machine had run out of water or somebody had forgotten the biscuits, or Claudio was pretending he would kill another manager, there would have been some tension. But instead, there were smiles, it was cordial.

How was he getting so much out of these unheralded players? That was the question that prompted his player Danny Drinkwater to talk about Claudio's methods. Which included a little *bell*. Ranieri was asked about this. Good question! Look for the joy, not just the jeopardy. There's a time and a place for good news, to be uplifted. This was it.

"I tell to them Dilly Ding, Dilly Dong! When they are sleeping. And then I buy for them a little bell," said Ranieri in his endearing Italian-English with occasionally misplaced words, far better than my English Italian.

The bell story fitted perfectly with the quiet eccentricities we'd heard about when he was Chelsea manager 13 years earlier. And it prompted something extraordinary. One of the reporters did something he might not have dared to do to Claudio's predecessor, or some of the grumpier managers that populate the world of football management. He actually handed Ranieri a little bell! Inspired!

"Hey, you are sleeping, come on!" said Ranieri smiling, and pressing the bell as if asking for service at a hotel. But there was an undercurrent of awkwardness, or reticence, as if he also realised his achievements, Leicester's achievements, should not become a novelty act. Or something to be trivialised.

The reporter persisted: "Do you think you have this aura of a head teacher about you though, with the players?" He was trying understandably to continue exploring the use of the bell. *"No, no"* said Ranieri and by now he was relaxing into the exchange and was chuckling. He hadn't gone looking for this, but he knew the media game, and it wasn't a problem for him to play along:

"Because from the beginning when there something was wrong, I say: Hey Dilly Dong, Dilly Dong! Wake up wake up. During all the training sessions sometimes Dilly Dong Dilly Dong. And so, on Christmas Day I bought for all the players, for all the staff, everybody, I bought a little bell. Dilly Ding Dilly Dong. Just a little joke!"

Ranieri was known for small motivational acts of generosity and togetherness, like taking the entire squad out for a pizza as a reward for not conceding a goal. But who of the players at the time felt the message *wasn't* serious? It's seriously clever. Were the gifts just for the players? No. Ranieri bought bells for *all* the staff. This was a man demonstrating what it was to show kindness.

When he entered these conferences, long before the pandemic changed society. Ranieri would make a point of shaking the hand of everybody in the room. At the back was a row of television cameras on the podium and hidden behind them were camera operators. Every single one of them would be offered Ranieri's hand. I didn't know about this until I found myself in that room. To this day, this simple gesture makes me smile. A football manager second, and a human being first. Respect, respect, respect. Wisdom, perspective, grace. Kindness. Qualities that bring the best out of people around you, whether or not you use a 'Dilly Dong' bell.

Chapter 16: A DRESS TO MATCH HIS TIE

When Claudio Ranieri addressed the media in Leicester there were five or six women in the room at most. It would be the same at Liverpool, Luton, Leeds. Throughout football and most sports events and conferences.

I regularly attended large conferences designed for people across sport to 'network', for people to talk themselves up to others eager to talk themselves up. I always felt my job was to find the sports news within, the story that represented what was under the surface in sport. We'd listen to grand speeches and watch slick marketing films about inclusivity, integrity and fairness, about the *good* that sport does. But nobody appeared to be talking about the vast gender imbalance at the conferences and at the top tables of decision-making. There were a lot of men in suits swapping business cards though.

In recent times, the number of journalists who are female is growing and to some, that is an end in itself. But is it? Have pay discrepancies, subtle prejudices and favouritism been eradicated? Do female journalists constantly feel the need to prove something, because the undercurrents of sexism are usually close to the surface? When I ask female friends in the industry, they say yes, the problems are still there, and there is poison on social media to deal with for 'daring' to talk about sport to an audience or readership that is predominantly male.

It can be uncomfortable as a man to raise the subject of sexism in the industry. I once 'pitched' a programme on the subject and it was thrown back in my face, with the softener that it was a 'good idea'. But the idea was rejected because it wasn't "personal enough to me", because I am a man. Ironically, the programme did have a significant personal element. As someone who had been a boss, I wanted to revisit whether I'd done enough to bring through female journalists. I had planned to interview former employees, to *listen*.

If I'm honest, I wasn't expecting a rough ride. I was opening myself up in an attempt to expose the men who don't think hard enough about this, who don't try to do the right thing. It wasn't hard to see the misogyny in sports journalism over my first couple of decades in the industry was destructive.

The way I think about it, it's less about gender or management. It's about kindness. Does somebody feel comfortable with you? I would estimate over 90 per cent of the bosses at the time were men. Many of them had a more-intimidating style than me. What did they do to make people feel more comfortable? Or were they actively using and abusing their aura?

Some football managers like Claudio Ranieri, like Jürgen Klopp, make people feel better about themselves. Support and encouragement. The only 'fear factor' players and the support team feel comes from potentially letting these managers down. Other football managers use a big booming voice and lots of swearing. You know the sort. The authority male figure.

I've tentatively had conversations with female friends about the behaviour of the male authority figures in newsrooms and offices. I know what intimidation in the workplace looks like. And I know how difficult it can be to stand up to bullying. But I know I can't know what it feels like to be them. It upsets me when I see friends who remain affected, entrapped psychologically by the effect of the overbearing male authority figure. It's toxic.

Some *still* seek the approval of the bullish male boss, years after leaving their organisations. This frustrates and saddens me - they are *still* being oppressed. These oafish, boorish misogynists still have a hold, still have an influence, still have a *surface* reputation as leaders who are mainly firm but fair. But their victims often look to them for approval rather than finding validation within themselves. Perhaps this is a throwback of learning how to best handle the original situation, and to keep the boss on side.

Why am I so passionately engaged by this subject? Is it virtue signalling? No. I cannot bear obnoxious male figures, cagey to their peers and superiors, but 'punching down' to those below. We've all suffered from this approach, male or female, and I've always been lucky to have the strength to fight back against it. I'm not easily intimidated and have been mentally equipped to handle it when it happens. But I do ask myself the question - is male confidence and female competence a generalisation? Or is it a quiet truth of many workplaces?

'Sportswomen' continue to have to manage two battles in their careers. One is to be the best at what they do, as far as possible. The other is to push for the recognition they deserve, the pay, the equality, more.

Tennis champion Billie Jean King has been doing whatever it takes to improve life for women in her sport, and all sport. At one stage she orchestrated around 60 colleagues as they barricaded themselves in a London hotel room, waving legal papers that led to the formation of the Women's Tennis Association.

Part of King's anger was a tournament in Los Angeles where the women's champion earned a sixth of the men's event. The daughter of a firefighter, she was a trailblazer. She even agreed to take part in the 'Battle of the Sexes'. This was an exhibition tennis match in 1973 in Houston against Bobby Riggs, a 55-year-old male player twice her age. An estimated television audience of 50 million viewers in America, and 90 million worldwide, watched King win in straight sets. Much has changed in tennis, but not without the female players having to fight for better pay, battling like Monica Seles scrapping on the baseline.

In 2007, the jewel in the tennis crown, Wimbledon, finally agreed to equal prize money for men and women, presumably leaving many in the best seats at Centre Court hot under the blazer at the novelty of female players being given equal footing. But tennis was an anomaly. Eight of the top ten best earners in women's sport a decade later were tennis players, and other sports were slower to catch up to the earning power of female players, or maybe didn't have the forehand and foresight of King, Chris Evert, Martina Navratilova and others, who ensured tennis wasn't a sport where women could be treated unfairly.

Tennis was taking one step forward, but there was the danger of a 'foot fault' and a big step back. Because glamour was usurping sporting prowess, something that was also prominent in sports broadcasting. I remember in the late 1990s being sent out to interview the world's most famous and marketable tennis player. A Russian woman, but I won't name her, because this is not about her, it's about a system. You see, she wasn't brilliant at tennis. Sure, she was good enough to play professionally but only just. And it didn't matter how many games she lost because she was so marketable. That sold tennis gear, and on this occasion, expensive watches. My interview with her was no *'Frost/Nixon'*.

Around that time the Williams sisters emerged, two of the most significant and fascinating sports stars in history, their achievements reaching way beyond hitting a ball with a racquet. *'Straight outta Compton'*, though the one in California not New York, and facing three major forms of prejudice as they forged their paths to trophy after trophy. Racism, sexism and class. To say it wasn't easy for a Black girl from a non-privileged background to succeed in a sport like tennis is possibly the mother of all understatements. To make it, Venus and Serena had to be so much better than the rest, but also to keep on *proving* it.

Venus, a year older, was the first to make it big, winning Wimbledon and the US Open in the year 2000. Eventually, it was Serena who would go on to become world number one and break record after record. And Serena who would provide the most intriguing narrative. But at the height of her success, Serena was still not getting the recognition and popularity she deserved. Sure, she had her fans, but others were getting more, to use a tennis term, love. Why? Why was blond-haired, blue-eyed, slim Russian, earning more from endorsements, despite far fewer trophies?

Often the play of leading female players would be described as graceful or classy. Complimentary analysis for Serena was harder to come by, backhanded compliments if she was lucky, and we'd constantly hear about her power and strength, as if she was always winning by blowing her lesser-built opponents off the court. As if she never played a drop shot, or expertly placed a second serve out of reach, or manoeuvred opponents around the court. As if she never showed the mental fortitude to dig her way out of a losing situation with smart play. It's not easy winning a 'Grand Slam' tennis tournament, and if Serena ever made it seem like that, shouldn't such ability be celebrated?

Something happened. And considering the barriers she faced, it was a shame to see it unfold. I'm talking about her infamous meltdown at the 2018 US Open. I take issue with those who quickly defended her behaviour to be *seen* to defend it. But I should also hold my own hand up. For the first and only time in my career I 'bottled it'. I was away on another deployment, but closely watched the incident unfold and was about to tweet on it. Then I considered the lack of sophistication and understanding on social media, where everything is overly simplistic. For me to criticise Serena could be misconstrued as prejudice against her. Social media doesn't do nuance. So, I kept my views to myself on an incident that *did* need properly exploring. It's not straightforward.

Umpire Carlos Ramos warned Williams for "receiving coach" as she struggled to contain the brilliance of Japanese player Naomi Osaka, in her first Grand Slam final. Williams *reportedly* said to Ramos: "I don't cheat, I'd rather lose," and the unravelling started from there. Serena cracked her racquet in fury, was deducted a point and called Ramos a "thief' for deducting it.

The final was completely overshadowed by Williams' behaviour, it was headline news, and when Osaka, the better player on the night, completed victory, she was in tears. Not of joy. Of upset. The crowd were booing, showing support to Serena against the umpire and the system. The situation was overwhelming. And when Serena comforted her, it was too late. She could have thought about Osaka earlier. This night should have belonged to her opponent, and it didn't. Never has, and possibly never will.

After the match Serena stayed on the attack: "*I'm here fighting for women's rights and for women's equality and for all kind of stuff. For me to say thief and for him to take a game, it made me feel like it was a sexist remark. He's never taken a game away from a man because they said thief. For me it blows my mind. But I'm going to continue to fight for women*".

These words were followed by article after article, some near hysterical, defending Serena, describing the difficulties she has faced in life as a Black woman. Counter-productive and patronising words about her. The right issue, the wrong example. There were countless times to highlight the racism and sexism suffered by her, by Venus, by other Black players, by other female players, by Black women across sport, across society. On this occasion, Serena got it horribly wrong. On that night, she threw a tantrum. The tantrum of a top tennis player. This felt to me like it was more 'John McEnroe' than Billie Jean King. Reminding me of the open frustration he used to display. Forgivably so? It was inadvertently disrespectful and damaging to her opponent on what should have been the best night of her life.

Serena, like most tennis champions, is prone to frustration when things aren't going her way. On this night she was being fairly and rarely beaten. Tennis umpires can have an air of pomposity and his manner could be adjudged lofty, but in an intimidating way? Sexist? Racist? Bullying? In my judgement, on that night, no. Serena's reaction was more explicable and excusable as arising being from a cumulative effect.

I did actually see lots of people online calling out Serena for her behaviour. Depressingly, many of them opportunistically used the incident to air their racist, sexist views, and in-built negativity around Serena and her temperament. I wish she hadn't lost it on that night, because it was a setback to an important issue, male entitlement and tone. Tone being the key word. I hate the way I've heard 'important' men speak to women in offices. And indeed, speak to anybody they consider junior and inferior. Strange how you don't hear those sorts of men using a tone like that to their bosses.

On that night in New York, common sense, my eyes, my ears, my sense of fair play, told me that my sympathies were unapologetically with Naomi Osaka, waving meekly and sheepishly to the booing crowd. And that rather than defending Serena, who happens to be my favourite tennis player since Seles, it would have been more sensible to use this occasion to draw light to the struggles she faced *away* from this night. Her 'case' here misrepresented the struggle women face in sport, in life, every day. Some friends have a slightly different view. One, a sports journalist, said to me that *"When you are a Black woman like me, and go through what we do, you don't get to analyse so deeply. You quickly support Serena. You get why she acted that way."*

In sports journalism, it can be easy to see a sportswoman, or sportsman as a competitor, a brand, a subject. But there is a human there. Serena, Naomi. To try walking in their shoes, to try to understand what they have been through individually, and their actions, to not be one-dimensional and throw around hot takes. It's the very least we can do.

There is a lot of room between where coverage of women's sporting events has progressed to, and where it should be. Witness the biggest women's sports event in history, for female competitors only. The 2019 football World Cup in France.

As you know by now, I love a football World Cup. I pushed hard to cover this as a priority over other major sports events 21 years after reporting on the men's World Cup in France. See how easy it is to offer up constant comparison to men's sport, and not let women's events exist on merit. Even the category 'women's sport' doesn't work – there is a world of difference between the Women's Football World Cup and a domestic rugby match that happens to be a women's fixture. So why bracket women's sport together and expect women, or men, to watch? This happens in media a lot. A 'womens' sports section or programme. It screams *clumsy male executive in charge of inclusivity, who is trying to keep up*.

The World Cup of 2019 was the biggest event for many reasons including size of crowds, audiences, broadcasters and sponsorship money. Social media consumption, inevitably, played an important part. Over a million tickets were sold, and over 58 million viewers watched a match in the last 16 between Brazil and France. 14 of the nations were sponsored by Nike alone. But what about the prize money? It doubled to $30 million, but compare that, as it's right to do in this instance, to the men's prize money of $400 million. FIFA's welcome response was to announce another doubling of the women's event prize money for next time, via an extension of the tournament from 24 to 32 teams. MY kind of extension, growing the *game* as well as the finances, and making the perfect format.

The standard of the best teams in international women's football was not in question, unless it was tiresome 'blokes' online doing the questioning and comparisons. And the best team, the exceptional '*Team USA*', made a noise on and off the field of play.

They took apart their opponents (including a 13-0 win over Thailand - not for the squeamish - and which drew some criticism for their celebrations). But what was even more significant, was players taking legal action against their national association for equal pay. Part of their case being their success in *comparison* to the men's team.

The players lost their original case in a Los Angeles court. The reason given was that the men's game negotiated its own deal. But the players and their representatives say such a deal wasn't offered to *them,* and appealed. The simplicity of being able to concentrate on the football not being afforded to the world's best team, because they happen to be female.

'Front and center', as they would write it in the States, was a woman who had already changed the face of football, understanding the need to be prominent, to be outspoken where necessary, to make a difference. An exceptional player in the US women's team, Megan Rapinoe, had turned 34-years-old when the tournament in France kicked off, and achieved a lot in the game. By the time her team lifted the World Cup in France she was a superstar, transcending football.

On the pitch you couldn't miss Rapinoe for two big reasons – her pink hair, and much more importantly, her six goals and three assists. She received the *'golden boot'* for top scorer *and 'golden ball'* for top player.

When Rapinoe spoke about discrimination she was laser-sharp, as when shooting for goal. *"Don't settle for anything less, go for equal, go for more, don't accept any of these antiquated and BS answers. Until we have equal investment, and overinvestment really, we're not gonna have any meaningful conversation about compensation and revenues and TV viewership. At times you feel like you're banging your head against a wall. But it's a fact of life for us so we might as well fight like hell."*

How inspirational and influential Rapinoe has been, how liberating, with her words and actions. Since 'coming out' in 2012, she has used her platform to tackle issues facing the LGBTQ+ community. It is a tragedy that others cannot come out, and understandable. Inevitably when a sports figure comes out, their sexuality quickly defines them rather than their sporting prowess.

A male cricketer found himself with the prefix "gay cricketer" as if it makes a difference to his batting and bowling. While in English men's football, there are 'apparently' NO famous gay male players since Justin Fashanu, who tragically ended his own life in 1998 at the age of 37.
High-profile footballers known to be gay don't publicly exist, as 'coming out' remains such a difficult hurdle for an athlete to cross. What a de-

moralising, destructive and unacceptable shame this continues to be, and imagine the suffering it causes those who need to keep their sexuality hidden. How desperately ironic and sad. Because who should ever have to hide it? Justin's niece Amal Fashanu continues to raise awareness of the issue via a foundation in his name, and privately supports players who are still having to conceal their sexuality from their teammates and the world outside.

Rapinoe, intelligently and sensitively, did not specifically call for her fellow pros to "come out", saying that while it's liberating, people should do it in their own time. "We see you and we're with you" was her gentle encouragement. When she was named 'FIFA Player of the Year' alongside Lionel Messi in September 2019, she used the stage to draw attention to racism, long before the issue was given a fraction of the prominence it needed.

"*If ever there's an instance of racism, if every single player on the field is not outraged, then to me they are part of the problem,*" she told the BBC's Eleanor Roper in an interview at the time. She also went toe-to-toe, or rather *tweet-to-tweet* with Trump, and slotted him away like one of her many goals. If Trump possessed any shame, he'd have walked off the platform there and then. You sense Rapinoe is a natural in the spotlight, the distinctive hair being a clue she makes her own rules, and football, sport, society needs her. But not all athletes have her talent and eloquence. And not all have her global platform and confidence. She is doing her best to share it.

Before 'Rapinoe's World Cup', I researched the story of women's football, including Scotland. 2019 was the first time the Scottish women's team had qualified, but this nation had a long history of women's football, originating through churches in the 16th century. This seems so remarkable, preceding even the reign of King Richard III, that I didn't fully believe it until I saw the evidence.

For 50 years, from the early 1920s, there was a ban on women using the facilities at men's grounds. It was a deliberate attempt to drive the game from sight. Yet talented players like Nancy 'Cannonball' Thompson were showing their ability for Scotland *despite* the system, not because of it.

Scotland weren't qualifying for Women's World Cups, but technically nobody was. Unlike men's football, there was no official World Cup arranged by the global governing body. Women's football was – to the wider world - out of sight and out of mind. In Scotland in the 1960s, when the men's team had strong players, a special talent named Rose Reilly was achieving incredible things without any fanfare or spotlight.

As a child in Ayrshire, she swapped a present of a doll for a football. As an adult, her feats should have made her 'world famous'. A prolific scorer of goals, she headed to France to play for Stade de Reims, then to AC Milan. It was good decision-making by Rose. The Scotland team didn't qualify for the World Cup until 2019.

While playing and scoring in Italy, she was able to switch to play for the Italian national team, scoring 13 goals in 22 games. Her finest moment should be known to everybody who cares about football.

In 1984 this Scotswoman, who'd long been frustrated by the lack of opportunity in her homeland, was captain of the *Italy* team that won the *Mundialito Femminile*, the precursor to the official Women's World Cup. In the final she scored a vital goal, and when she eventually retired in the early 90s, her career had spanned four decades. Shouldn't the majority of global football fans have heard of Rose Reilly, and had the chance to celebrate her achievements?

*

The champions of women's football in Scotland are the formidable Glasgow City, FC winning the league every year for a decade and a force in women's European football too. They had the trophies, but not the crowds, nor the media coverage.

This became so frustrating they decided to send out a message. *"You can't be what you can't see."* And emblazoned it on the back of their shirts. You can imagine what Rose Reilly was thinking, about nothing having changed. Over 30 years after she was officially the world's best player, new generations were still having to fight for a spotlight.

Glasgow City's players – like the US team - weren't able to focus on football alone. Many were part-time, including Joanne Love, a scientist. Jo played a phenomenal 191 times for Scotland and was part of the Glasgow City team for their game against Hamilton, in a near-empty stadium. In the dressing room before the game, she held the hand of a small girl, the mascot on the day, and introduced her to the team.

The girl must have been around six years old. Looking for heroes, for inspiration. Like I was at her age, hungry for more. *You can't be what you don't see.*

In sport, momentum is crucial. Pre-pandemic, international women's football had some momentum, and there were good operators in the media and behind the scenes, pushing, hitting the right buttons to get more sportswomen seen, to celebrate what they are achieving. For every 'top ten' women's tennis player being paid well, there are hundreds, thousands of sportswomen fighting for the opportunities they need. The concern is that when sport stopped, the momentum stopped. That old habits *will* return, that women's sport will fall behind again.

After two full decades playing club football in Scotland, Jo's season was halted, like so much of life, by Covid-19. But ironically her talents were fielded in a different way. Jo has been carrying out vital laboratory work in Glasgow, putting football, and sport more generally, into perspective. While she was playing an important role in managing an unprecedented crisis, the men's game was often preoccupied by such things as a disallowed goal because of change to the handball law. That may sound like a crude comparison, but if female footballers are going to be constantly held up against the men's game, then why not switch it around?

One day, soon we hope, there will be a time when a female footballer doesn't have to hold down another job, or move to another country, or fight in the courts for equal pay. Or fight in an office to get their voice heard. Or wear an outfit in a television studio to match the colour of the male presenter's tie.

Chapter 17: A FOOTBALLER TO FEED A CHILD

On talent shows, when young singers strive to become famous, wanting fame with every bone in their body, then become famous, then complain about the downside of fame, they don't usually attract much sympathy. But why *shouldn't* a kid with a voice try and be star, and why *should* they have to put up with so much abuse, any more than the rest of us?

Sports stars will usually see fame as a by-product, a necessary 'evil'. Most of them hate interviews and grow into it, getting better over time. For every Peter Crouch with his dry humour and engaging personality, there are dozens of footballers who look like they'd rather be anywhere than in front of that advertising board full of logos. I have some sympathy considering the dubious quality of some of the questions they get asked.

Sports stars want to be musicians. How many times have we seen 'big hitters' in sport also try for a big hit in music? Musicians want to be sports stars. What platinum-selling musical genius doesn't also fancy being Michael Jordan or an incredible footballer like Lionel Messi? But there is a difference between the two professions – aside from the obvious. Sports stars are still expected to be *'role models'*. That's why rock stars 'raising hell' used to be shrugged off but England footballer Raheem Sterling buying a car is front page news. How dare he spend his money. And there's often a racial undertone, or overtone from critics. To be young, Black and rich doesn't sit well with everyone. But we'll get to that.

Role model. What does that actually mean? Who joins a football academy as a child, practices day and night, makes sacrifices and dreams of being a role model? Who kicks a ball to seek praise over their conduct instead of their ability to beat three players and score the winning goal in a World Cup final? If it worked like that, the wonderfully decent England manager Gareth Southgate would have been one of world football's 'all-time greatest'. But it's been wonderful to see him thriving in his humane leadership of the England national team. You win some, you lose some.

Expectations are put on people who make a living through sport, that most of us don't have to comply by. There are other quirks of this unofficial moral code. Such as how *we* are allowed to leave a job if we find a better one, and yet a footballer can be castigated for doing so. When you've been congratulated on a new role, has anybody questioned your loyalty? Well, it goes with the pay cheque if you're a high-earning footballer.

'Role model' can be a mythical, misunderstood term. It's often used for a misdemeanour, or a pattern of undesirable behaviour. *What kind of role model is he, swearing like that?"* To use my new catchphrase, *sport reflects society*. And in sport, to use one of Sepp Blatter's phrases, there are "bad apples".

Sport operates in a weird bubble though, and few things have confounded me and defeated me over 30 years of reporting on it as much as what I'll call *'sports law',* the punishments dished out within sport for offences that take place away from the sporting workplace.

Let's take the example of the NFL, the thrilling and enjoyable theatre of American Football played between September and February. I'm not picking on the NFL, or using them without good reason, because there is plenty they get right and the action is irresistibly watchable, but I remain dismayed by a regular problem *for* this league. Not a problem for the NFL only, far from it, but a recurring issue within this sport. Namely their punishments for criminal activity, especially domestic violence.

Players have been arrested and charged for such offences with depressing regularity, reflecting a societal problem. This is not always quickly dealt with by the law, and means the player continues to work. If this happened with a colleague of ours, we would most likely be unaware of the situation, and they would usually continue working until if and when they faced trial. But in sport, and when it's headline news, the 'story' unfolds under a spotlight. And this is what I can't get my head around - league executives or franchise bosses will then take action that is liable to include a *ban* for a number of games.

Take a step back. A ban. *'Let that sink in'*, as the social media phrase goes. A commission of sports administrators, usually men, gets to decide on a punishment for a player who is charged with domestic violence. Let's not sanitise it with that official term. Charged with beating a woman. Viciously and cruelly abusing their partners. In 2014, the NFL invoked a domestic violence policy, stating first time offenders would receive a six-game, no-pay ban. How did they settle on six games? Not eight, or four? Or a season. With respect, who are these men to decided how many games a brutal attack on a woman should be punished with? That is the job of the law.

I'm not singling out the NFL as better or worse than other sports governing bodies, but they have had to deal with this more than most. I am questioning how this is fair on anybody, including them. It does not feel right, it should not be their place to equate horrific crimes to the amount of time lost from the workplace.

It is undoubtedly an unwieldy situation for these sports bosses, and they shouldn't be having to make decisions as to whether a player takes the field, after offences away from the game. It turns the stomach when these franchises are grappling with how many missed games a beating is worth.

The annual *'Super Bowl'* is the showpiece game of NFL, and one of the main events of the year in the United States, sport or otherwise. In a recent Super Bowl, one of the 'star' players, an explosively fast runner, was running from the past. One journalist 'upset the applecart' by repeatedly asking why this man's backstory was off limits. But sports journalism has a horrible habit of thinking there's a time and place where talking about *sport* is all that matters.

And in Super Bowl such stories are swept under a 'red carpet' as the players enter the field of play to wild applause. The backstory was that the player had pleaded guilty, eventually, to punching and choking his girlfriend, while eight weeks pregnant with their son. He'd been dismissed from his college team for this, while the law of the land put him on probation for three years. When he finished the probation, he was *not* a convicted felon, that's how it often works.

Five years later, a district attorney, in a separate case with the same player accused, concluded that another crime had occurred. This was after an investigation into child abuse, involving an allegedly injured three-year-old. A County District Attorney concluded "the evidence did not *'conclusively establish who committed the crime'*. The player carried on playing for his franchise because the NFL wanted to 'wait to get the facts and not rush into any judgement'.

What does the franchise do with this guy? Damned if you ban him, damned if you wait for the law to take its course. But 'sports law' doesn't exist, and judgement should surely not be in the hands of these men. What they can do is–make a moral judgement in the first place. They knew exactly what the background of this man was when they hired him, a piece of knowledge not always open to employers.

Researching this story, most of which was well-known to me and those who follow the NFL, I read one article by a prestigious publication that read: *"The week before his arrest he returned a punt 92 yards for a touchdown that tied the game with one-minute remaining in the fourth quarter."* I find it incredible that a writer can effortlessly give that level of sporting detail in the same paragraph as the crimes. At least pause, like a prosecutor would tend to do in a court. Show some respect, some perspective. Sporting achievement and criminal activity are allowed to flow together too easily: *"Despite the murder, Player X managed to score TWO goals to win the cup for his team."*

Redemption for heinous crimes should not ever be seen to come from achievement on the sports field. And yet so often it does. And sports administrators should not be asked to do the job of a legal system. And yet so often they are.

It feels to me, like a subject that is complicated, evolving, and needs proper attention and intelligent debate. It can't be ignored. When we are asked to idolise sports stars, are we really meant to accept the sanitised version? I always prefer my recognition of the world's biggest sports stars to be *consensual*. We don't need to be told who to like, while their activities away from sport are whitewashed.

I'd been educated on the moral and journalistic issues around sports stars as a Deputy Sports Editor in the 1990s, when a famous England footballer was accused of domestic abuse. A female colleague asked to have a word with me, curious as to why there was no wider debate in the media around whether the England manager should be picking an alleged abuser for the World Cup.

It was a very good point, and there was no easy answer. Put yourself in that manager's shoes, with a player who hadn't been found guilty or convicted of anything. Or if they *had* been convicted but were clear to play. Do you pick on morals or ability?

If this was purely a sports decision, and one of the best players was available for selection, you'd be compelled to select him, back then at least. But maybe we have learned not to be so compartmental. Because as I sit here now, is there any chance I would take him? No. Maybe I would subconsciously use a 'loophole' to opt out of picking him. The loophole being the need to pick the 'right characters', not just the best players, to form a team.

Teams are now far more likely to be built around how their personalities blend, not just 'the best 11'. In long cricket tours, those who can 'fit in' and retain team spirit can be quietly favoured. This is another minefield, because 'difficult characters' can be conceivably discriminated against.

Where do you draw the line if you pick a team on moral grounds? Does the 'reformed' convicted criminal stay in, even if there's every sign that he hasn't actually reformed ? Second chances are a thorny issue in sport as in life. What about an alleged offender? They have rights, right? What about an aggressive guy, with an unblemished record, who has a threatening aura? Should he be left out on suspicion of being a 'bad apple.' What about the unknown offender? Are you running checks while picking this team? Picking sports teams on morals is near-impossible. Even with gut instinct and integrity.

This is why law is vital. Actual law. I don't think I'll even be able to accept *sports law,* via bans, suspensions and fines for serious crimes off the pitch. Sports administrators should never be comfortable with their ability to govern such serious matters because sport often fails miserably with its own crimes and misdemeanours – and even 'Independent' legal panels in sport are often unsatisfactory.

I was interested by the view of the chairman of a major Italian football club on the subject of the racism incident that reared up in the interview with Sepp Blatter. I mentioned it to this chairman during an interview ahead of a Champions League game, between his club and the accused player's club. The player in question had been banned by the Football Association's 'Disciplinary Committee' for a few matches, after a court of law cleared him.

How many games should a ban be for alleged racism? Football's attempts to deal with racism across Europe and beyond have been almost staggeringly ineffective. If it was up to me, when there is racism, I would remove the club from competitions. Let's see how popular the racists are then. I know that's an over-simplification, but it has to be a realistic part of a competition framework, something sport *does* control. Fines, bans, stadium closures. They don't work.

The Italian chairman, going against the tide, said that he felt the ban was wrong and that the accused player *should* be allowed to play against his own team. He said he was bemused that "sports law" was being used, as "it doesn't actually exist." The reason there was a discrepancy is that the Football Association's burden of proof is lower than a court of law. My own assessment of what happened on that day, and the punishments, has to be kept to myself for legal reasons. But law has to be respected and adhered to, and I've reported on enough questionable sports governance over the years to not feel sport should be 'above the law.'

*

An unwritten *metaphorical* 'law' of sport is that a footballer must not flaunt wealth gratuitously, that they must show 'loyalty' and that they must 'put a shift in'. Modern fans love players who appear to be working hard, and more suspicious of the 'lazy' modern maverick than fans were in the 1970s, when you couldn't move for charismatic, skilful, unpredictable showmen with long hair and socks rolled down provocatively, as if to say: *You can hack at my legs with your brutal tackles, but I will still flick the ball up, volley a goal and blow kisses to the crowd!*

134

The modern sports competitor also knows the importance of strong social media. The cleverest and best advised, will be using it wisely to ensure their reputation is protected, get their message across and understanding that it is something we all have to live with – the endless opinion, the never-ending tsunami of views on their ability and right to earn a living. It used to be only Saturday afternoons when footballers could hear the displeasure over their dissatisfactory performances from the crowd on the terraces.

Some players risk being more engaged with their profiles than their contributions to results. It is true that clubs now consider *profiles* when signing players, not just what they can do with a ball. It is an overall package. I hope it never goes so far that a player's FIFA console skills are factored in, so they can represent in both areas and please the marketing department. Engaging with social media is a delicate process, there are many with a 'bull in a giant china shop' approach. For all the good it can bring in connectivity, the poison and abuse is relentlessly damaging.

However - out of the quagmire of social media influence, came something truly precious. Unprecedented in impact, importance, message, influence. A footballer managing to do the job of government. By feeding hungry children. As a child taking his early steps towards becoming a footballer, Marcus Rashford was often hungry, as were his siblings, while their mother struggled to provide for them, working every hour she could and going without herself. By the age of 23, Marcus was scoring goals for Manchester United and England, a player of high skill and pace, and putting in the hard work to improve. Premier League, Champions League, World Cups, he had already made his mark in the world's major tournaments.

Like Megan Rapinoe, Rashford could have now decided to concentrate on his own progress, his own game, his own family and his own friends. Instead, he decided to make a difference. Few footballers in history have made such a difference, and few people managed to take on the ravages of a global pandemic so effectively. By feeding hungry children. Hundreds and thousands of them.

In April 2020, the UK's Health Secretary decided to use some of his time during the Coronavirus Pandemic to criticise Premier League players, jumping on a misjudgement by some football club administrators, who 'furloughed' non-playing staff to take advantage of the UK Government's emergency scheme. The huge furlough operation was designed to save jobs and businesses, to ease the pressure on rich football clubs, but that wasn't the fault of the players.

Politicians pounce on the chance to criticise sport, when the wind is blowing in that direction, like Jamie Vardy, or indeed Rashford, would pounce and score. In the politician's case, usually their shots are opportunistic but missing the target and the point. Flip it around and see how quickly a grinning Prime Minister or President will invite a victorious sports team for a photo opportunity. These are men, nearly always men, who wouldn't know Marcus Rashford from Marcus Wareing the chef, until there's a bit of reflected glory to be had.

With the UK in the grip of the first lockdown and all football activity suspended, Rashford helped deliver food to families who relied on free school meals. But before the summer holiday, it was announced there would be no extension for these meals. Whatever your political views, the Government's Members of Parliament were being 'whipped' to vote against a motion to extend the scheme. Which means that they were effectively, in fact literally, voting not to help hungry children.

An over-simplification? Again, it is always more powerful to not think of 'hungry children', but instead a 'hungry child'. Such as a young Marcus Rashford, whose Christmas dinners came from a food bank or soup kitchen. And sometimes the food was not there at all. Every vote, every policy, every decision, affects *individuals*, and during a pandemic, widespread poverty was taking a grip, not just serious illness and death.

Marcus Rashford, taking brilliant advice on top of his own instincts, wrote an open letter to MPs, imploring them to reverse the decision and protect over a million children, and their families, from hunger. "*This is about humanity,*" he wrote, "*Looking at ourselves in the mirror and feeling like we did everything we could to protect those who can't, for whatever reason or circumstance, protect themselves.*"

The UK Prime Minister claimed to have been unaware of Marcus Rashford's campaign when he announced a £120 million 'Covid food fund'. Infuriatingly, this was being called a 'U-turn', one of those empty clichéd political terms favoured by journalists, along with calling disputes 'rows'.

Calling the scenario a U-turn turned it into a political story alone, rather than calling it what it was. A decision to *not* help feed hungry children, that became a decision to feed hungry children because of public pressure ignited by a footballer. 'U-turn' sanitises this horrendous misjudgement about the importance of children starving or not. This is not your politics, it's about compassion.

By autumn it happened all over again. No scheme in place, and Marcus Rashford challenging it again, only this time something even better happened, worthy of the old phrase 'restored our faith in humanity.' This time, rather than just supporting the campaign, people took practical action. Individuals, businesses, communities, sought ways to help provide food, deliver food, and this while signing a petition to 'end child food poverty'.

By now, the message had finally properly landed in Downing Street. A 'Covid winter grant scheme' was announced to support the vulnerable. It was being called a second 'U-turn' of course, and Marcus Rashford was being called a hero. By most of us.

The actions of this quietly-spoken and polite Mancunian, growing in confidence in his interviews and showing huge dignity, weren't to everyone's taste. One notorious newspaper, and its enabling readership, reported that the "*campaigning football star bought five luxury homes worth more than £2 million*". Another way of looking at that story could be that a high-earning and sensible young footballer took advice to invest in property. That should be his own business. Stopping children going hungry? Now that's all our business.

Some supporters of his club, and other armchair experts, weren't entirely happy with Rashford, questioning his 'form' on the pitch, and suggesting the 'campaigning' was a distraction. As if it's not important to Rashford to keep showing what he can do on the pitch for club and country. Would it be inappropriately flippant to ask a football fan whether their team winning a match or feeding a hungry child is more important? Perhaps it's worth considering. How many games without scoring is his act of humanity worth? You see how absurd the bubble of 'sports opinion' is?

Then he missed 'that' penalty in the Euro 2020 final 'shootout' which England lost to Italy, who became European Champions. Criticism from some over his 'non-football activities' re-emerged. And some of the overall abuse to him, and two teammates who also missed, was racist. This is England.

On a wall in Manchester, as England's team progressed in the Euro tournament and a wave of optimism returned to the country, was a mural of Rashford. Defaced after his 'crime' of missing the penalty. Hundreds flocked to the mural. And left notes of support. One was yellow post-it. *"Thank you for all our dinner"* signed with a heart from *'Reggie, 6'*.

We can all have an opinion on Marcus Rashford's ability, his actions, the UK Government's actions. The majority held him up as a beacon during the pandemic. You suspect his work off the pitch is far from done. My opinion, I like to think, is something helped by being older and wiser than the kid that walked through the door at Hayters 30 years ago.

As a child, as a young man, I hated his club, Manchester United. Dislike is a big part of sport, and when it stops short of abuse, it has a place in the narrative, sometimes it's at the epicentre. But when football returned from a pandemic, and Rashford scored, I smiled. In fact, I cheered. I wouldn't begrudge that man, and those around him, anything. Because sport has to have perspective. If you want to use that term *role model*, then he is the best example of a player using the appeal of sport to change society, and he continues to do so.

I humbly put forward Marcus Rashford as the most extraordinary and important figure in the history of British sport, the closest British sport has in historical significance since Muhammad Ali. You read that correctly. No goal he scores, or anybody else scores, is as significant as using his status to feed hungry children. It took a *footballer* to feed a child.

CHAPTER 18: NERVE

"If I only had a brain." Many of us remember the Scarecrow in *'The Wizard of Oz'* singing that. We also remember the Tin Man didn't have a heart, much as he wanted one. But the character that interested me was the lion, who a sports commentator might describe as having *"Joined a team facing a difficult journey on a yellow brick road."*

This lion was introduced to us as a coward, aware of his own lack of courage and dolefully singing *"If I only had the nerve"*. In football, on the *'Road to Wembley'* such behaviour would send a red flag to a manager – it's unlikely the Lion would be selected as one of the five guys sent to the penalty spot and asked to take one to decide the outcome. Often in sport, and in life, holding your nerve isn't easy.

*

In stressful *work* situations I'm lucky in not suffering from nerves, but that doesn't make me immune in other circumstances. So traumatic was one experience, helpless in a hospital while an emergency was unfolding, that I was hit with an involuntary consequence. Months later, with all mercifully fine, I nevertheless felt I was going to pass out three times in the same week. There had been no problem before that, at any stage of my life. I had some brutal checks, *'tilt tests'* they called them, and was told I wasn't susceptible to collapse. But I suspected I had a form of PTSD, *Post Traumatic Stress Disorder*. Doctors didn't disagree, and when I spoke to friends who are veteran war correspondents, they took a few seconds to assert that's what I was suffering from. They pointed out that suppressing a deep trauma can become physically damaging, and you don't have to have witnessed the horrors of war to be affected.

Rightly or wrongly, I decided to take my own course of action, that wouldn't work for everyone. I took reassurance from the diagnosis I *wouldn't* pass out, and that my family wouldn't be in danger while I was driving. Using a rational approach to the situation we'd been in and the delayed physical effect, I would try to put it in to perspective, put the incident behind me and get on with life. Not everyone will feel they can do that. People deal with crisis in different ways, or don't deal with it, and that's why psychological effects of the pandemic have been a quietly devastating part of the global crisis.

In work situations, I just don't feel nervous. I don't know why. It's not just experience, I was the same as a young reporter. Maybe I've felt with my background, I've got nothing to lose. That if I don't believe in myself, why should anybody else believe in me in a cut-throat environment? In a television studio, my feeling is 'What's the worst that can happen?' The worst hasn't happened. Yes, there have been many times the sound into my ear hasn't worked and I've been left cut-off from the studio, so I've had to busk it, or people have sworn at me while broadcasting live 'on air' in the street. But I've never sworn on air myself. Even that can be forgivable, one of the UK's favourite newsreaders, a lovely man, once stumbled on the words 'Kent countryside'. If only he'd actually said Kent. And the politician Jeremy Hunt frequently poses problems too.

If I had a pound for every sports stadium I've stood outside surrounded by boisterous fans shouting over the top of me, I'd have so much money I could build my own sports stadium and stage my own World Cup. There are simple methods I use to concentrate. Firstly, know what you're talking about. If the subject was alien it would be far harder. I think of little bullet points and expand on each one, rather than try to memorise scripts or stick to pre-prepared speech. Expect the unexpected, don't be tense, relax your shoulders and keep your cool. We still see experienced reporters gripping the microphone for dear life, more rigid than the Tin Man, and I wonder if it's worth the stress for them. Be prepared for the worst that can happen, and everything else is a bonus. When you're in with the public, anything can happen so just go with it. You have no choice.

'It's their world not ours' is my favourite line from an underrated film called *The Paper*, with Robert Duvall playing a wise old newspaper executive. The moment a reporter thinks it's 'all about them', and thinks they are important, and gets irritated with the public, they are already compromised. I see it all the time. It almost angers me, but it's actually funny. *It's NOT about you.* When you remember that, and relax, you can get on with your broadcast.

Mental wellbeing in the workplace, in society, has taken on great significance, constantly talked about, assessed, analysed, in some cases improved. In sports competition, the psychological side of elite sports performance has increased exponentially in the past couple of decades.

The world is changing. In the past, sportsmen and women were just expected to 'get on with it'. How many times did we suspect a prodigiously talented character in sport failed to 'fulfil their potential' because they couldn't handle the pressure? Conversely, there were others who 'squeezed every last drop' out of their limited talent by being able to cope with the expectation and demands.

Cricket, Test cricket particularly, encapsulates life more accurately than anything else, sport or otherwise. Ups, downs, pressure, application, decision-making, adversity and resilience for starters, and the developing narrative is often dictated by weather conditions, the subject that dominates British life. Five days of each Test match, and a series of Test matches, unfold as life unfolds, and create unrelenting mental demands. It's why you so often hear that what counts is *between the ears*.

Imagine a cricketer, perhaps one who isn't socially comfortable or confident, on a long tour (some can last as long as three months) spending hours in a hotel room away from family and friends. That player is expected to go out to bat for the team, while possibly lacking form and confidence, being criticised by the media, criticised on social media and with his or her place in the team under threat. Add in some vocal criticism by opposition fielders (commonly referred to as 'sledging') as the player themself questions their own place in the side. All of that is happening before they have even begun their job of trying to score some runs for the team. This scenario is commonplace. Careers have been seriously hampered, and ended, by anxiety, and in some cases acute stress.

Sometimes in cricket, a player and a team can be having to toil through difficult conditions. Maybe there is cloud cover overhead so the cricket ball is swinging around when it's bowled, maybe your team is well behind in the game, and the batters have to defend, defend, keep defending, stay batting, avoid getting out, cope, survive. Having protected the wicket, gradually the opportunity to score runs can start to materialise.

Confidence starts to build. Momentum and power balance start to shift from bowlers and fielding team to the batter. Maybe the sun peeks through the clouds, and the batter is still there batting. In a partnership perhaps. And now runs are flowing. Later in the day, with a much better position on the scoreboard, the ball softer, the bowlers tired and the confidence building, the batter may start to attack, to accumulate quickly, to dominate, to assert, to *flow*. Batting, cricket, life has suddenly become much easier.

My approach to life, not just working life, is borrowed from cricket. Defend, protect when necessary, by all means, but don't become *too* defensive because you might lose yourself, lose the chance to impose yourself, and fail. On the other hand, don't be hot-headed and reckless, overconfident and injudicious. Get 'on the front foot', literally in cricket, metaphorically in life, and be positive. Look to build, accumulate, encourage your fellow batters. Be alert, busy, lay foundations. Then look to thrive. Back yourself, believe in yourself, while protecting yourself. *Positive, not defensive, not reckless.*

Psychologically, I'm a rank amateur of course, but professionals are employed to get the best out of competitors in sport, and increasingly to protect athletes from themselves. This is now commonplace, but I do recall some of the strategies that were used in major events of the past, before every top team started to employ somebody to look after the mental aspect of working in sport.

In golf, the Ryder Cup places a unique strain on players. It is a team tournament between the best golfers in Europe and the best from the United States that takes place every two years and there are clear reasons the tournament generates so much pressure. The Ryder Cup grew in competitiveness, status and popularity in the 1980s and didn't stop growing, becoming a prestigious event that many sports fans, not just golf fans, look forward to. The format leaves no place to hide - every point appears to be important, every game precious, making participation coveted and significant.

The main reason for the intense pressure comes down to the responsibility the golfers feel to the other members of their team. Week in week out the golfers are used to representing themselves, with only their caddy at their side, life's best-paid bag carriers (providing valuable assistance and advice). But in the Ryder Cup, there are eleven other players to consider, with thousands of unusually raucous fans on the course, and millions watching on television. The golfer is desperate not want to let his team down. Whether playing in a pairs match, or in the singles matches on the last day of the three. It could all come down to the point *they* win or lose, and sometimes does.

The ice-cool German Bernhard Langer once missed a short 'putt' to tie the Ryder Cup, which would have retained the trophy for Europe, at Kiawah Island near Charleston. Trust me, nobody was doing the *'Charleston'* and smiling during these three days of competition. The match was called *'The War on the Shore'* with traditional sporting hyperbole. There was a lot of antipathy. Imagine being Langer that evening. No matter how understanding his teammates were, no matter how well he played, no matter how good his temperament, the blame was on him. He knew what it meant when he stood over the tiny dimpled ball and tried to knock it in the hole. And just happened to fail on this occasion.

I was once told a story from behind the scenes at a Ryder Cup 20 years ago. A Welsh golfer was playing in his first one for Europe, a massive moment for any player, but he faced a familiar problem. The three days are split into five sessions, but the captain only needs to pick eight of his 12 players in each session, in four pairs, for each session. Subsequently, four golfers from each team are *left out* from each section of play.

It's possible that a player will not be risked and have hardly played before the crucial individual matches on the final Sunday, where everyone definitely plays. This can lead to a build-up of nerves for the omitted players. I can't imagine that leads to a great night's sleep, and on this occasion, the Welshman wasn't selected for the first day. He was only selected for *one* of the four sessions, and he narrowly lost that match with his Swedish partner. So entering the decisive final day of one of sport's biggest events, he'd not contributed a single point, or even a half a point.

The overall match was tied at eight points each, and the Welshman would have to play a match in the singles against a brilliant American golfer. No pressure. But, behind the scenes and away from the greens, the Welshman was holding his nerve. This was thanks to a psychologist or a 'life coach'. The idea was to protect the golfer, in a bubble of sorts.

You see, the Ryder Cup is as close as golf gets to a riot - every point and putt seems to be fought for with a raucous crowd. Scores are constantly being analysed and compared, contributions assessed, and nerve having to be held. The most successful Ryder Cup golfers are not necessarily the most successful in major individual tournaments. Englishman Ian Poulter is an unstoppable, fist-pumping force of nature in the Ryder Cup, nick-named '*The Postman*' for 'always delivering' and his repeated success in inspiring Europe to the trophy. Others don't take to the pressure with a fraction of his gusto. But the Welshman, on this occasion, was kept away from the scoreboard and the pressure. And told to concentrate on his own practice. '*Manage the manageables.*' I've always liked that phrase.

Come the final day and our golfer was *still* kept waiting, because his 'singles' match was the second-last to start. Considering his lack of participation over the first two days, it's not unreasonable to conclude his team captain was hoping and expecting Europe would have enough points from the other, more experienced, players in earlier matches. But he won his match. A deserved victory, an emphatic victory, a precious point. And as this was his only Ryder Cup, he has a 100 per cent winning record that can never be taken away from him. With the help of his psychologist, this golfer concentrated on his own game, his 'manageables', not the size of the event. And prevailed.

Aside from professional psychologists, sheer experience can be vital in keeping cool. In the Solheim Cup, the women's golf team cup between Europe and the United States, Norwegian Suzann Pettersen absolutely nailed it. After a successful individual career and aged 38, she'd been away from golf for 20 months on maternity leave before this competition in Scotland. The captain Catriona Matthew had shrewdly, though not entirely with the approval of golf pundits, picked Pettersen for the 12-woman team as a 'wildcard', which meant she didn't have to qualify through a points system. That's because, while on maternity leave, she *couldn't* qualify through the points system.

If you don't know golf, you may still be able to guess what happened. Pettersen knocked a vital long putt into the hole to beat her opponent and clinch the trophy by a single point. It was dramatic, wonderful and typically downplayed by the Norwegian, who said she wasn't aware her putt was to win the event. Either way, I'd have wanted Pettersen standing on that green with a putter in hand, and nobody else.

A vital putt feels like a penalty kick in football. Nothing in sport raises the subject of nerve like penalties. So much of it is about pressure and mental strength. During a game, taking a penalty could and should be seen as an opportunity not a hurdle. Rather than feeling the responsibility of taking it as a burden, it's actually a perfect opportunity to score, the objective of football, and you can be a 'matchwinner'. The best penalty takers look hungry for the ball, to place it on the spot and emphatically smash it in the goal. Some of these are blessed with the ideal amount of ability and control, such as Southampton's Matthew Le Tissier, who famously only missed one in his career.

Le Tissier always looked like he had the ball under remote control, guiding it in with power, swerve, accuracy, whatever he liked. But he and other penalty- taking maestros also have confidence and a clear mind. They know exactly where they want the ball to go, there's no self-doubt or indecision, they hold the ball with an absence of fear and if the goalkeeper then does something to compel a change of strategy, they react accordingly, making a clinical, controlled, last-second adjustment to shoot in a different direction. The opposite is the player that looks like he or she has the weight of the world on their shoulders as they walk from the halfway line to the penalty spot, and in a major competition they *do* have the hopes and dreams of a nation resting upon them. And they can be defined for a failure from the penalty spot. As Gareth Southgate was for 20 years after missing with that less-than-emphatic penalty in the semi-final between England and Germany in Euro '96, a tournament the host team England had looked like winning.

Happily, Southgate found his redemption as a manager. On that night I felt Southgate had a 'miss face', a ludicrous piece of armchair analysis but one that some of us can't help. Does a player look like they 'fancy' the penalty? Do they look likely to score? Do they really have a '*miss face*'? Maybe you've put your hands over your own face when such a player steps up and your club or country's chance of glory is resting on it. My own face was hardly that of a 'winner' the next morning at 6am, stood outside the team hotel in Buckinghamshire being asked live on television "*What's the latest?*" The latest was that the players were sleeping, and the country was 'gutted'.

Most footballers and most fans would rather be a goalkeeper in a shootout. With the chance to be a hero, but without the blame attached to the taker, who only gets one chance and has the onus on them to score. There is a famous piece of psychology which garnered widespread approval that I take issue with. Netherlands manager Louis van Gaal was lauded as a genius for substituting his goalkeeper before a World Cup quarter-final shootout against Costa Rica in Brazil.

Van Gaal removed his goalkeeper Jasper Cillessen, substituting him with a 'penalty specialist' named Tim Krul. It was deemed to work. Krul saved two penalties and the Netherlands progressed to the semi-finals. I heard plenty of people claiming the Costa Ricans were 'psyched out' by the switch, though I'm not sure if that's true. I can't help but suspect van Gaal's handling of the situation was psychologically questionable, and ultimately backfired. Because Cillessen was not happy. The whole thing had been a shock to him and clearly affected his confidence. That was the crucial mistake. He could at least have felt part of the strategy. Cillessen was assured he remained the keeper for the semi-final against Argentina, but how was his confidence, crucial for a goalkeeper? It can't be measured, but the evidence was there. The team's *next* game also went to penalty kicks. And the Netherlands didn't have any of their allocated substitutions remaining on that occasion, so Tim Krul had to stay sitting on the substitutes bench and Cillessen was now in the spotlight. He didn't save *any* of the four penalties he faced.

The Netherlands missed out on winning a World Cup yet again, having beaten champions Spain 5-1 in their opening match. Was van Gaal right? That Cillessen just wasn't good at saving penalties? Or had he inadvertently given him psychological baggage? Either way, I think empowering and supporting your first-choice goalkeeper, and improving his penalty confidence, feels like a better approach to me. While it's easy to judge from a studio or armchair, some football coaches seem to overplay their importance and interfere *too* much, removing some of the natural decision-making skills of the players. There comes a point where players have to take responsibility for their own actions.

The most famous penalty in history is Antonin Panenka, chipping the ball as if in slow motion to win the 1976 European Championship for Czechoslovakia over West Germany. And I still can't decide if this was nerves of steel or madness. The technique was new, and it was the surprise element as well as execution that made it so effective. But what if this fearless footballer had messed it up? I still wince when others try what became known as a 'Panenka penalty'. It feels like they are asking for trouble.

There is another example of extreme cool from the penalty sport that I witnessed in Saint-Etienne during the 1998 World Cup I reported on in France. I was there when England were beaten in another famous penalty shootout. England were a little unlucky to lose the match, a disallowed goal from Sol Campbell away from beating a fine Argentina team, and refereeing decisions *still* debated. But then they fluffed their lines from the penalty spot. One player, David Batty, didn't even rehearse his lines. Apparently, he'd never taken a penalty in a proper match before, and his poor effort was saved. Van Gaal's 'over-thinking' is definitely preferable to this under-preparation.

It's a *successful* penalty I remember from that day, but it wasn't an Argentinian or English one. It was from a World Cup game earlier in the day in Bordeaux. In a lull before broadcasting in the afternoon, I watched Croatia v Romania on a tiny monitor in the satellite track that accompanied us, shading from fierce sunshine. It was a match that was settled by one goal, a penalty, that took Croatia into the quarter-final stage. The penalty was taken by the leading scorer in the tournament, Davor Suker. He took this penalty shortly before half-time with his left foot, striking his shot emphatically low into the corner of the net away from the diving goalkeeper's left hand. Goal! Actually no. The referee decided there had been an infringement and decided the penalty had to be retaken. A few minutes of dispute and disruption on the pitch took place, which could have seemed like hours to a nervous player on the penalty spot. For all my confidence and my own happiness to take penalties when I play football, I'd hate this. To score, and then to be asked to do it again. Would you not feel a little rattled?

How did Davor Suker react? He stood motionless. With his fingers on the pulse of his neck, keeping calm. Blocking out the protestations and chaos around him. And then, when finally invited to retake the kick, he took exactly the same penalty, put it in exactly the same place, successfully evading the goalkeeper's left hand again, and won the match for Croatia. Suker had held his pulse, held his nerve and simply refused to let unpredictable events unsettle and defeat him. Considering the subsequent game in Saint-Etienne was one of the most memorable in World Cup history for English people, it's perhaps quirky that Suker keeping cool remains my stand-out memory of the day, and indeed that tournament. He was effectively using a *'Lion Mind'*.

The Lion Mind is a philosophy in a book published that year, Larry Rosenberg's *Breath by Breath*. Based on the behaviour of real lions, not a cowardly lion on a yellow brick road. Rosenberg asked how a lion would react to you waving a bone in front of them, as compared to a dog's reaction.

A dog would follow the bone, but the lion is more likely to ignore the bone and keep focused. A 'Lion Mind' encourages you *not* to follow the distractions and stay focused. To not waste energy on contemplating events, thoughts and circumstances that may be inconsequential or beyond your control. To hold your nerve. To *manage the manageables*. In sport, in life.

Chapter 19: THE MIRACLE OF LEICESTER

As the finishing line approached, no longer could Leicester City's quality as a football team be questioned. The intriguing thing now was whether they could hold their nerve.

They were five points ahead at the top of the Premier League after that significant win at Manchester City in February, and they had also developed a vital trait for a successful team, quickly shaking off setbacks. After losing to Arsenal again, only their third defeat in this extraordinary season, they embarked on yet another run of matches without defeat.

The clubs they were beating were not high in the table; Norwich, West Bromwich Albion, Newcastle, Crystal Palace, Southampton and Sunderland, but not so long ago all these clubs were at Leicester's level, or higher. The improvement had been immense and it was now the sound of praise ringing in their ears, not just Claudio's little bell.

My friend and colleague Richard headed with me to Leicester at the start of April to tell the story of Leicester's mystifying, magical rise, and their incredible backstory. Richard was armed with a television camera, where his namesake once brandished a sword.

If there had been enough time, we could have made an entire series that started with the exhumation of the bones of King Richard III. Lest we forget the accusation that that he killed his nephews in the Tower of London in the 11th century, a notorious accusation, and prominently explored in the work of Thomas More and Shakespeare. This is refuted by some historians, and not a popular tale in Leicester.

The claims are dismissed by some as a 'Tudor besmirching of the last Plantagenet King', with many in the city campaigning against a performance of Shakespeare's Richard III, close to where his body now lay. Methinks this horrific story is something that will still be argued about by future historians, but it's important to remember that this is not a king who'd been regarded as a heroic figure. To many, he is quite the opposite.

Such a bloody and dark royal history puts football into perspective, but the point about rise of Leicester City FC is that it won't be forgotten either. By Easter 2016 at the end of March, many non-believers had accepted it *could* happen, and realistically now *would* happen. Leicester would actually win the Premier League.

Others, including me, were still not sure. Was it weary cynicism? Had we seen too much? Been disappointed by sport too many times? Suffering from a pragmatism that makes you a bit of a killjoy? I just couldn't see them doing it. The highly regarded journalist Osasu Obayiuwana would playfully bait me on *Twitter*, asking me when I would accept that it was going to happen.

I'd never spent time in Leicester, but I quickly became very fond of the city, with its love of sport and palpable friendliness. Leicester Market is a centrepiece, over 800 years old and the largest outdoor covered market in Europe. I was conscious of the cliché, a vibrant market with salt-of-the-earth market holders and a friendly atmosphere. But it's true. If fruit and vegetables can ever be described as glorious, then this is the place. For my small part, I'd decided I couldn't be that typical sports reporter in a blazer, thrusting my fluffy microphone over the tomatoes with a patronising question about what it all means. On my first visit here, I just soaked it up, we couldn't have been more informal, and the shoppers and stall-holders were just delightful. Within two hours of being in Leicester, I was a fan.

The people we spoke to, from lifelong Leicester season ticket holders who attended every match, to people who never watched football, had a sense of excited disbelief that was enchanting. Life wasn't usually like this. There was a magic in the air, something to be embraced. Do you believe in magic?

In the new *'King Richard III Visitor Centre'*, which opened next to the spot where his remains were found, people wondered if there was something strange awoken by the incredible excavation, and whether this was the influence of the King. The Mayor of Leicester Peter Soulsby, one of those lifelong Leicester City fans who attended every match he could and was in the role through this extraordinary journey, spoke to us with excitement and pride in his city. That pride was starting to embolden and energise. Could a city really be affected like this by sport? Hell yes!

A BBC radio sports reporter who embodied Leicester's energy and increasing national recognition was Ian Stringer, who was generous with his time for me in a ridiculously busy period for him and his colleagues. Ian's commentaries and reporting on Leicester's rise became part of the narrative, his commentary on Jamie Vardy's sensational goal against Liverpool would send shivers down the spine of the coldest curmudgeon. He didn't have the room or inclination to step back and approach Leicester's rise cautiously, he was caught up in capturing the noise, and the euphoria, and holding his own nerve. Which he did with aplomb.

After leaving Ian we talked our way into one of Leicester's highest buildings and filmed the city on a warm early spring day, with light clouds and a blue sky. Leicester was resplendent, the calm before a final push for glory. Richard (the ace *Director of Photography*, not the risen king) and I ate the finest curry, maybe the finest *meal* I've ever had, in a restaurant in the heart of the city named *Kayal.* I'd never been one for seafood curry before, but these dishes of Keralan speciality, were as good as food gets. With spices dancing on the taste buds and coconut at the heart of the dishes. Why am I telling you this? Because that day was good for the senses, and good for the soul. They say an Englishman never admits he's happy. I do. I just wasn't *quite* as happy as those Leicester City FC fans!

If there was a time for rational doubt, reasonable doubt, even for '*Lion Minds*', it came in the middle of April with five games to go. Leicester played West Ham in a Sunday afternoon match at the King Power Stadium and all was going to *their* script. They were leading by a goal to nil, the goal scored by Jamie Vardy. But suddenly there was trouble.

Vardy had received a yellow card, football's warning card, for a mistimed tackle. It looked a little harsh and was to prove important. Later in the game Vardy seemed to tumble theatrically. The referee gave him a second yellow card. Meaning red. Meaning Vardy was sent off and would also miss the next match. On closer inspection there *was* some initial contact from a West Ham defender. Vardy was unlucky, twice. To compound this, he reacted badly, complaining bitterly as he left the pitch. And when the referee reported him for this, his ban was extended to a second game, the vital match against Manchester United. There was probably no party at the Vardys' that night.

West Ham seized on their opportunity and equalised, then scored again and led the match by two goals to one. On incidents like this, in games like this, the fortunes of a team can turn, and momentum can be lost. The history of sport is full of teams who 'snatched defeat from the jaws of victory' and ended up empty-handed. It's a familiar story. Sport and life. Another famous example happened in the 1956 running of the world's biggest horse race, The Grand National. A horse named Devon Loch had cleared all the fences, all the obstacles and was charging up the home straight at Aintree.

Suddenly, inexplicably and unchallenged, the horse fell on its stomach. No glory for the jockey Dick Francis (who went on to become a best-selling author), nor the owner, a 20th century royal, The Queen Mother. Nobody was more aghast than her to see Devon Loch suddenly hit the Aintree turf. It's why Devon Loch's name is mentioned so regularly when a sporting team approaches the finishing line.

In the case of Leicester's match against West Ham, there was one more twist. Leicester were eventually awarded a penalty, in the last minute of the match. It was another disputed decision, but this time in the favour of the boys in blue. The regular penalty-taker Vardy was off the pitch fuming and so it was Leonardo Ulloa who stepped up. The replacement held his nerve from the penalty spot. Another successful Argentinian penalty taker. 2-2. One point gained, or two points dropped? Depends on the mentality. It's moments like this that manager Ranieri's wisdom, his *sangfroid* under pressure, would be precious.

The next night, worrying developments for Leicester. Tottenham were now the only team who could stop them, and they were playing very well. They won by four goals to nil at Stoke, a performance of high quality that looked ominous. Tottenham fans were hardly full of expectation and entitlement though. *"It's the hope that kills you"* was a familiar line from their fans, as they hadn't been champions since 1961, despite being one of the biggest clubs in English football. They'd believe they could over-haul Leicester when it happened, and not before.

Tottenham were held to a draw by West Bromwich Albion in their next match, which just wasn't enough. Because Leicester had beaten Swansea City four-nil at the King Power Stadium, despite being deprived of Vardy. Ulloa scored twice. What a team, what a squad. When the dust settled,

Leicester were eight points ahead of Tottenham with three games to go. Three points for a win meant if Leicester won at Manchester United on 'May Day', they would win the Premier League and be English champions for the first time in their 132-year history. English football had been turned on its head. And remember, the world was watching.

The dilemma was where I needed to be to report on this? In Manchester, the scene of a potentially historic match, or Leicester, the scene of the story? For me, it's always about the people. It had to be Leicester.

We headed to the King Power Stadium. It was eerie and misleading, there was no sense of the epic nature of what was unfolding as we sat in Richard's car and watched the match on our phones (decades earlier the only way to follow such events would have been a transistor radio – at least there were choices in 2016, though the nostalgic in me remembers them fondly). It was tense, it was weird, it was strangely disconcerting. Like a huge battle was taking place and you were pacing the grounds back at the castle.

Leicester fans across the globe were watching. From sports bars in the United States, to the headquarters of the chairman's *King Power* organisation in Bangkok where there were several hundred excited supporters in blue shirts. Thailand was gripped. And playing a significant part in this incredible rise.

At the Old Trafford stadium in Manchester, a few thousand lucky Leicester fans, beside themselves with excitement, roared their backing when the teams walked out. A chant of "*Dilly Ding, Dilly Dong*" started.

Manchester United scored first. It would have been unthinkable during Alex Ferguson's 27-year reign as Manchester United manager, an extraordinarily successful reign, that Leicester City would visit this ground. Even more unthinkable that the only team capable of winning the Premier League title that afternoon *was* Leicester City. Even six *months* earlier the scenario would have seemed outlandish, almost daft to contemplate. After eight minutes of the match, Manchester United scored a goal. Was this some normality creeping into the season at the final moment? No. Within ten minutes Leicester had equalised. Their captain scored the goal.

There is something wonderful about the feats of Wes Morgan. He played for his hometown team for a decade from 2002, Nottingham Forest, a club whose glory days under Brian Clough were long gone. For them and for him, life in the *second* tier was a reality. As a central defender, heading, tackling, blocking, doing the dirty work. For over 400 games. Morgan was respected but 'under the radar'. In January 2012, Morgan signed as a player for Leicester City for what's called an *'undisclosed fee'*. It would not have involved millions of pounds.

Morgan *did* make an immediate impact in the Leicester set-up though. After a few months he was made 'Captain Morgan', and in his first full season he led the team into the Premier League as Champions, missing just one game. And this led to international football at a relatively late age, called up by Jamaica when he was a few months from turning 30 in 2013. He made his debut in Panama City, imagine that! Then a year later made captain of Jamaica. *'The Reggae Boyz'* as they are called, beat Canada three-one. Morgan went on to represent Jamaica 30 times, including two major continental tournaments, Copa America and the Gold Cup. Quite an adventure for the second half of a football career.

And there he was at Old Trafford in the spring of 2016 in a Leicester shirt, statuesque, powerful and quick-witted, meeting the ball with his head from Danny Drinkwater's cross and scoring a precious equalising goal. For 75 tense minutes, plus a half-time break, there was an extreme tension, but a deadlock. And the match finished 1-1. In the car outside it was anticlimactic. I started to dream of the food at *Kayal*. At least Wes Morgan was getting a small portion of the credit he'd always deserved. He played every minute of Leicester's amazing season. Every single minute. If only everything in life was as reliable as Wes Morgan.

Leicester hadn't quite taken their first opportunity to win the league, but blue fever still hung over the city. The next day, May 2, 2016, could be the one. If Tottenham failed to beat Chelsea, a difficult match against last year's champions, *sans the sacked Mourinho*, then Leicester would win the Premier League.

On that May Bank Holiday in the city centre, a giant pause button had been hit. There were no signs of what the city was on the brink of, no buzz. People shopped, grabbed coffee, got on with life as it was before the pandemic. I left my hotel for a late morning walk through the city. As always for a walk I put on music, I usually remember the songs for the big events. In this case it was an unusual one. '*Why Does My Heart Feel So Bad*?' by *Moby*. I don't know why, but I just remember that song so clearly as I walked through Leicester. It captured a strange tension.

On a television screen, through a shop window I saw Gary Lineker, the UK's most famous sports presenter. Easy to see him now as a TV star, as new generations do. Some of us remember his goalscoring for England, at vital moments, in World Cups. Against Poland, Cameroon, West Germany, arms raised and smiling. But I also remembered 1985 and a cold night in south London watching Millwall FC with my friend Peter. In the beaten Leicester City team that night was Gary Lineker, playing for his hometown club.

As a small boy from Leicester in 1969, Lineker cried when watching them beaten in the FA Cup final at Wembley. They could never quite fulfil their dreams back then. Could a schoolboy from Leicester ever imagine a story like this, a day like this, something as magical as this?

Past the famous bronze 'Sporting Success' statue of a cricketer, rugby player and footballer I walked, and stopped to take a photo of the clock tower. At 11.14am on May 2, 2016. Also in shot was a *Pizza Hut*. Above the Pizza Hut was a single blue flag. The only sign. I remember feeling nervous. Have you ever had those times? On a big day, you feel a knot in the stomach. Like you're looking down on yourself. I wondered, genuinely, if there was a higher force at work. I felt a little strange. A bit disorientated. I didn't feel like a man who'd covered sport across the globe for nearly 30 years. I felt like a little boy lost. I'm not telling you this to represent anything other than that's how it felt that day. I don't know why. It was weird.

The whole day was strange, tense, ultimately momentous. The King Power Stadium stood empty. The match was at Chelsea's Stamford Bridge ground in London. Correspondents in Leicester had a choice. Broadcast from outside an empty stadium, or from a local bar. Trying to broadcast from a packed bar is a wretched aspect of the business ordinarily, but in this instance, the noise, the reaction, the colour, it needed capturing. The Leicester fans would prefer to win it in their own stadium, with a goal by their own team, but it was their time. Right here, right now. Even if they weren't playing on the night.This was Tottenham against Chelsea – and what happened this evening could change everything.

The mood in the bar was dampened by the first half, with Tottenham scoring twice in the match they had to win to retain a chance of stopping Leicester. But in the 58th minute at Stamford Bridge Chelsea scored, and now they were only losing two-one. Chaos. Beer flying in Leicester, frazzled reporters holding their earpieces in and trying to make themselves heard above the fans. Their team, their day, their world.

And then, with seven minutes of the scheduled 90 minutes left at Stamford Bridge, the decisive moment. With a sweep of the right foot, Chelsea's star player, Belgian Eden Hazard, sent the ball high into the Tottenham net for the goal that made it real. The score was 2-2. A drawn game was not enough for Tottenham.

Pandemonium in Leicester. And Jamie Vardy really was having a party. Some of the Leicester City players gathered at his house, and later that night, social media footage appeared of their wild celebrations, first for Hazard's goal, then the final whistle at Stamford Bridge.

In Leicester, and wherever Leicester fans were dotted across the world, the wait was over. They had done it. The most remarkable Premier League triumph, and an unprecedented achievement. Sport's biggest shock. Ever.

We headed to the King Power Stadium, feeling there was an inevitability Leicester fans would head there to celebrate. This once-in-a-lifetime joy was not best confined to their own homes. This story was being followed everywhere the Premier League was devoured, and there aren't many places on the map where it isn't. If any!

At first, late on the Bank Holiday night, there were a few blue flags, and a few horns being sounded. Then more cars took to the streets like we see in a nation that has just won the World Cup and the noise level rose. People were spilling out on to the streets, slightly dazed, sharing their joy. I stood 'wired-up' to the camera and ready to talk into the glass, to try to add some perspective to what was barely making sense. And then, as I was about to talk, unstoppably, they came.

Running towards the light of our camera position, the first base towards the front of the King Power Stadium, the Leicester fans. Correction, the *people* of Leicester. I'd seen hysterical football euphoria many times before, but not like this. This was different. Within a few seconds of speaking, I was surrounded by people, but not a typical group of football fans. This was *litmus Leicester*. Next to me was a man carrying a baby, who I suggested "should perhaps be in bed", though not grumpily. I expected people with large flags, but not babies. The baby, to be fair, looked delighted. The excitement and delirium of the flash mob, now over a hundred of them, was taking over. While I tried to carry on it was a like a blue sea and I was submerged, leaving the important thing: scenes of utterly infectious, unrestrained joy. Pure joy.

Eventually, knowing I was still broadcasting live despite not being able to hear a thing, I battled my way forward using a word for the first time that even King Richard would have rejected as old fashioned. *'Gangway please'*. I'll never know where that came from, but I promise that deep inside, it was said with irony, I knew how bizarre this wall was. It was chaos, but if you lose self-awareness, you lose yourself. Still chanting, still singing, still shouting, the people of Leicester did give me the opportunity to resume speaking, this time in a croaky voice, with staccato statements. It wasn't a time for Shakespeare.

"Leicester City. Who would have thought it nine months ago? Five-thousand -to- one outsiders. No wonder thousands have come to the stadium. A team of journeyman. A manager who was dismissed. And yet Leicester have found a way to win the Premier League. It's on the front page of the New York Times, it's everywhere, you can't move for journalists. There's a sea of blue, they will celebrate for hours and hours, they've got work tomorrow, they've got school tomorrow, they don't care."

My words in isolation are far from poetic. But the scenes? They are beautiful. Because I am surrounded by the most diverse crowd you could see. Female, male, young, old, Black, white. Wherever these people descended from, right here, right now, they were Leicester. Leicester. The proudest people in the world that night, and long after. The two minutes that unfolded manage to be both funny and moving.

When I give careers speeches to children, and I feel they may be bored, I quickly show them this. And they get it. They laugh hysterically and they too overflow with joy. The clip went viral. I was once confronted in a lift in Brazil by a man who jumped in as the doors closed. I'd been robbed the day before so seized up. The man looked me up and down and smiled. "*Leicester guy!*" he said. What a privilege to be amongst the thousands of people who ended up at the stadium in Leicester that night. Not a 'privilege' in modern social media, humblebragging terms. I *mean* a privilege.

When I got back to my hotel room exhausted at 3am, I thought of Claudio Ranieri. He hadn't been in Leicester that day. He'd been in Rome. Apparently taking tea with his elderly mother. A civilised approach to overseeing the biggest triumph in sports history. I hope she was proud. His team shook the world that day, and for nine months.

Six days later, Leicester City returned to the King Power stadium to be officially crowned. Before the game Italian tenor Andrea Bocelli performed, having been invited by Ranieri. The two Italians walked on to the pitch together, with Ranieri gently guiding his blind friend. And then Bocelli, wearing a Leicester shirt, sang "*Nessun Dorma*" and "*Time to Say Goodbye*", changing the words to "Time to *Win Again*".

The Leicester fans were so excited in their singing and chanting, they failed to settle for the opening bars. Ranieri raised his hand, orchestrating calm, not ordering it. This is his way. His other hand had been placed gently, reassuringly on the back of Bocelli.

This moment transcended Leicester, and football and sport. It was life-affirming. Leicester fans wept, many uncontrollably. Many of us wept. This wasn't about football. It was about dignity. Mortality. And living your best life. Nothing's impossible. Find it. *Find it.* Hold your nerve. *Believe*!

The match was played against Everton and Leicester won by three goals to one. Jamie Vardy scored twice. The other goal scorer was a king. *Andy King.* Do you believe in magic? When the game finished, Wes Morgan lifted the Premier League trophy, surrounded by miracle men. Ranieri spoke to the Leicester fans, to whom the day will have felt like a dream, like utopia.

"*Keep dreaming*," he said softly.

Chapter 20: LONDON

Leicester's triumph was unique, but the joy we saw in the people of the city did ring some bells. Four years earlier, the London Olympics had created an atmosphere in Britain that felt almost impossibly optimistic. British reserve and grumpiness were suddenly tossed away like a hammer or javelin.

A few weeks of sunshine and medals generated a glow that was precious, and more than that, seemed to change the national mood, the national character. This is not a generalisation or an optical illusion, it really did. We shed the famous British reserve and 'turned those frowns upside down'.

The organisers always insisted the London Olympics and Paralympics would be a great success, led by Sebastian Coe, the man who won redemptive gold in Moscow, won another Olympic gold in Los Angeles, and was now in charge of the whole thing. But there were others whose job it was to challenge this. Such as me. And I did. For years.

In 2005, the Games were awarded to London by the International Olympic Committee, despite Paris having been considered favourites to host until very late in the procedure. So late that my 'Plan A', as a producer of substantial coverage for BBC radio, was for a Paris victory.

When IOC president Jacques Rogge opened an envelope at lunchtime and said "*London*", the entire office cheered. Yes, part of me was pleased, but mainly I knew this would be an intensely frenetic day, with me in the evening programme producer's hotseat. Plan B wasn't exactly easy to implement!

The programme was a few hours later, and it was 'lively' to say the least. British athletes were turning up at the studio straight from the celebrations in Central London, some having a had a rare glass of something alcoholic and fizzy. Which had 'gone to their heads'. "Let's hold on to her and hope she sobers up" I remember saying to an assistant producer about one of the guests, a brilliant athlete who wasn't sobering up quickly enough.

The big challenge was to remember this story, this decision, wasn't *just* a celebration. Was bringing the Olympics to London a wise move? Was it worth the money? Would there be potentially adverse effects? One of the studio guests was making these points and was very well researched, but another took umbrage to him and was so aggressive I had to physically go into the studio from behind the glass partition and warn him. Olympic fever wasn't quite flowing through me yet.

In the next seven years, as a Sports Editor then a global sports correspondent, I needed to find the balance between the *good news* story of Britain hosting the games, including regenerating a significant part of east London, and holding the organisers, Government and IOC to account over costs and benefits. I could see both sides, balanced as if on the high beam.

On one hand it was ludicrous when people complained about the transformation of land that was toxic sludge, often for the sake of complaining. On the other hand, there had to be a *legacy.* It was the key word used by the organisers, but it couldn't afford to be an empty promise. This couldn't just be two parties – Olympics and Paralympics – followed by years of clearing up a mess. It needed to *change* London, regenerate the landscape and make a difference to the health and wellbeing of the UK public.

Using the patience and fairness of precious 'contacts', who accepted my need to challenge the IOC, I pushed hard on the 'legacy angle'. At one media conference, I overstepped the mark with uncharacteristic rudeness, which I can't usually bear in journalists. When I asked about how a legacy is measured and monitored *after* a Games ends, it was explained to me that it can take at least a decade to fully assess. "I'll see you here in ten years," I said spikily to the assembled panel of organisers.

The London Games were only a few weeks away, and there was still plenty of pessimism in the UK. This is to be expected wherever an Olympics takes place, as was once explained to me by a veteran organiser. There's initial excitement at the hosting rights, followed by years of disapproval of money being spent, then finally a successful event that is embraced and enjoyed so much that the public say: "*That was great, can we do that again?*" While that's a deliberate over-simplification, there is a lot of truth in his summary.

The cost, ultimately billions of pounds, was being regularly criticised. An Olympics and a legacy don't come cheap. But it wasn't the only concern. Three other aspects had started to dominate talk around the Games. One was security. There was an inescapable feeling the Games would be targeted by terrorists. Nobody in Britain had forgotten the attack the day after the hosting decision in 2005, where 56 people were killed by bombs on the underground system during the morning commute.

Another issue was far less grave but wouldn't go away. Traffic. Many Londoners were saying how "*travelling in London during the Games would be a nightmare*" rather than looking forward to hosting them. The mealy-mouthed grumbling had become irritating, with lots of chatter about "*getting out of the country and going on holiday*". In hindsight, such energy-sapping negativity must have been a nightmare for the organisers to have to listen to. It turned out to be a completely unjustified concern, with Olympic lanes running smoothly, and moaning exiting via the fast lane. The Games proved to be safe.

The third repeated concern was the Opening Ceremony. For every queen and king of the dancefloor, some Brits are slow to get in to party mood, standing on the perimeter clutching a bottle of beer or glass of wine and hoping someone brings out some nibbles to distract them. How much will it cost? Who's meant to performing? It's going to be embarrassing. We never get these things right. If you're British and don't remember this negativity, you've either got a short memory or managed to ignore the '*Eeyores*'.

I was to report on every day of my 'home' Olympics, but on the night of the Opening Ceremony, my role was reporting amongst the public outside of the Olympic Park, one of many large gatherings with giant screens around the country. After finishing one broadcast I returned to the satellite truck to watch the start of the ceremony on a small monitor, as I'd done with that retaken penalty by Davor Suker 14 years earlier, and many times in between. An inauspicious start to the Games 'fortnight' and still no Olympic fever from me. The crowd had been more attracted by the warm summer's evening and refreshments than the promise of the 'night of their lives'. Few truly believed in the Opening Ceremony. Oh ye of little faith, oh *me* of little faith!

The track record of ceremony director Danny Boyle, whose cinema credits include renowned films *Trainspotting* and *Slumdog Millionaire*, provided some grounds for cautious optimism of what might be in store, but not more than that. What Boyle and his team had been developing turned out to be majestic. Better than that. It was life-affirming. His genius, and the creativity of those around him with their hard work and ambition, managed to make us laugh, cry, think, feel and be proud of being British. It was a lost concept to many of us, worn down by the hijacking of patriotism by bigots and xenophobic 'Little Englanders'. Our inability to grasp a sense of pride in our country had meant an erosion of our culture, a failure to celebrate being British. And there didn't seem there was much to celebrate. Even our national football teams had disappointed us for decades.

And the tone for the entire few weeks was set by those first few minutes. At 9pm on that night of July 27, 2012, there was a countdown on our screens, from 60 to 1, simply but smartly using visually striking numbers from street scenes, busses, nameplates, capturing London. The best ideas are often the simplest. And then a two-minute '*Journey along the Thames*'. An underrated and beautiful piece of exhilarating, perfectly observed, clever, insightful, film-making. The best I've ever seen, truly.

In the film we journey rapidly along the River Thames, observing British life. A gentle 'village cricket' scene, a family having a day out, London landmarks, a pause to recreate the *EastEnders* title theme using the humour that characterised the ceremony, then into the London underground and whizzing through tunnels joined by the ghosts of Victorian times. Visually it was stunning. But it was the *sound* too. So effective, so restrained, so perfect, so moving. By now a small crowd had gathered, 100 metres from the giant screen, to stand alongside me looking into the satellite truck's small screen.

I was agog, mesmerised, I had shivers up and down my spine and goosebumps on my arms. This was what it was like to be proud of London, a city I am still not in love with but just happen to be from. We were only seconds into the Olympics, and Boyle and his team were nailing it already. How bloody brilliant! 'Oh, *us* of little faith'!

As the film reached its conclusion, the viewer had been taken away from the Thames and we approached the Olympic stadium. It wasn't forgotten that the world was watching, and the show needed to be inclusive, so this was also a showcase for the UK and there couldn't be too much navel-gazing. An archive collection of Event Programmes from previous Olympics appeared in a montage while the music had become the sublime *Map of the Problematique* by Muse. Boyle and co absolutely nailed the music choices for the arresting, rousing intro, as we were all swept into the stadium for the *Isles of Wonder* show. And they continued to get it right.

The next three-and-a-half hours were stunning, leaving the vast majority of the UK public excited, happy, reassured and optimistic about the next two weeks and beyond. If that sounds 'happy clappy' - well that's the point. It felt, it feels, weird to say it out loud. Our mood had been transformed like a click of the fingers. And yet this was deeper, searching for our souls. There was plenty, unashamedly, that Boyle was doing aimed for the people of the UK, not the global audience, asking them to celebrate their own people, their own land.

From the ambitious depiction of the Industrial revolution, appearances by influential Brits like Tim Berners-Lee, the *World Wide Web* creator, to the celebration of the NHS. Eight years later the British people stood and clapped the doctors and nurses again, in as different circumstances as imaginable. And the Web helped us stay in touch with each other in the most challenging of times.

Boyle's team made a shrewd and loving selection of British culture and movies, with a soundtrack that reflected the influence of the nation's music far beyond these shores. And underpinning it all, and risking losing the TV audience overseas, was that humour. The failsafe was a sequence involving Mr Bean, one of the world's favourite characters and never lost in translation. More risky, unlikely and unforgettable was the sequence involving The Queen and James Bond, aka Daniel Craig. It's still a remarkable feat to persuade *Her Majesty* to act in a scene, then be represented by a stuntman jumping out of a helicopter with Bond into the Olympic Stadium. It was jaw dropping. And still raises a smile.

Years later, I watched an enlightening documentary on how the ceremony was put together, under financial and logistical pressure and with a public thinking 'impress me', while bracing themselves to be underwhelmed. The running theme of the documentary was the leadership of

Boyle, of which I had no preconceptions. It turns out his style was to em-power people, make them believe, encourage their own decision-making and support their vision and creativity. Moreover, he didn't micro-manage for the sake of it. When he *did* feel strongly, such as an issue with the hiring and using of certain drums, then he fought for the money and imposed himself.

From the top downwards, the volunteers - and remember that's what they were, *volunteers* - felt included and valued. We can't conclude they all *felt* like this, but this was the vibe from the documentary. What had been set is a tone. A tone 180 degrees removed from a father setting an intimidating tone in his home, or a middle-manager's uncomfortable office atmosphere, or a sulky football manager suddenly setting a lighter mood just because *they* feel like it. Boyle created an environment for people to feel better about themselves every day.

Then, rather wonderfully, the volunteers took the baton and set the tone amongst the visiting public. Something that can raise suspicion in London is friendliness. Like a lot of major cities, everybody can appear in a rush, and caught up in their own bubble. My forty-five years of living there gave me enough evidence that in Central London particularly, this is too often the case. But in their purple outfits, and clutching information leaflets, the enthusiasm of the vast army of volunteers was infectious.

There was a dignity about the friendliness that made you stop and think, to question your own behaviour. Because none of us were used to it. Visitors to the UK lucky enough to have tickets were getting the best of Britain, perhaps unprecedented Britain. It was like being on a different planet. First out of shame then more naturally, we started to be *nicer*. And as if that wasn't enough, the sun was shining. Yes, the weather. The key to a summer event in Britain and talked about endlessly, was behav-ing itself. So *this* is that they mean by a 'feel-good factor'.

*

That special feeling across London and the UK, a special brand of magic, reached Leicester in May 2016.

One month later, that nation was divided. Brexit. The word that dominat-ed for years in Britain, and much of Europe. 17,410,742 people voted to leave. 16,141,241 voted to remain. The people who had come together to celebrate every medal, every performance, every special effort for those glorious six weeks in London in 2012, were now split into two large camps. So damaging, so debilitating, so bitter was the arguing over Brexit, that the term became toxic and stayed toxic. The political opportunism and sleight of hand behind the scenes were stomach-churning, whatever bus people preferred to be on.

Brexit coincided, and perhaps accelerated, a poisonous culture of opinion 'sharing' in Britain, largely through social media. Newspapers with agendas retained huge influence, so hadn't quite handed the baton over to the digital world. But whether in print or online, airing an opinion was part of daily life, minute-by-minute, insult-by-insult. It was difficult to stand back from it, and see what Britain had become, but one element of the Brexit process, and social media, was barely being considered.

Who is *changing* minds? The purpose of airing an opinion was no longer to appeal to the consideration of others. Perversely, opinions were only being used to reinforce one's standing amongst one's peers and fellow believers. Sometimes a form of showboating, grandstanding and intellectual muscle-flexing, and at other times pure stubborn ignorance. 'Echo Chambers' are one of the biggest dangers to society, with people becoming entrenched in their beliefs. It's okay for us to have strong beliefs, and to air them. But to *change* a mind, to change *your* mind, to give something full consideration but then stick with your view, to *listen*? Those who are prepared to listen, to be educated or enlightened, whether on Brexit or anything else, are becoming depressingly rare.

In May 2016, between Leicester winning the league and the Brexit referendum, I happened to be on a tube train, in east London, and two young guys, maybe mid-20s, were talking about Brexit. One of them said that while he was adamant Britain should 'remain', and would himself be voting to stay, he was worried at the tone of some fellow '*remainers*', because he felt it was coming across as condescending. "Many leavers will dig in," he said. "Because they feel patronised. They won't *listen* or even *consider* changing their view." Whatever your political views, however you voted, was he wrong about the entrenched, uncompromising nature of debate, which we saw from *both* sides?

Woven undeniably into Brexit, are entrenched views about race, about national identity, about what the Union Jack means when it's *not* being raised in a sports stadium. Rather than a civilised debate about this concern, the debate was taken over by a feeling amongst British people that they had a right to an opinion, and a vote, and why should that be challenged? No longer were people actually considering facts and issues, it was about people demanding to be listened to. Maybe if he'd have known what was coming, Boyle could have used the incredible and prescient 1980s song *'Brilliant Mind'* by *Furniture*: *"I'm at the stage, where I want my words heard and no-one wants to listen cos everybody's yelling."*

*

What is often critical for any Olympics, and most major sporting events, is home success. Britain needed golds, plenty of them. Silvers and bronzes too. Whether it's Korea, Brazil, the UK, anywhere I've reported on these events, you notice a tension until the first gold is won, then a relaxation and then a sense that the nation is enthused, engaged and expectant. There is then a buzz for when the *next* gold will be.

The sports authorities in the UK, and the Government, were all too aware of this. Money had been ploughed into many sports, much of it from the *National Lottery*, which had helped transform British sport into a powerful force in multi-sport Games. Even sports where there was no tradition in Britain and no hope of a medal, were getting teams together. Such as handball. So unfamiliar was handball to British crowds I half-expected cries of 'handball' when the event started, and a demand for a penalty!

There is a trade-off during a 'goldrush' though. A lot of the sports involved were only highly popular during Olympic games when Britain was *winning*, and yet received more funding money than sports which offer more for communities and opportunity to all. Certain sports suffer from not appealing to a high enough 'class' of person. The one I highlighted, which too many of my peers have neglected, is basketball. It's no use leaving such an important sport in the shadows between Olympics.

Basketball is the second most popular sport amongst diverse teenagers in the UK. It has been for many years, but suffers from a lack of funding. Why? Put simply, medals. There is only *one* Gold available in Olympic basketball, in what is a highly competitive world sport. Standards are extremely high. The British League is competitive, but not strong enough to produce world beating players. When handfuls of medals can be won by Britain in selected individual sports, with the reflected glory that comes with it, money doesn't reach team sports that can't offer success in the medal table. There's not a limitless pot of money, but what's more important? Medals or participation? Legacy.

Basketball was suffering from a lack of funding, and I felt the story needed telling when the London Olympics had long gone. Is it right that a sport so popular with a young, diverse, urban and traditionally poorer background isn't funded properly? While sports with a high proportion of 'public school' competitors were receiving money because they had won medals. A vicious cycle for the poor sports, who needed to achieve better results to receive the money to achieve better results.

Leicester's team are the *Leicester Riders*, and they are the best basketball team in the UK. When I visited them under the guidance of their long-serving chairman and energiser Kevin Routledge, it was encouraging to see their players devote so much time to the schoolkids of the city, striving to do as much community work as possible with limited resources.

The crowds at their games weren't huge, but diverse, just as I'd experienced outside the football stadium when Leicester City FC won the Premier League. It's still rare to see hijabs in some British sporting crowds, but there were Muslim families courtside in Leicester, and a wide age range. Remember, the London Olympics were not just about London, they were about sport and legacy across the whole of the UK. The funding of Olympic sports across the country, in Leicester and all over, should not be ignored. Kevin could not be doing more to push them, but without enough help from outside, Leicester Riders are a *quiet* success story. Too quiet.

It says something that my attempts to promote British basketball, because of its youth appeal and diversity, can prompt the response: "Yeah but it's *not* the NBA." I know! But it could and should have more attention. It needs a revamp. One day I hope British basketball's popularity surges, and I would love to help it succeed.

Back in 2012, basketball did not grab our attention, but that is partly for a positive reason, because of the extraordinary memories being created in the new Olympic Stadium and the other venues. Britain won three golds within the space of 46 minutes in the stadium on the middle Saturday. *Super Saturday* as it quickly became known. The golden girl heptathlete, Jessica Ennis, the flame haired long jumper who rose and extended to the big moment of life, Greg Rutherford, and the north London distance runner who was once a refugee from Somalia, Mo Farah.

I was there, at the finishing line. All those times I've been stood outside, and suddenly I was one of *The Lucky Few*. I say few, but there were 80,000 people inside the purpose-built stadium at the heart of the Olympic Park, and whether you were watching on TV, on a large screen, in the stadium, or competing, it was a special night. Once in a career, once in a lifetime. The noise was a beautiful cacophony, with Union Jacks being waved. Like The Last Night of the Proms. But for all classes. We felt we *belonged*. Isn't this what happens to other people and other nations? It was happening to us.

During those Olympics, the Great Britain team won 65 medals, 29 of them gold, the country's biggest total since London hosted 104 years earlier. The performances and victories and medals and ceremonies were being greeted with daily and nightly fervour. Do you believe in magic?

Two weeks later the London Paralympics took place, and the magic still hung in the air. Great Britain had a strong team, and the medals flowed again, but the effect of the event went far beyond sporting success. Perceptions of disability were being challenged, changed, not just with sporting prowess, but the *stories* that were being told. Connections were felt, and this was in no small part in Britain due to the extensive, innovative coverage on Channel 4 in the UK.

An inspired decision was made to use the majestic theme tune '*Harder Than You Think*' by Public Enemy, and the most notable part of the Paralympic broadcasting coverage was a TV show that played out in the evenings after the action, *The Last Leg*. It was grown-up sports coverage, an exception to the norm, where excellent event broadcasting can sometimes be dragged down by inane studio analysts and presentation.

The nightly programme wrongfooted us with its sharpness, irreverence and bold approach, getting laughs from unlikely lanes. There was chemistry and comedy between the presenting team, the Australian Adam Hills, who was born without a right foot, Josh Widdicombe, and Alex Brooker, whose physical disabilities are more obvious than those of Hill's. The programme was so successful that it continued to be an essential part of the channel's prime time coverage on Friday nights for the following decade. And by the following Paralympics in Rio, this broadcasting team had become seriously powerful communicators.

Brooker, who had lived with arm and leg deformities his entire life, suddenly became serious, and emotionally explained why gold-medal winning racing driver Alex Zanardi gave him strength and dignity as a disabled person. It was broadcasting at its most important, powerfully moving and clearly affected his friends, colleagues and the audience.

It was never forgotten by *The Last Leg*, and the overall coverage, that the Paralympics is sporting competition of a very high quality. And ultimately, being desperate for a competitor to strike gold for your country is what stirs the public. In London, hundreds of thousands more people were getting to experience the Olympic atmosphere, a sense of excitement that had a touch of Disney's 'Magic Kingdom' about it. People wandering from event to event, smiling in the sunshine.

*

The noise in that Olympic Stadium on that Saturday night, August 4, 2012, will never leave me. It was one sound, voices together in unity. That is what sport can do.

The sound of society a decade later can be overwhelming. There is no old-fashioned sound control, on an old-fashioned television, where we can moderate noise and focus on what is important. Do we allow ourselves enough respite, do we edit enough as we keep turning on those devices and going back to say more? Are we actually listening to what is important? The sound is tumultuous, and the warning bells are not being heard. The 'Olympic Spirit' of London 2012 seems a long, long time ago.

Chapter 21: LEAP YEAR

There was a boy who I went to school with by the name of Patrick Wheeler. He is a cult hero in our house.

When my son was eight-years old, I casually referred to Patrick because of his unusual birthday. Patrick was born on February 29, 1972, Leap Year's Day. At school in 1980, we therefore celebrated Patrick's *second* birthday.

"What does he do about his birthdays when it isn't a Leap Year Daddy?"
"Well, he probably celebrates on February 28, or March 1. The Queen has two birthdays, and one is just for official reasons. So maybe Patrick has an official birthday, just like the Queen. Two of a kind."
"Can you ask him Daddy?"

I don't know where Patrick Wheeler is. I haven't seen him since those schooldays. I've no idea how his life turned out. I hope he's somewhere smiling. What I remember most is his smile. He was usually happy be-cause he'd scored a goal. Patrick was a goal machine. There weren't many better ten-year-old football assassins in south-east London. Our Paolo Rossi. 1982 was a vintage year for the Italian national team and *Marvels Lane Infants* team, south-east London. Our school team won many matches thanks to Patrick. He was small, fast and very talented.

I was the lucky one. My job on the pitch was easy, I just gave him the ball. I was the *other* goal scorer, for what that's worth. He probably scored three to every one of mine and I was decent at that age and played for three teams; my district, a good Sunday team called Riverside FC, and alongside Patrick for Marvels Lane school. He never made a fuss. He just used to stick the ball into the net, turn and smile. Considering he was 'so much younger' than the opposition, two and a half years old while they were ten, Patrick was our matchwinner. He deserves his legendary status in my house. When we think of Leap Years, and birthdays, and goals, we think of Patrick.

Patrick happens to be Black. When my son asked me to describe Patrick, the first thing I thought about was him scoring. Then the smile. Then that he was Black. I grew up with race not being as big a deal as it was for some, with two of my three closest friends being Black. 'Some of my best friends are Black' etc. Can you believe anybody actually says that? But you're never too old to listen and learn lessons. I thought it was enough to be easy-going about race. To smile when people ask where I'm from because I'm lightly olive-skinned (it happened every single day at school, which feels utterly bizarre now). To feel pity for those with prejudice, or who make a big deal about skin colour. But a few years ago, it transpired a work colleague, a cameraman named Devron, had been a pupil at the same school as me. And he educated me on something while we sat having a curry in Newport on a freezing January night (living the dream). *"Your Black friends were protecting you Lee"* said Devron "Protecting me from what? I know there was racism around, but me and my mates didn't have to deal with anything serious, even though some of them are Black. *"It affected them, but not you Lee. They were going through it every day. Getting on the bus and watching people hold their bags tighter. The little comments. Every day"*.

Had I become so hardened by life on a south London estate, that as long as me and my mates weren't being battered, then all was fine? As long as the guy that came into school and picked a fight with my good friend Ian, carrying a sock full of snooker balls into the playground, wasn't *overtly* racist, then it maybe wasn't racism. I think about Stephen Lawrence a lot, maybe you do too. The 18-year-old schoolboy murdered for being Black in suburban south London. OK, maybe I think about it slightly more than you. It happened one road away from where I lived, when I was barely older than him. A close friend, Mark, often used the same bus stop, that chilling murder scene, when travelling home from my house. We never really spoke about it, until recently. Just too close to home. I think of Stephen's dignified parents, and the tireless work they've done to make sure his death makes a difference. He'd be in his forties now.

Within the debate about *taking a knee* in sport, I think of Devron's insight, of my friends' experiences, and of Stephen Lawrence. The debate around the knee eventually became too hollow, too flippant, and with wilful ignorance about why a player or team would feel the need to do it. The word 'politicised' being used, without that accusation necessarily having any substance.

Taking a knee is not a straightforward subject though. When it became an 'obligation', the danger of apathy set in. It felt uncomfortable listening to commentators 'getting a mention out of the way'. We should feel it, like those who truly believe in doing it, for it to have the right impact. Some people celebrated the gesture, while simultaneously doing nothing to change a *culture* of racism. Were too many people using a knee to cover another part of their body – their backs? How engaged were they in fairness *before* the killing of American George Floyd on May 25, 2020, when a police officer knelt on his neck for more than nine minutes?

As so often happens, it took sport to take a major issue to the next level of public consciousness. In 2016 an American footballer, San Francisco 49ers quarterback Colin Kaepernick, and his teammate Eric Reid chose to kneel during the national anthem, to draw attention to issues of racial inequality and police brutality. "*I am not protesting the anthem or the nation, I'm protesting organised brutality. To me this is much bigger than football and it would be selfish to look the other way,*" said Kaepernick at the time. Other players, other teams followed suit and took a knee. It had become a major story. There was a perception from some Americans, stoked by a man of an '*orange colour*', the President of the United States, that the actions were disrespecting the flag. Kaepernick chose to sit during the anthem, which wasn't sitting well with some 49ers fans, including a former serviceman named Nate Boyer. It is their correspondence, their conversations, which led to Kaepernick deciding Boyer's suggestion was a respectful and appropriate protest. Which led him to take a knee instead. Kaepernick had assured Boyer there was no disrespect intended to the military or the flag. They came to an understanding of each other. They listened. Profoundly, Boyer said: "We didn't even have opposing opinions. We had opposing *experiences.*"

Knees continued to be taken across the NFL, to the considerable discomfort and chagrin of some of the figures in authority of the league. These included team owners who regularly played golf with the man in the White House. In 2017 the amateur golfer, businessman and reality TV star who was voted into power and was kept there by his enablers and excusers, said with customary 'charm' that NFL owners should 'fire' players who are taking a knee: *"That's a total disrespect for our heritage. That's a total disrespect of everything we stand for. Wouldn't you love to see one of the NFL owners say: Get that son of a bitch off the field right now. Out! He's fired".*

Kaepernick's mother Teresa responded by saying on Twitter: *"I guess that makes me a proud bitch."*

Kaepernick's last game as an NFL quarterback was on New Year's Day 2017. He reportedly 'didn't fit' into the new plans of the new coach of the 49ers and was released. A few years on, NFL franchise owners publicly expressed regret at not signing him. The league's commissioner said he'd wished he'd "listened to Kaepernick" earlier. But why were NFL bosses, why was the world of sport, suddenly expressing regret, and backing Kaepernick and the many other players taking a knee? What changed in 2020? George Floyd.

When historians try to make sense of the year a pandemic terrorised the planet, the impact of his death will be interwoven. Imagine something, *anything*, being of such gravitas, that it temporarily overshadows a pandemic. No longer would millions, hundreds of millions, stand for such racist brutality. A callous, hideous murder of a man with a knee on his throat. And to think how many millions objected to the taking of a knee on a sports field.

The *Star-Spangled Banner* had been the backdrop to civil rights protests before, protests that are still talked about but evidently didn't change things *enough*. At the Mexico Olympics in 1968, medallists Tommie Smith and John Carlos both raised a clenched fist in a black glove to give a Black Power salute, standing on the podium as the anthem played. It was a few months after the assassination of Black civil rights activist Martin Luther King Jr and they wanted to, they *needed* to, highlight racial injustice. The image is one of the most striking and famous of 20th century. Smith said he cried when he saw Kaepernick's protest, nearly 50 years later. How much had changed, since they stood on that podium in Mexico?

At the time the most famous sportsman of the era was one of the most famous men on the planet, Muhammad Ali. *His* actions, his words, carried a similar impact to his heavyweight punches in the boxing ring. He won Olympic boxing gold as Cassius Clay in 1960 then changed his name four years later, having converted to Islam.

"Cassius Clay is a slave name," he asserted. *"I didn't choose it and I don't want it. I am Muhammad Ali, a free name. It means beloved of God."* Ali died in 2016. We can imagine what he would have made of Kaepernick's

stance later that year, the death of George Floyd four years later. How much has changed? Like Smith and Carlos, like Kaepernick and Reid, Ali felt he *had* to use his platform to speak out.

In the aftermath of the killing of George Floyd, sport played an important part, proving yet again the power it has to make a difference, the platform it gives, and the responsibility on the shoulders of Black athletes, who didn't enter the game to make a stance, but feel compelled and proud to do so. Many were angry, many were heartbroken. In some cases, they were scared. Watching a man losing his life in that way had a profound effect on them, on most of us, and on the world.

In August of 2020, NBA players took an immediate and powerful stance to on-*another* incident of apparent police brutality against a Black American — the shooting of Jacob Blake. It happened approximately 40 miles south of Milwaukee. The city's NBA team, the Milwaukee Bucks, refused to take the court for their match that night. "*The baseless shootings of Jacob Blake and other Black men and women by law enforcement underscores the need for action,*" the NBA Coaches Association said in a statement, and further games were called off.

The biggest stars in basketball, including the most successful current player Lebron James, spoke out. Enough was enough. This was a sport where people were listening. Emergency meetings took place, and the players were supported, not chastised. This took place while the NBA season had resumed inside a 'Covid-secure bubble' within the 'Walt Disney World' complex in Florida. Sport was dealing with the realities of life, not the 'Disney' version.

Also sending a powerful message in the summer of 2020 was Naomi Osaka, who wore a mask to enter the arena at the US Open tennis in New York. On the mask was the name Breonna Taylor, the medical technician fatally shot in her Louisville home by police in March of that year. "*I'm aware that tennis is watched all over the world, and maybe there is someone who doesn't know Breonna Taylor's story. It's just spreading awareness.*"

Across the sports world, it wasn't always clear how authentic gestures were, however well-meaning. *Taking a knee* made an impactful start and became commonplace in the summer of 2020. It was happening in rugby, cricket, hockey, in most sports you could think of. It was a gesture of solidarity and togetherness, a message that racism won't be tolerated. But then there was a danger that apathy set in.

Football, including the Premier League, typified the impact and the dilution. At first, two squads of players, officials and managers, kneeling respectfully in silence in an empty stadium, had a powerful resonance. After many months, it became customary and less impactful. A bit forced. Something well-meaning, that was *losing* its meaning. Is this what is meant by a token gesture? Was some of sport's response to racism, and of sports broadcasting's response to racism, cosmetic? Ultimately, to look at a footballer on one knee and think it is overtly political seems a stretch.

In 2015 I had made a documentary about the lack of coaches in world football who are black. When journalists tackled the subject, not nearly often enough, the focus was usually on the *Rooney Rule*, where positive discrimination is used in the hiring process of coaches in the NFL system in America. Blatant racism was being talked about. But *'unconscious racism'* where a coach isn't getting a job in sport because of subtle prejudices and preconceptions in employers, wasn't always explored forensically. And when there aren't Black talents in the manager's seat, or boardroom, it's hard to break through. *You can't be what you can't see.*

In my programme, I explored why so few of the 92 English football league clubs had Black coaches. At the time there were three. THREE. Once, Black players in England were exceptions, and suffered horrendous prejudice and abuse over their perceived contributions and qualities. Over many years, the issue had reached the dugout, and the boardroom. How much representation of ethnic minorities is there in the actual running of these clubs? We also explored African football, and the culture of employing coaches who are white. Three coaches of the 16 nations in that year's *Africa Cup of Nations* were Black.

The former Arsenal and England captain, Sol Campbell was one of the guests, a man who can generate a lot of opinion on his character without any of us actually knowing him. Why is this? I'd been a pitchside reporter when he was captain of his country and was in little doubt as to his leadership skills, which he was finally given a chance to prove as manager of Macclesfield Town FC. He kept them in the league to muted praise. What are some people seeing when they comment on Campbell? A racist stereotype of a Black man with a 'chip on his shoulder'? I've heard that phrase used repeatedly about people who are Black and vocal about lack of opportunity and call people out on it.

The Football Association representative Heather Rabbatts was another guest on the programme I made. A former chief executive of a London Borough Council, Rabbatts was the first person from an ethnic minority to be an FA Director when she was appointed in 2011, and the only woman on the board at the time. Nobody in sport has nailed racism more effectively than she did on a BBC programme about Anton Ferdinand, who spoke about his guilt at staying quiet on his racial abuse. The very abuse I had raised in that Blatter interview. Some journalists pompously questioned Ferdinand's silence, which is easy to do with white, middle-aged, middle-class entitlement, and not excused by the fact Anton blamed himself while some of his friends and family admitted they wanted him to take a stance. Not Heather. Who asked why do we "blame the victim"? Indeed, why do we do that? The case had eaten away at Ferdinand, and seemingly ruined his playing career. Watching him grasp, successfully, for the right words, was intensely moving. It was an important programme. It probably wasn't *my* place to be angry, but I was, I am. Did people actually notice the difference between Heather's words, Heather's *tone*, and the words of those who questioned Ferdinand?

Some of us couldn't help but notice that broadcasting executives were scrambling to cover their backs with on-screen representation. How many of them addressed the lack of diversity on screen and at senior level *before* George Floyd's killing? Must it take a brutal murder on the streets of America for chances to be given to those overlooked? Some of these bosses were lauded for their programming and content on the subject of race in sport. And yet many of these bosses will still find a way to hire many of the wrong people, of all races, and fail to properly support and empower those they have hired. If we don't hold *these* people to account for their track records, then the current positive discrimination *is* cosmetic. But we won't. We don't. We should.

My suspicion of bosses in sports broadcasting, in journalism and in many industries, on their track records in hiring and supporting employees from diverse backgrounds, does have a disclaimer. That it's more important to *listen* to those affected by poor and disempowering or discriminatory behaviour, than to be personally outraged about one's own industry, and the people that run it. I can emphasise. But as Heather would put it, the victims have to live, be defined by interpretations of them based on race. Listening to Black friends in my industry, they have educated me on the importance of getting opportunities whatever the circumstances. Their work can then open other doors from within. Again, *you can't be what you can't see.*

A Black employee shouldn't be asked to consider whether they have benefitted from positive discrimination, while they are busy doing that job well. And imagine what it's like to be *asked* if you got a job through a beneficial system. How demoralising and destructive. This is something I need to take care over when criticising executives. That the benefits of them increasing diversity possibly usurp the feeling that they should have done it earlier.

And there have been cases of sport's *Black Lives Matter* coverage getting it spectacularly right, memorably before the first Test match between England and West Indies in that strange summer bubble of 2020. We had a lot to be grateful for from this West Indies team, for their brave decision to fly in and play the series during the pandemic, the cricket they played and the manner in which they carried themselves. When they took the knee, raising a fist in a single black glove in reference to the Black Power Olympic 68 salute, you *felt* it. It really meant something.

In Sky's broadcasting team, two of their pundits were asked to speak on their experiences of racism - West Indian cricket legend Michael Holding and former England cricketer Ebony Rainford-Brent. Two fine broadcasters, and in both cases their finest moment. The impact of *individual* stories is priceless, it makes a connection with us. Rainford-Brent, who demonstrably would rather have been living in a world where she could focus on cricket, wept as she recounted the racism she had suffered. And the point was how routine, even mundane it was. The little comments about her hair, her food, her clothes. Chipping away at her dignity. She spoke so eloquently, so movingly, and educated us in a way we'd never forget.

Holding also cried. This is one of the all-time great bowlers, a man whose bowling was fast, effective, successful, graceful and so quiet in the run-up he was nicknamed '*Whispering Death*'. He is now better-known for his integrity. Holding talked about the racism his parents had faced in detail, his distinctive treacle-coated Jamaican voice trembling with anger and upset: *What people need to understand, this stems from a long time ago, the dehumanisation of the Black race is where it all started,"* Holding said, *"History's written by the people who do the harm, not by the people who are harmed."*

I had the privilege of speaking to him on the phone after the death of Richie Benaud in 2015, and he spoke generously about how much he'd learned from the greatest of broadcasters, the master of restraint in words. On the subject of racism, Holding was showing again how he'd taken the baton for eloquence, his words were landing with customary precision, each one making an impact. He managed to shock and enlighten. *"Do you know how it feels to be followed when you enter a shop on Oxford Street because of the colour of your skin?"* he said tearfully.

Michael Holding's fame doesn't make him immune from racism. With a microphone or cricket ball, he becomes more 'acceptable' to those who shouldn't be judging him. When Devron carries his expensive TV camera people relax around him. What would you first notice about him?

And what's important in a description of Patrick Wheeler, who was born in a Leap Year?

Chapter 22: CHEAT?

With great power comes great responsibility. Sport really *does* have a significant influence on society, whether or not you think it should. But what happens if we can't trust what we are seeing? The pursuit of winning, of glory, can still be pure, but the rewards and glory for winning have ended up poisoning many events. Do you still believe in sport?

Whether an approach is considered cheating, 'gamesmanship', rule manipulation or simply unfair can depend on the sport, the era, the circumstances, the setting or the exponents.

Some don't like the way success can be 'bought'. It's not cheating, but it's not popular either, unless your team or nation benefits. And those who do the spending benefit too. That's the point. 'Throwing money' at a player, a club, a sport or prestigious global event can improve a nation's reputation, or create a softening, a diversion, from the actions of those of power. This is sometimes called *sportswashing.*

This is where a nation-state, group or individual uses sport to improve its reputation. At its worst, the move into sport whitewashes and distracts from disreputable, or even criminal, behaviour. A regime can be ordering a murder with one hand, while shaking the hand of a sports' governing bodies with the other.

Then there is 'soft power'. From the hosting of major events to the purchase and transformation of football clubs, spending billions to ensure some success can be an effective 'reputation management'. Or not. 'Soft power' can be confounding, because it's not easy to see the benefits when the spenders are criticised, or even ridiculed.

Reputation management is a tightrope. The buyer of a sports club or event wants to be *known* to be associated and behind it, yet not directly in the firing line. No wonder rich countries spend so much on 'spin doctors', though not always successfully.

We have seen a succession of major sporting events being hosted by countries with questionable reputations. They have the money to take the risks, and the money to have the right connections in sports governance. This is something that has been under the microscope, and rightly so. It should be scrutinised even more closely. As should what happens in sport *on* the field of play.

Within sports events, cheating can have a major influence on outcomes, trophies, medals, livelihoods and reputations.

There is downright cheating, and there is also manipulative, sly rule-bending, which is sanitised and legitimised with phrases like *'marginal gains'*. Like life, very few hold their hands up when they are caught cheating. Bend the reality, style it out, brazen it out, go for gold.

Systemic doping for political gain has turned sport into a dark farce. The method is actually quite simple. Put the corrupt system in place, win the medals and look tough, effective, successful, powerful. If you're found out deny, deny, deny. Who's going to stop you?

Those in charge of sport often fail to deal with doping. They will half-stop the cheats. They take some action, but don't go far enough, so as not to compromise their own positions. The classic fudging and avoidance. The courage of the 'whistle-blowers' provides the sharpest of contrast with the administrators, who are desperate to put their fingers in ears and say: "I can't hear you, please make the problem go away before we have to deal with it." If an entire event can be poisoned by systemic, state-sponsored doping, is there actually a point to the event at all? I feel sorry for those who still believe the sport they are watching is clean. Actually, I take that back, I envy them. Maybe ignorance is bliss. You think in a 100-metre final, all the athletes are clean?

The sport we watch in good faith can be an 'optical illusion'. Many times I watch races and quietly shake my head. You think I want to feel like that? You think I don't want to believe? I've just found out too much, seen too much, heard too much, reported on too many sport stories that became news stories for the wrong reasons. I'd love to believe in fairy tales beyond Leicester City FC, but I don't, I can't.

You want me to name the cheats? Sadly, I can't. They are protected, their lawyers are better than mine, and better than yours. I have my suspicions about many who haven't been caught yet. Him? Yep. Her? Yep. Even *him*. I'm sorry, but yes. People ask me all the time whether certain athletes are 'clean'. Please not *him* they say. I'm sorry, he's definitely cheating. I became *The Grinch Who Stole Christmas*. The joy killer? I honestly don't want to be.

I was educated in cheating by experts at the sharp end. One was very senior in *anti-doping* and oversaw the 'busting' of a famous athlete. When that athlete made his comeback from serving a ban for a major doping offence, I invited her on to a programme, and before broadcasting we discussed the subject.

"I sympathise with those who want him banned for life" I said to her. She looked at me as if I was mad. *"He's one of the good ones, Lee"*.
"Eh?" I said incredulously.
"How do you think we catch people? You think anti-doping is enough? They have a head start on us".
"So why is he a *good* guy?"
"Because he accepted his wrongdoing and he's working with us now. Most don't, they just continue to deny. This man has informed on others. Intel, not doping tests, is what catches the cheats".

Think about how much sense that makes. Incredible cyclists who never failed 'dope tests', but had a network around them too sophisticated for the anti-dopers. In a sport where it's not whether you need medical assistance, it's whether you can *stay within the rules* with your medical assistance. It is usually 'whistle-blowers' who expose cheats. Anti-doping regimes are valuable, necessary and a deterrent, because it would be a 'free-for-all' for dopers if the system didn't exist. But there are ways and means for dopers not to get caught, and to circumnavigate rules. Little windows where the anti-dopers can't touch them.

"Why not just let them get on with it, may the best chemist win," said a boss to me once. I realised he wasn't joking. This is the weariness and cynicism the manipulation of sport causes. Apathy could end up destroying some sports.

Systemic doping turned some sport into farce. How can we believe any-thing that happens if an entire event was used to make those in power look even more powerful and successful? Costing many billions of dol-lars, and costing sport its credibility. Because in sport, as in other areas of big business and corruption, the justice doesn't come swiftly and cleanly. It becomes political, there are vested interests, compromised sports leaders. When nations are awarded sporting events, the leaders of regimes get closer to the leaders of sport, and when it goes wrong it shouldn't be left to sport to dish out justice. I repeat, what *is* sports law? The amount of fudge and avoidance that comes from sport's governing bodies becomes crushingly predictable. Strict punishments are excep-tions.

The danger to sports bosses, as I've said in my work on air many times, comes from the public simply turning their backs. How much cheating can people take? In the age of the limited attention span and a multi-tude of distractions, will the public actually care about doping?

Once people stop caring, well what is sport there for? So widespread and depressing is doping in sport, there is a danger of becoming too disillusioned, too angry. Alternative perspectives on cheating are worth listening to. You could get so self-righteous you ended up hating sport, so it's worth at least contemplating whether some forms of cheating are more acceptable than others, given none of it is going to go away. And worth looking deeper into whether they are universally condemned, or in some cases celebrated. It does occur to me that if *our* team's player handles the ball to win a match for *us*, our celebrations aren't muted. In some ways the celebration is enhanced. Some of us are sporting hypo-crites, because we tolerate forms of cheating that don't affect our own chances.

Scotland football fans, with a keen sense of *schadenfreude*, love Diego Maradona, and not just because he's the greatest footballer of all time. They love his handball which helped bring down England at the 1986 World Cup in Mexico. For some English football fans, time has healed the pain from that infamous bit of cheating, and instead helps them fo-cus more on the greatest *goal* in history a few minutes later, where he dribbled around the England team as if they were drunk. A lot of the antagonism for Maradona and Argentina came from the Falklands con-flict four years earlier. It was proper hatred, as stirred up by Blatter's mate three decades later. The 'cheating' part of that famous game in 1986 was only part of an extraordinary match and backstory. Much as sports journalism likes to distil stories down to one banner headline. *"CHEAT!"*

*

For most NFL fans, time *hasn't* healed the New England Patriots being found guilty of deflating balls strategically in 2014, supposedly making them easier to catch, which became known as *'Deflategate'*. It's almost funny, but the Patriots are 'serial winners' with a perceived air of smugness, fans of other franchises didn't want to forgive them and their 'golden boy' quarterback Tom Brady. It was a perfect excuse to throw shade at them. Sometimes we're selective about how bad an incident is depending on the perpetrator. And in Brady's case, by the time he reached 43-years-old and won the 2021 Superbowl, it felt churlish to *still* dislike him. The guy's seven successful Super Bowls, longevity, durability and yes, nerve, means keeping the focus on deflated balls seems a little mealy-mouthed.

When players and teams cheat, and people choose not to forget, they 'only have themselves to blame', to use a line adored by sport commentators. There was hardly any sympathy for Australian cricketers who tried to make an old cricket ball more responsive, by one of them hiding sandpaper down his trousers and secretly rubbing it on the ball. We like to pretend cricket is still noble. It's not. But there was an outcry because the cheating appeared to be particularly sly and the characters involved originally seemed to do it with disdainful cockiness.

It was such a big deal 'Down Under' that the country's Prime Minister waded in, by which time careers and reputations looked beyond repair (so did the ball) and the fans of opponents South Africa had a 'pile-on'. England cricket fans were vocal in condemnation too, disregarding how our own players have been found to have tampered with balls from time to time. It's what us sports fans do. We have selective memory! So best not to encourage us!

The smugness of the little cheating set-up in that Australian team initially meant their comeuppance was pleasing to see. Apparently, the bowlers 'didn't know about it', despite bowling with a ball that looked like a dog had been at it. But then some felt sorry for the captain Steve Smith breaking down in tears at the 'shame' he'd caused his family. The rivalry between England and Australia at cricket is pretty intense, sometimes toxic, but there comes a point you have to remember this is sport, nobody was hurt.

A few months later I interviewed the man who actually hid the sandpaper down his trousers, Cameron Bancroft. He spoke to us candidly and with contrition, and by that stage booing his appearances on a cricket field felt somewhat unworthy of the effort. When people in sport cheat, we tend to need contrition and apologies, which some cheats still don't bother with, during their 'confessionals' to talk show hosts.

There's also a blurred area where cheating is softened to *gamesmanship*, which can sometimes be passed off as a 'skill'. What an old fashioned and strange word it is. I don't see gamesmanship as something to be pointed to with admiration and respect, especially by those who revel in sport's darker arts.

Did Real Madrid player Sergio Ramos cheat in the 2018 Champions League Final against Liverpool FC? Ramos appeared to hold on to the arm of Mo Salah, the opposition's main threat, as they fell the turf. The tangle resulted in Salah leaving the pitch with a dislocated shoulder. Ramos denied it was an intentional piece of sabotage. Some believed him, others felt it was in keeping with his style of play, and some revelled in the speculation he had used the dark arts to stage an intervention to change the course of a big match.

The incident and subsequent injury also ruined Salah's hope of a successful first World Cup with Egypt. Salah showed remarkable grace, far more than I'd be capable of, when he was reunited briefly with Ramos at an awards ceremony later that year, accident or not. Ramos, self-assured and slick to those who cast him as a movie villain, put his hand on Salah's shoulder. Cheat? Hero? Villain? Deliberate? Accidental? Depends on your levels of cynicism, your morals and which team you support.

Unsavoury behaviour my extensive sport-watching has served up too often are champions who use subtle intimidating psychology when things are not going their way. A bit of ever-so-gentle bullying wrapped up as banter. I'm thinking of a darts player who used to put his arm around the shoulder of the guy who's beating him as they leave the stage for the interval, in a patronising 'good on you' way. Get off him! Because you can rest assured if the underdog *keeps* doing well, the champion will soon be snarling and shouting.

There's also a really good player, who looks like a small fridge with an angry tortoise's head. For years he seemed only able to flourish by screaming very close to his opponents faces after getting a successful throw. Then 'playing innocent' in the interview afterwards, as if to say: "What did I do?" To be fair to him, he eventually started beating players without needing histrionics, and became one of the best in the business.

My friend and former colleague Simon enjoyed creative cheating in sport and celebrated it, so we used to argue about it like a pair of grumpy old fishermen in a quayside pub. But I do take his point – there can sometimes be something comical about creative and bizarre rule-circumnavigations. A 'veritable smorgasbord' of them, to use another example of a phrase with words that have become attached together!

Managers who send spies to watch the opposition team's training sessions, or who hide in laundry baskets and pop out suddenly to conduct a 'team talk' when they are meant to be banned, or water their pitch excessively because a marshy bog will hamper the other team more. That last one was popular in the 1970s before grass came into fashion.

In 2009, came the most astonishing of cheating attempts, which stained the reputation of London rugby club Harlequins. A player used a blood capsule to feign injury near the end of a European Cup game, which allowed him to leave the field, and for another Harlequins player to return to the action in his place.

The plan didn't work, they lost the game, and the blood ruse was rumbled. Cheats never prosper and all that. What compounded the subterfuge was the realisation they had been found out, which led to a team doctor agreeing to make an actual cut. This came to light too, and the situation developed into an unprecedented rugby scandal.

An investigation concluded this wasn't the first time the club had used such dark methods of cheating. You could flippantly joke that it went *egg-shaped* for them, but the repercussions had a seriously drastic effect on careers and reputations. The player was given a one-year ban, reduced to four months, while the Director of Rugby responsible was given a three year-ban - and the chairman resigned. The physio was banned for two years and the club doctor who administered the cut was suspended by the General Medical Council. These weren't light punishments, and inevitably, it damaged reputations. While blood injuries, genuine or otherwise, can quickly heal, the stigma of being a cheat can last forever.

Which brings me to the Pakistani cricketers, a court case I reported on extensively in 2011, and stands out as the story that taught me most about the difference between a snap analysis and a forensic, exhaustive understanding of the humanity within sport. The *story* behind the headline. In late 2011, I spent six weeks at Southwark Crown court beside the River Thames, covering the court case where three Pakistani cricketers and a fixer were found guilty of corruption offences. The players had already received long bans from cricket, sports law, for a combined total of 22 years. Now they faced jail terms. It wasn't hard to see they *had* cheated, but the court case meandered like the Thames. It was almost reassuring to see the evidence considered at such length, and for those on the jury who didn't understand cricket to be so meticulously educated in what had transpired.

The players had cheated for money in a Test match against England a year earlier. The crimes took place at Lord's Cricket Ground, the darkest day for the 'home of cricket' in its 200 years. They engaged in what is called *spot fixing,* which is different to *match fixing*. Spot fixing is where the players receive money for manipulating small, often inconsequential parts of the game, in this case what is called '*no-balling*'. Deliberately putting a foot over the bowling line at pre-agreed moments. This is unlikely to cost a team anything more than one run at the time, but in this case, it cost the players their careers and their liberty.

The reason such cheating occurs is the appetite for gambling in parts of the world where it is illegal, and bookmakers offering the chance to bet on parts of cricket that really shouldn't available. Such as how many runs will be scored off a set of six balls. It's an invitation for corruption, a metaphorical pitch laid out for players who decide their wages are not enough. There are players who will have done this, remained lucky, and aren't yet exposed.

Do you believe in cricket fairy tales? If so, we can take it on trust that entire cricket *matches* haven't been fixed. There have been times I've watched international matches and some quirky behaviour has aroused suspicion. I remember once seeing a player defy science to not 'run out' an opposition player, finding a way for his gloves holding the ball to miss the stumps and let the batsman survive. And you realise it is *match* fixing going on. Not just spot fixing, which is bad enough. The issue was discussed a length in court but under legal restrictions not to report. "It's just not cricket" remains a well-known phrase. How quaint that cricket somehow clings on to the reputation for fair play in wider society. Depressingly ironic.

The longest cricket ban for the three players in the Pakistani cricketers court case I covered was ten years. The longest *jail sentence* was two and a half years. Both of these handed down to the Pakistan captain Salman Butt. He was in charge of the team *and* helping facilitate the spot fixing actions of two bowlers - Mohammad Asif and Mohammad Amir. It was Amir whose case received most attention. An 18-year-old with a long mane, he ran to deliver the ball with the athleticism of a racehorse. An unusual 'left-armer', he was one of the most talented young bowlers I've seen at that age, perhaps *the* most.

When the news emerged that the game was being investigated after a newspaper corruption sting with Pakistan bowlers involved, an ashen-faced television panel tried to react, and it was Michael Holding who nailed it again, immediately showing humanity rather than making empty noises: *"Not the kid, please not the kid"* he said with his voice cracking. Both times I've seen Holding choked on TV have stayed long in the memory. And it proved to be a typically sharp instant take. Because Amir was an indisputably naïve teenager, new to the team and heavily leant on by team-mates, and to do the right thing by them. Stupidly and corruptly, he did the wrong thing. Would I have done it? No. Was it horribly damaging to sport? Yes. But do you just condemn him as a cheat, black and white, cut and dried, or is there room for any compassion too?

Amir was sentenced to six months in prison, eventually serving three. He looked shellshocked and terrified. Amir's defence showed the jury footage of his unmistakable joy at getting England batsmen out legitimately in that match. There was a context here. Amir thought, wrongly, that he could cheat with the no-balls, take the money, keep his teammates and fixers happy, and still win the match for his country. This was an education for me. If I was outside of the court for that case, I would have probably felt no sympathy for Amir whatsoever.

That doesn't mean I expect you to have sympathy, or that he should be excused. I'm saying that what took place was actually a human tragedy, and that some of us came to understand that by the privilege of being in the courtroom. I believe we have a duty to try and express that, to colour in the picture, not leave it as black and white. As a former England cricket captain-turned-newspaper-writer did. He publicly rebuked the banter-fuelled childish comments of the ex-England cricketers who think they are comedians. One flippantly said that 'Wandsworth Prison' cricket team would now be stronger with Amir. But I was watching a frightened kid who messed up, getting a jail sentence. It really wasn't funny.

Amir's five year ban from cricket ripped the heart from his career, but it felt like an appropriate punishment. Ultimately, the integrity of the sport was in tatters after this case, and Amir and all three players had to be made an example of. Ultimately. and worryingly, it took this controversial sting from the disgraced and defunct 'News of the World' newspaper to get evidence strong enough to expose cricketers.

What was uncomfortable, and questionable, was that the newspaper's investigation hadn't *captured* the fix, it was their own *staged* trap to put a spotlight on what was going on. In a way, the three Pakistani cricketers were unlucky to be the ones that were caught up in this intricate sting. Amir eventually returned with some success five years later, including star performances at the 2019 World Cup eight years later – also in England. Sport has a habit of throwing up such ironies and nuances.

Corruption, cheating and greed have caused considerable damage to cricket, and to many other sports. Forgiveness for those involved who harm the game and kill our trust should be hard to come by. But we also need to consider how sports fans and media see things in binary terms. Cheat or not. Ban or not. Jail or not. They are decisions. But an understanding of a backstory takes more work, is more challenging. If your view on something doesn't evolve, doesn't adapt to circumstance, doesn't listen to the backstory, watch the effects on humans, then your response will be more akin to the Tin Man than a character with a heart.

The need for redemption for individuals who corrupt our precious sports has been explained to me. My opinion continues to evolve because I actually take a *harder* line on cheats than many. The most frustrated I've ever been as a sports journalist, was when many of my peers attacked the public for booing a notorious drugs cheat at a World Athletics Championships. Their point, expressed pompously by some, was to doubt the legitimacy of *one* of his bans. They held up this evidence like proud prefects who'd done some homework, but their judgement and common sense was underdeveloped.

Fact is sacred, comment is free, but sharp instincts have a place too. What about the time this same athlete was bang to rights, admitted guilt and received a long ban? Do we know for sure these are the only times he cheated? What we saw in the stadium strongly indicated he was *still* untrustworthy, to phrase it carefully, and this exposed how out of touch those who don't pay for tickets can be. The public are entitled to express how they feel about being cheated, rather than carry a list of people they are allowed to boo or not.

We (the fans) decide if a reputation can ever be repaired, not a court of sport or a court of law. The organisations, the regimes, the enablers, the systems often escape censure while the front men or women take all the consequences. So then it is down to us to use our judgement. Contrition from those who ruin things for us is the least we expect. And when it's not forthcoming from serial cheats, and the cover-up continues, us sports fans *do* have more power than we think.

One day, we may decide we no longer care either way. Can they hear how loudly that particular bell has started to ring? Sport is in danger.

Chapter 23: THE BELL TOLLS

Leicester City winning the Premier League didn't create a sense that *other* clubs could now do it to. Or indeed that Leicester would repeat the feat. This underlined the surreal nature of their triumph. They were the best team, played best, deserved it, sustained it and remained strong. Yet it felt like a one-off.

Their opening match of their defence of the Premier League title in August 2016 was a trip to Hull City, a game they certainly wouldn't have chosen themselves. Claudio Ranieri summed it up when he was asked about the chances of Leicester holding on to the trophy. "*It is more likely that ET comes to Piccadilly Circus,*" he said with a smile, and added mischievously that the odds, 5000-1 a year ago, should be *6000-1* this time!

One of the most important players to the cause had already left. Every player has contributed something precious, but N'Golo Kante's tireless protection of the Leicester defence had attracted the attention of richer clubs, who knew such a player could be invaluable to hold their own team together. The world's most expensive glue. Chelsea, now managed by Italian Antonio Conte, bought him for a fee of close to £30 million. They went on to win the league, in no small part through this small, likeable midfielder. Partly known for his humility, he was still driving his Mini to training. Though it's perhaps not ideal that the new champions sold such a prized asset. That's football. It's far from perfect.

Ranieri himself had signed a new four-year contract. As had Jamie Vardy, who played for England in the 2016 European Championship in France, scoring in a 2-1 win over Wales. And the other star player, Riyad Mahrez? Ranieri said he would "*Kill him before letting him leave.*" A good sign for Mahrez was that Quique Flores was *still* ok, but perhaps to be on the safe side, the Algerian ended up staying with Leicester for two more years. Manchester City eventually bought Mahrez in a £60 million deal. £59.6 million profit. Football is a strange 'business'.

Hull beat Leicester by two goals to one. Jamie Vardy didn't score. Leicester won only three of their first fourteen matches. It was clear by early autumn, perhaps even before the summer of 2016 was out, that Leicester would be handing over the trophy to one of the 'usual suspects'. But what did anybody expect? Lightning can strike twice, but over 38 games? That's where a miracle is needed. Never mind magic - do you believe in reality checks?!

Had Leicester become a bad team, a soft touch? No. They were punching closer to their normal weight. Win some, lose some. Problem is if a team loses too many then the spectre of relegation looms. And people lose their metaphorical heads. Panic sets in. On December 10, 2016 Leicester beat Manchester City 4-2 at their King Power Stadium. Jamie Vardy scored three goals. So things really weren't so drastically different.

Simultaneously, Leicester were playing in the Champions League for the first time As the English *champions*. The fans were living that dream, a European tour. To Bruges, Copenhagen and Porto, the Leicester fans travelled. And the team did enough conquering to qualify for the final 16. They were unbeaten in the first five games.

This meant Leicester would resume a challenge for European glory in February 2017 with a match against Spanish team Sevilla FC. They had already made the world sit up and take notice. Now they were in the latter stages of the continent's top club competition, in fact the *world's* top club competition. They *couldn't,* could they? Not according to what are sometimes called 'football folk'.

Football folk are the combined forces of studio pundits, armchair pundits, social media pundits, anybody with an opinion on football. The consensus was that Leicester had 'lost their way'. Their league form had become a growing concern. Five defeats in succession early in 2017 had left the club perilously close to the relegation zone, the place at the bottom where three clubs -eventually lose their places in the Premier League.

Lest we forget that Leicester, champions or not, had no divine right to a place in the Premier League, the tip of the pyramid. This was the same group of players whose first miracle had been to somehow retain their place in the spring of 2015, that magical time of King Richard's reburial. What would have happened if they *had* been relegated? We would never have experienced the unique joy Leicester's triumph generated. But relegation happens, it happens to the clubs of other fans. Bigger clubs, smaller clubs. Perspective is needed. If Leicester had been relegated the world would not have fallen off its axis. The sun would still rise.

So let me ask you something. When a club are challenging to be champions of Europe, do *you* think the manager should be sacked?

In February that year, the noise started to get louder. Not the roar of the fans at the King Power Stadium this time, but the noise *about* Leicester and Ranieri. You see, patience is not a virtue in football. False expectation is more of a trait. Irrational demands to win games is another trait. And speculation over manager's jobs is the fire that is stoked on a daily basis. So much so, it generates more interest than the actual matches. Football has become theatre. It has become Shakespearean. There can be tragedy, but in this story there was also farce.

There was substance in the rumours about Ranieri's job. Moreover, the media, and many football fans, loved it. They always *love* the drama. If the speculation about Ranieri could be distilled into a sentence, it would come from one of the football writers holding court on a TV discussion show, across a table and a bowl full of plastic croissants: "*It will be sad if Leicester sack Ranieri, but he has to go. He's lost the dressing room.*" Losing the dressing room is one of the favoured phrases of the speculator, who isn't always as close to the players within the dressing room as they'd like us to believe.

There was a time when newspaper sports writers like Nigel Clarke were genuinely good friends with footballers. Nigel taught me a lot as a young journalist and it was privilege to feel part of his family. In the 1970s, when he was at Hayters Agency, and then a writer on national newspapers of Fleet Street, players and journalists would drink together, holiday together, spend time with each other's families - and there was a bond of trust. Little unwritten rules about what they'd write, and more importantly what they *wouldn't*. Football changed, society changed. It's different now, and not unknown for a reporter to have their photo taken with players who don't know them personally at all but humour them, and post pictures while describing them as friends, in the era of 'clickbait'.

I watched the speculation on Ranieri's job grow with a mixture of incredulity at the farce, and weary realism he *was* going to be sacked. Sometimes a good result can save a job, most famously helping prolific trophy-winner Alex Ferguson survive as Manchester United manager after failing to win anything in his first three years. A player named Mark Robins scored the goal against Nottingham Forest that kept them in the Cup and supposedly kept 'Fergie' his job. Not a bad decision to keep him, as it led to 24 years of spectacular success.

Regularly in football, another manager has been lined up and a good result for the current manager comes too late. Or they are perceived to have *'lost the dressing room'*. So, what does the phrase actually mean? It's a phrase that suggests the players no longer believe in the manager's methods, no longer understand the tactics, no longer respect the tactics. It suggests the manager can no longer get the best out of them, with a bell or not. There can be truth in the phrase, the claim - players, managers, owners admit as much. But it is overused.

The suggestion was that the Leicester City players, including the big names, *particularly* the big names, were agitating for a change. That the coaching staff, some with the little bells still on their shelves at home, were frustrated by Ranieri's tactics. The things that had enchanted were starting to grate, after the years they had spent together. My apologies, I mean 18 *months*. Football is a fickle, fickle, business.

I had an opinion, for what it was worth, and it was consistent with my views of football, of sport, of life. I think that perspective was being missed, vanishing like a puff of magic in the air. That if Leicester City's owners didn't give Ranieri time after his miracle work, it underlined that the *game* was, is, misguided. That was my private view. But there was work for me to do. And that work meant telling the story, meant explaining that Ranieri was fighting to save his job, and that it might already be too late. It's my job to try to give context to those looking in to football from the outside bewildered, while those inside the game were saying emphatically: *"Leicester can't afford to go down. He's got to go."*

Many people I know, who are not big football fans, were bemused by how the game works and the fact Ranieri's job was under threat. I think their views are instructive and fascinating. I decided to collate them before Richard and I returned to Leicester in February 2017. It wasn't a scientific poll, but I didn't use 'leading' questions. I simply asked if they had heard about Ranieri: I kept getting the same answer: "Yes I heard they might sack him. That's *madness* isn't it?!"

This is not about right and wrong. This is about how football operates, and how those who report on it are largely operating for fans and enthusiasts. But the Leicester story transcended football, and so I had a duty to make the coverage relatable to all. 'Football folk' knew Ranieri had to go, but the general public didn't. I tried to operate in the middle of that Venn diagram. I can see what the Leicester City FC Executive Board were thinking, but I can also see how desperately unfair that is on Ranieri. What bothered me is the sheer dismissive certainty of some of the pundits analysing the situation, it felt like a little more grace was necessary. It didn't occur to them to step back, step away, breathe, think, and ask themselves properly "Does this man *deserve* time?" and secondly, "Isn't what Claudio Ranieri achieved at Leicester worth more than this? Isn't it a special case? And if they are relegated, wouldn't he then deserve a chance to try and bring them back?"

But such sentiment would seem bizarre, naïve and misguided in a media room, or television studio, or even the boardroom of a football club. Football is not a 'normal' business. It is attractive, influential and successful. But running a football club, league or competition as a business is not straightforward. Huge losses can be incurred. And knee-jerk decisions are more commonplace. Long-term thinking can be an alien concept when a team loses a few football matches. We are fixated on football finances for three reasons. Because we care about football, because of the imbalance, and because footballers being paid hundreds of thousands of pounds per week remains startling. The Premier League has been an astonishing and enduring success in global business. And even the smaller clubs within the 20 have more financial muscle than champions in some of Europe's biggest leagues. But football clubs running up large debts is commonplace. And trying to balance business decisions with ambition to success in football can prove unsustainable for many club owners. Managing the team is such an important job in football that success is usually demanded, not just expected. And while some managerial departures are sudden, there is usually a painful scenario of a 'dead man walking'. There were months of nonsense before the sacking of David Moyes as Manchester United manager, the replacement who struggled to fill Alex Ferguson's shoes. Many social media 'sages' claimed to have it 'on good authority' from a contact at the New York Stock Exchange that Moyes was about to be sacked. Never was one man 'sacked' so many times! But football and its followers don't do patience. And another day of rumours would unfold. Nobody considered the NYSE might have more important things to worry about than football!

In Leicester, Claudio was clinging on. We awaited his appearance at his weekly media conference. These scheduled 'pre-match' events were still routine and mundane, there weren't many journalists in the room from outside of the 'Leicester bubble'. They may still have been champions, but they hadn't developed the 'airs and graces' of one of the biggest clubs. This was another thing that made the speculation about their manager losing his job unsettling. *Dilly Ding Dilly Dong*! Please don't go Claudio. He walked in the room looking smart and relaxed in a blue sweater and white shirt. I was dressed identically having *'not got the memo'* as people used to say awkwardly in some offices when they inadvertently wore the same clothes. But he didn't shake my hand because of the outfit. He shook the hand of *all* of us in the room as usual, despite the tension he was clearly carrying within. He knew exactly how precarious his position had become. But if Premier League points were handed out for humility, Leicester wouldn't have lost a single game of his reign.

At the conference, after a few questions from the floor about minor team matters, I addressed the elephant in the room: *"You will be aware of the speculation over your job. Don't you think you deserve better after what you've achieved?"* Ranieri gave a wry smile and a shrug: *"This is football,"* he said. But he was hurting. It wasn't hard to see.

A few days later Ranieri took his team to Seville for the long-awaited Champions League match. It was a much better performance from his team, and despite losing two-one to a strong side, Leicester had scored a precious "away goal" (by Jamie Vardy), to bring back to the King Power Stadium for the second leg. These goals counted double if the overall match ended level.

The next day Claudio Ranieri was sacked as manager of Leicester City Football Club. The man who had overseen sport's biggest miracle had been dismissed nine months later with his team still competing to be Champions of Europe. That's the business football had become. In a statement the club's vice-chairman Aiyawatt Srivaddhanaprabha, son of

Khun Vichai said: *"This has been the most difficult decision we have had to make in nearly seven years. But we are duty-bound to put the club's long-term interests above all sense of personal sentiment, no matter how strong that might be."* The decision they made, in the world of football, made sense to the world of football.

Managerial changes offer no guarantees. Often a sacking has a positive short-term effect. But long-term? The majority of 'football folk' still think it was the right decision. In football, dressing rooms are 'lost' and magicians are told they are no longer magic. The pyramid, that precious tip of English football, is considered more important than the fairy tale that made Leicester famous and showed the world what the people in the city already knew. It's a special city. There was plenty of sympathy for Ranieri. Liverpool manager Klopp said it was as 'mystifying as the election of Trump'. José Mourinho, whose team were on the way to being the new champions, wore a training top with Ranieri's initials to show solidarity and spoke with humility about the decision. The antipathy that flared up years earlier was long gone.

Of all the names for the new Leicester coach to have, the new incumbent was called Shakespeare. Craig Shakespeare. A man not accustomed to facing the media, he looked like a nervous man in a big spotlight. By all accounts a fine coach, he denied there had been any plotting or agitating behind the exit of his boss. And said that Ranieri had phoned him to thank him for his support. But it was horribly uncomfortable to watch him in media conferences answering questions about Ranieri.

Under Shakespeare, Leicester won their first six matches, and beat Sevilla 2-0 to reach the quarter-final stage of the Champions league. They were then knocked out by another strong Spanish team, Atletico Madrid, but more importantly to 'football folk', they avoided relegation from the Premier League. The precious, vital aim of English clubs, apart from the most powerful at the tip at the pyramid. Survival. *The King is dead, long live the King. This* is what Claudio Ranieri said when he was sacked:

"My dream died. After the euphoria of last season and being crowned champions, all I dreamt of was staying with Leicester. Sadly this was not to be. My adventure was amazing and will live with me forever. My heartfelt thanks to everybody at the club, everybody who was part of what we achieved. But mostly to the supporters. You took me in to your

hearts from day one and loved me. I love you too. No-one can ever take away what we achieved together, and I hope you think about it and smile every day the way I always will."

Shakespeare was soon getting out his quill to sign a three-year contract. But by October that year *he* was sacked. Leicester's next manager Claude Puel was sacked after 16 months. One of the world's best coaches, Mourinho, was sacked by Chelsea twice. Quique Flores was sacked by Watford, then re-hired and sacked again after three months. It's not a job for life. Nobody receives a clock for long service. In football, only *the lucky few* are given the precious gift of time.

As he flew into Italy, Claudio Ranieri looked down at his hands. "Dilly Ding, Dilly Dong" he said to himself with a wry smile.

There was no bell. It is amazing what you can do with a bit of imagination, a bit of belief. In yourself. In others.

Chapter 24: DIE TWICE

Some football managers can't get a job. There are far more football managers than jobs. And many of these jobs give the manager precious little chance of holding on to it. But renowned managers do not struggle to find new work, often with a large cheque from the club that sacked them in their pocket.

When Claudio Ranieri, the miracle man, was sacked by Leicester, he didn't struggle to find new work. Within the last few years, years he has managed FC Nantes in France, came back to the Premier League with Fulham, returned to his birthplace to manage AS Roma, and then moved to another Italian club in Genoa, Sampdoria. Then Watford FC! Football is strange, and management is a rollercoaster as well as a merry-go-round. But a football manager in his sixties with a strong CV can be in his prime with all that accumulated knowledge and experience. They have been there, seen it, done it, managed it.

For a player, an athlete, a sportsman, a sportswoman, their playing career often ends at a young age. As fans we move on to their successors and new generations and thank them for the memories. *'The King or queen is dead long live the new one'*. But the effects on the athlete are usually profound, and sometimes devastating. It is said that athletes 'die twice'. The first time is the day they stop competing.

The loss that is suffered by a competitor when that day comes takes many forms, not just the likely loss of earnings. For the elite athlete, there is a loss of identity, an adjustment to living of past glories rather than the potential to write chapters. It is why so many attempt an ill-fated comeback, when the body can no longer get them to the podium.

There is also, critically, a loss of routine. What we see being achieved by top athletes is a result, a small piece of the whole picture, and nothing like unglamourous work behind the scenes. Someone responsible for the welfare of athletes at the top of English sport, once asked me to imagine what it's like to be a hero for a two-week Olympic window, but then to disappear from view. *"We don't see the blood, sweat and tears,"* she said, as we watched Britain's exceptional women's hockey team train. It goes out of the public's view. Out of sight. Out of mind. Us onlookers move on with our lives. But what about the players? In the case of the athletes we were watching train, she was helping to prepare players for new careers after hockey, as well as other sports. It had become a potentially life-saving part of their training, much as they would love to be able to concentrate 100 per cent on hockey.

When the training schedule isn't needed, and elite fitness is lost, the physical effects can sometimes be obvious. But the mental effects are where the bigger problem lies. When I explored the subject and talked to competitors, a pattern was clear. Playing sport for a living can be mentally challenging, and if anxiety and stress are already part of their life, the effects of retirement can have debilitating and dangerous consequences. The psychological stability of current athletes has become a more open process, part of the conversation. Duty of care exists where once it was ignored, sport reflecting society's better understanding of mental health. But what happens when the athlete is left to care for themselves and the career that has gone?

Many English cricketers can be thankful for the Professional Cricketers Association, and the advice of a certain Graeme Fowler to help their mental health. He offered support to players who are struggling when playing and in retirement, and was one of the first to bring the matter into the open in sport. If anybody has an insight, it's Graeme. In his pomp in the 1980s he was a dashing batsman, the opening batsman for Lancashire and England, wielding his bat like flashing blade and bravely scoring runs against the most fearsome bowlers in cricket history. The West Indian quick bowlers at the time were terrifying, and Graeme, whose face was once rearranged by a ball, just got on with it. Usually relished the challenge in fact. There was a swagger, a verve to his game. But Graeme has had to come to terms with his mental health.

Darkness can creep up on him, as he told me in his garden in Durham over a cup of tea, a warm man with an engaging Accrington twang that used to soothe listeners to BBC radio's cricket commentary. He has a long grey beard and the hair on top has gone, but there is a twinkle in the eyes when he talks. It is a truly beautiful summer's day, perfection. The birds sing, the sun shines, and darkness stays within. He explained that in retirement, depression can take hold. It's what happened to him.

When he finally sought help he said to a doctor: "*I can't sleep. I'm not interested in anything, everything is pointless. I've no appetite*." The doctor asked if he'd had suicidal thoughts: "*No because I have a nice life. I have a great job, a great family, lovely wife. But I can't get to it. It's over there*" he said gesticulating to somewhere out of reach. "*So, am I going to kill myself? No. But do I wish I was dead? Yes*."

Graeme invented a scale for himself to cope with his depression and has made sure he passed it on to others. A scale of 0–20 in which 10 is neutral. Anything above 10 is good, and below bad. When we spoke in 2017 his lowest overall was five. He told me his best at the time was sixteen. He shares the scale with his family to help their understanding on a daily basis. The insight and help given by Graeme can be enlightening to younger cricketers.

The PCA have been extremely proactive in recognising the specific mental pressures on cricketers of the past and present. Andrew Flintoff, the most famous cricketer of his generation, the last of the heroes when cricket was free on television and now a broadcasting personality, spoke candidly about his mental health struggles in a campaign. A key figure in setting up the PCA was my close friend Matty's father, Fred Rumsey. He wanted to look out for others. It's so often the most powerful tool we have. In cricket, in sport, in life. And there is humour. How often do we see the brave face, the facade, the tears of a clown? In Graeme's case, the thing we did most on that summer Saturday – Richard, me and his family - was laugh. He lit up when talking about his exploits in the 80s, a time when another good friend of mine, Andy, had a poster of him on his wall. His wife said to him: "*You know you always tell me how you had less than a second to react to that fast bowling from the West Indians? How come your brilliant eyesight still can't help you find the milk in the fridge?!*"

*

Once a cricketer retires they usually stay retired. But in boxing, 'comebacks' are a familiar narrative, and often to be watched through your fingers. Money is usually the main motivation, and it's not hard to see why. A retired champion, perhaps 'retired' with a soft 'r' and looking for the right fight, would take millions of dollars to get back into the ring. In that same summer I visited the Fowlers' house, in 2017, a champion boxer came out of retirement in Nevada for a fight that took "doing it for the money" to a new level.

Floyd Mayweather Junior had a record of 49 fights and 49 wins before taking on a mixed martial arts fighter from Ireland, Conor McGregor. It was a boxing match in Las Vegas being billed as the biggest fight in combat sports history, with McGregor 'learning on the job' when it came to pure boxing and having to adjust his skills to fight one of the 'all-time greats' of the ring.

Rarely have two nicknames been more appropriate. *Notorious* for the outspoken, unpredictable, abrasive Irish fighter, and *Money* for Mayweather. If I was one of the great fighters, I'm not sure I'd like that nickname. But there are far worse things he could be called too. Boxing is another sport where actions out of the ring are often tossed aside like towels. Mayweather has been found guilty of domestic violence offences and served time in jail.

According to Forbes Magazine, he made $275 million from the fight with McGregor. It wasn't as one-sided as many expected. McGregor coped with the switch of disciplines and lasted to the tenth round. But Mayweather's technical knockout took his record to fifty wins, no defeats.

In 2021, Mayweather's relentless money-making show brought a new fight against 'YouTuber' Logan Paul. The exhibition bout took place in Florida and reportedly sold more than one million pay-per-view buys. The fight went the full distance with no winner announced. Logan Paul was seen by many, including Mayweather, to have acquitted himself well. Mayweather threw approximately half the punches and landed over three times as many. If the 'fight' was in my back garden, I'd have pulled my curtains together and left them to it.

A return to the ring can be extremely lucrative, but they are not often this smooth. The greatest, Ali, suffered horribly when he returned to the ring after two years away in 1980.

Ali was 38-years old, not nearly as old as other great champions who have trodden this treacherous path of resuming a career after years away. But there had already been signs of the Parkinson's disease symptoms which gripped the second half of his life. Being 'granted' the right to fight Larry Holmes was a decision that encapsulated the dark nature of the sport. Money comes first. This was too lucrative for too many people, not least Ali, *not* to happen.

Ali was paid $8 million for the Las Vegas fight and in 1980 that was a mighty cheque. I watched as an eight-year-old in south London. The first and only time I saw the greatest sportsman in history in action. But he was brutally tortured by a man who didn't want to hurt him. "*I worry for the man, I love him*" said Holmes of Ali, with whom he'd once been a junior sparring partner.

The fight was in a temporary stadium in the car park of *Caesars Palace* hotel and casino. And there's nothing that says classy like a fight in a car park. It lasted until the 11th round. But unlike that Mayweather v McGregor construct, this wasn't a fight people wanted to see more of. Ali had suffered terribly at the hands of Holmes, a man doing his job, earning $6 million, and wishing it was any other boxer than Ali at the end of his punches.

Sylvester "Rocky" Stallone at ringside is reported to have said it was "*Like watching an autopsy on a man who is still alive.*' If only this was the movies. Holmes went back to his dressing room and cried.

Ali fought *again* 14 months later, losing in ten rounds to Trevor Berbick in The Bahamas. By the end of his career *The Greatest* is estimated to have absorbed 200,000 punches. And remember he was so fast he "*turned off the lights and was in bed before it gets dark.*"

In a documentary about Frank Bruno's two fights with Mike Tyson, Bruno said his beloved trainer George Francis had warned him the hardest fight would be his retirement from boxing. When the training, the routine, the hunger, the purpose is removed, then the boxer often feels they no longer *matter,* their existence has changed profoundly.

Bruno spoke movingly of his time in mental institutions as he tried to adjust to life outside of the ring. And the man who had been Britain's favourite sportsman for years wasn't in demand in the media either. Broadcasting can be a hard business in different ways. The people who are chosen to be handed the microphone can be baffling, especially to some of those left out of broadcast booth. It's fickle, judgemental and often random. Ex-athletes often need the right name, the right achieve-ments, and *then* have enough to say to hold on to a position. Some flour-ish. Some even find they have more talent in broadcasting than they did in their first career. The lucky few.

Most of those who forge successful new careers in their sport, whether in the media, officialdom or managing, still desperately miss the chance to *play*, the freedom to express themselves. Being responsible for their themselves only comes with challenge. How often do we hear football managers talk about how they miss playing in a big game, or any game, or the feeling of being part of a group of players with a shared goal, of *belonging*? Managing can be a lonely place. And a retirement outside of 'the game' is far worse. That's why managing is often called 'the next best thing' Not 'the best' you'll maybe have noticed.

It's often noted how many of the best football managers, remembering they are now the superstars of the Premier League, had modest playing careers. Is their success down to having more time, more focus, more to prove? Four of the five most successful managers of the Premier League era have been Ferguson, Wenger, Mourinho and Klopp. None of whom had a glittering playing career, all of whom were making significant in-roads into management before they reached the age of 40.

The exception is Pep Guardiola, a player of distinction for Barcelona and Spain before becoming a coach. He spent further time honing his craft and philosophy in Catalonia and then thrived at Bayern Munich and Man-chester City. A serial winner. He always looks absorbed in concentration to the point of tormented. I'd like to get the chance to ask him one day if he actually *enjoys* managing as much as he enjoyed playing in that Barce-lona midfield.

Claudio Ranieri had a reasonable playing career as a defender in Italy but never hit the heights with Roma, making just six appearances for the club before leaving for unheralded club Catanzaro. How much did that shape his determination to succeed as a coach, to make a distinct mark on the world of football. How much of what Ranieri achieved in Leicester, was born when his playing career died?

There were rumours of Hollywood's interest in the story of Ranieri and Leicester. Maybe they would have a slimmed down Stallone playing him.

Stallone's Rocky Films ended with him invariably bloody, bruised and victorious after an unlikely comeback to win the title and the glory, having his rock bottom in his life in Philadelphia. No matter how old he got, he still found a way into the ring for a money-spinning new shot at the title, a new movie. But what opponent remained. I used to joke that I'd like to see *'Rocky v Rocky'*, where a cloned Rocky fought himself. The tagline would be *'He's beaten the best but can Rocky beat the opponent he knows best*?!"

It's true isn't it? Our biggest opponent really is in the mirror. The retiring athlete too often doesn't recognise or like what they see. What they are suffering from is a form of grieving, for a career that has passed. For their mortality.

Chapter 25: LOCAL HERO

Not every footballer has the 'luxury' of it being their full-time profession. Such as scientist Jo Love, and her fellow Scot, a firefighter named Frank McKeown. Telling Frank's story took me deeper into the difference between telling a story and *feeling* it.

On November 29, 2013, a police helicopter crashed into *The Clutha*, a pub in Glasgow. Seven people in the pub and the three crew on board were killed. 31 further people were injured. Frank spent the night amongst the carnage with many of his friends and colleagues, doing his job, a job that presents numerous physical and mental challenges. The day after the tragedy, actually the *same* day for Frank, Stranraer FC played at Clyde in the fourth round of the Scottish Cup. Frank was the captain of the Stranraer team. The match finished as a draw. Which meant a replayed match in Stranraer ten days later. I couldn't imagine what that day, that night, was like for Frank. It seemed an extraordinary piece of resilience, and a story that needed telling.

I phoned the club and had my first experience of the kindness and co-operation of Stranraer FC. That led to a phone call with Frank himself. He was polite and he was helpful. But what he wasn't, was someone who regarded himself as a hero. And this presented an issue in telling the story, because that's clearly what he is, and how others see him. I asked If I was welcome up in Stranraer for the team's 'replay' against Clyde. Frank was reluctant, as he didn't want recognition when his firefighting colleagues were equally brave, and families were grieving. It was sensitive and it was understandable. But he took a leap of faith and we got to meet. Telling this story was going to be a challenge, and I headed to Glasgow uncharacteristically nervous. Having earned trust from Frank, I couldn't bear the thought of him regretting it.

Stranraer is on the south-west coast of Scotland, a couple of hours by road from Glasgow, where most of the players live and worked. The club is over 150 years old and accustomed to playing in the lower divisions of Scottish football on a semi-professional basis. It is a club whose every match I now follow, a club with a spirit, and a soul.

This could be found on the team bus as we travelled with Frank and the players. Camaraderie and unity that could seem like a football cliché. But it's real. Stephen Aitken was the manager. He explained to me how Frank assured him he was OK to play, and that he knew how much he wanted to, as well as the team needing him. "*That's the kind of man he is,*" said Stephen, a man whose warmth permeated on a bitterly cold November night, not unusual in this part of the world. The thermals were wearing thermals.

Vice-chairman Iain Dougan also had a welcoming manner, and an effervescence when talking about his club, and about Frank. A pride. "*Frank is a leader. He connects with people and his teammates look up to him,*" Iain told me. Iain had become hooked on the club from his first visit in 1971. And found himself eventually running them. I felt like everything I loved about sport, about football, was in these people, on that coach, in that club. The coach was being driven by a guy named Stewart Marshall. He'd taken Stranraer's players to their games for 40 years. *Forty* years. His father did the job before him. This is what underpins football and keeps the game going in a country with a rich history, a country that played in the first men's international game in the 19th century, and whose women played in the 16th century. While the players and staff got off and headed into the ground at Stranraer, the cameraman Akhilesh and I stayed on the coach to sort out some equipment. Stewart came over to my seat. We hadn't been introduced yet. After a few polite words he said to me quietly: "Frank. He's a great lad." It was Stewart's way of gently telling me not to let him down, to do him justice. He needn't have worried. That feeling on the coach hasn't left me. Stranraer is better known for ferries than football. To me, and my generation, it had been just another name on the 'Football Pools', with the results of matches read out at 4.45pm on Saturday afternoons. Stranraer one Stenhousemuir nil, or the tongue twister East Fife five Forfar four.

The ground is named Stair Park. It's a modest pitch exposed to the elements, but over 4,000 fans can pack in and make a noise. Next to the main stand there was a tiny club shop in the corner, selling blue shirts and bobble hats. It's beautiful, and it's home to them. I remember '*Roar*' by Katy Perry blaring out of the speaker while we filmed the stadium. I remember the children in blue hats and scarves smiling. I remember Andy Stirling on the ball, with a sweet left foot crossing into danger. I remember the half-time sausage rolls and soup in the small director's room we were invited into and the little heater on the floor. I remember how friendly, how kind these people were.

Stranraer and Clyde were drawing one goal each after an hour of the match. And then Frank scored. As a defender this wasn't necessarily part of his duties, but there he was, taking responsibility and heading the ball past the goalkeeper. His team won four-one and reached the fifth round, with only 16 teams left, the cream of Scottish football. The glorious unpredictability and opportunity that is the Scottish Cup, the same ability to dream the English FA Cup provides. The distraction from life's stark realities. A football club is the best thing a lot of people have.

After the return to Glasgow late that night, Stephen the manager insisted he drive us back to my hotel from the drop-off point on the outskirts. He wouldn't take no for an answer, despite needing to get up for his early shift a couple of hours later. We met Frank the next morning by the river, and I was relieved that he was clearly so relaxed, despite the television camera that accompanied us. He spoke insomuch as he could, about his role that night at The Clutha. I knew that Frank wouldn't want to say much. That he'd want to give us what was needed, but no more. His actions were speaking louder than any words, and he remained mindful of the victims and his colleagues. *"You're there to do a job like anybody else has to do. You're thinking of the victims and the families, but you need it to make sure the job goes as smoothly for the sake of everybody involved."* What time did you actually leave The Clutha on the day of the game? *"About 7.30 in the morning."*

After a night dealing with the horror, Frank then led his teammates on to a football pitch. It's barely conceivable to us on the outside. For him, it was about being a professional, twice over.

How could I meet Frank's wish to not be treated as a hero? The answer had been all around me, from the moment I approached Stranraer FC. All around him, is support, is respect, from the people he leads into those football matches. And into emergencies. The bond helps him and helps them. There is a trust and that means Frank doesn't need to be anything other than himself. Nobody expects him to "talk a good game". When he speaks, they listen. They are lucky to have Frank in their lives, but he knows he is lucky to have them.

I was deeply moved by the story behind Stranraer's victory in the Scottish Cup. In the scorebook, it said Stranraer four Clyde one. That is all some people get to see. I saw similar qualities in Frank that I'd seen in Graham Price when I told the story of Pontypool Rugby Football Club earlier a few weeks later. On the surface it was the story of a Welsh rugby club. But sport is just the starting point. This simple tale was about community, togetherness and belonging.

Graham grew up in this Welsh town living and breathing rugby, the national obsession. And signed for the club, revered through Wales and beyond. New Zealand's mighty All Blacks were one of their opponents. Stocky and powerful, built like a brick wall, Graham played in the front row, getting down and dirty each week. Pontypool won more often than not. Beside him were two more local lads, Bobby Windsor and Charlie Faulkner. The front row. The three of them played alongside each other for Wales, the aim of any schoolboy of the era, and many youngsters growing up there to this day. Three friends, living the dream.

So good were they individually, collectively, they were picked for the British and Irish Lions for the 1977 tour of New Zealand. The Lions are the best players in the British and Ireland coming together to make a team that has special status, for special players. And undertaking some of the toughest missions in rugby. A few months away from their families and the town. It wasn't a typical job and wasn't technically a job at all. They were amateurs.

Like Frank McKeown, like Jo Love - Graham and his teammates also needed a job that actually paid them an income. He told of how grateful he was that the fibre-glass company in Cwmbran he worked for showed understanding when he was clobbered on the pitch during an Australian tour. He had to temporarily push his jaw back together with thumb and forefinger, looking like something from a horror movie. It can be a brutal sport, and these were uncompromising times. Price could dish it out too. There was no need for fake blood capsules. Price, Windsor and Faulkner made Pontypool proud.

The rugby club was everything to the town, it was the focal point, the famous point, the hub of the community, the heartbeat. But when rugby turned professional in the 1990s, the traditional Welsh rugby club changed. The focal point became the national team, and a feeder system of strong regional teams. No longer were Pontypool mighty. And there were many other clubs suffering the same fate.

When I reached Pontypool, the Welsh national team was thriving and had a hint of glamour. It remained a tough sport, but after the game some players would be as likely to have gel in their hair than mud. Rugby was reflecting the change in how heroes look, and what we consider heroic. I remember meeting Ben Jeffreys, a businessman trying to protect Pontypool Rugby Club, to *evolve* Pontypool Rugby Club, to continue the work his father had started, to retain Pontypool RFC's purpose. This is a club who are over 150 years old. But they want to create new stories, not just rely on a proud history. It's thanks to Ben and people around him that Pontypool continue to compete, win matches, attract a crowd. But no longer is the rugby ground the place the community come, the place of worship on a Saturday. And reflected in the shift away from the traditions of the rugby club, and the Saturday match, we see the ghost of the British high street. We see life changing. And we aren't sure it's for the better. Vandalism almost forced the club to leave their ground in 2019. Would anyone do this in Graham's era when the place felt sacred?

Graham spoke to me in the deserted dressing room of the deserted Pontypool Park ground on another freezing winter's night. Into his seventh decade, still a man of stature and presence, and if you caricatured his features, with some of the distinctive marks and ears of a rugby forward you could imagine a friendly giant holding a bewildered beanstalk climber in his huge palm. For nearly two decades, he would have put on the shirt in this room and returned with it caked in blood and sweat. I wasn't here to talk about his exploits on the pitch though. I wanted to know what his town meant to him. "It's where I'm *from*," said Graham softly. Graham is another man who doesn't want to make a show, a fuss. But the *way* he said it, I knew exactly what he meant. He'd lived his life here, it defines him, it's in his blood. It's not just a rugby club, or a game. The town of Pontypool represents who he is. Where he grew up and where he'll die. A town that has seen better times but is within the DNA of the people.

I tried to ask another question and I realised I couldn't speak. I was choked. Feeling it, not just telling it. I was seeing into the soul of this man, sat in a room that felt like a cell, a quiet echo around us, the polar opposite of the roar and buzz of a crowd with a purpose that filled the stands outside in the 'glory days'. The sense of belonging the match can bring. The pride and dignity that a successful sports team can give to a town or a city. Like Leicester. Drink in the good times, cherish them, for life won't always be so good.

Chapter 26: SISTER JEAN

What happens when the magic goes from sport? When you really have seen too much, when it's worn you down. The corruption, the cheating, the greed, the incessant hyperbole. When the noise is not natural, when it's forced into you through the smug men in shiny shoes and shiny studios, and wave after wave of social media 'content'. Views you wish had stayed private. How do you find it again? How do you rediscover the *joy* sport can bring?

The answer is likely to be that YOU will step towards to *it*. You will return to it. You will suddenly be drawn to sport like the flower that catches your eye on a woodland walk, the song that hits a chord, the atmosphere that draws you in. Don't believe the hype. Believe in magic. Sometimes, it draws you in. Out of the corner of your eye, it unfolds.

*

Houston, I have a problem. It's a great city but I can't sleep. My chances of sleeping are pretty non-existent. I've been to all corners to work but this is only my second bout of jetlag ever. I couldn't be more awake. You know when you're not just awake but *awake*. Zingy, lemony fresh awake. Like a spring bunny, when you want to be a hibernating bear.

I get up and iron my shirt in case Lady Gaga notices the creases. Sorry did I say Lady Gaga?! We were both in Houston for *Super Bowl* in 2017. One of us would be performing to a packed stadium with millions watching on screens across America and the globe. I had more chance of being launched into space from Houston than getting to interview her one-on-one ahead of her Super Bowl performance. But I was to be allowed into her media conference the day before, and one likes to have sharp creases when close to pop royalty.

I can't say ironing at 3am massively appeals. Or at 3pm. But in a small American hotel room it's particularly soul-destroying. Can somebody please invent a travel spray that sorts these creases out, or tell me where to find one? Or maybe I should buy better shirts. I switch the hotel TV on. The original jetlag I suffered back in 1999 in Japan was brutal. Back then, the TV provided a trippy, alien experience, like the film *Lost in Translation*, that had me pinching myself to see if I was real and alive. Honestly, it was terrifying. This second jetlag was made slightly less daunting by the wonders of American TV. Some will never like it, but I've a soft spot for the ebbs and flows of their news and sport coverage. The rat-a-tat-tat. It can be strangely soothing.

On came a basketball documentary. Bad news, I couldn't give a toss about basketball at the time. Good news, it was an *'ESPN 30 for 30'*, the benchmark of slick sports documentaries. This was promisingly called '*I Hate Christian Laettner*' about a college basketball star of the '90s. I gave it a chance. It was mesmerising. Laettner was hated. HATED. Like the villain kid from the '80s teen flicks, the tall, blond, arrogant 'asshole' who sneered at the hero and the girl they both pursued. Think '*Pretty in Pink'*. Think '*Karate Kid'*. In Laettner's prime, 'college hoops' was huge. Tens of millions would be absorbed by *March Madness,* a three-week last-team-standing competition featuring 68 teams. He played for Duke, the University they love to hate, and in the 1992 regional final of March Madness, he cemented his 'hate-figure' reputation. Laettner accidentally-on-purpose stood on the opposition's star player Aminu Timberlake, a Black player. Was it racist, or was his uncompromising style indiscriminate in its brutality? Truth is, he could be obnoxious on the court, whoever the opponent, and years later he apologised. Doesn't make him evil. But you don't need to like him either. What made it worse for Duke haters was that, with time about to run out in the game, Laettner won the match for his team. He called for the ball to be thrown from the far end of the court, pivoted, and coolly sunk a winning basket from considerable distance. Without looking for a moment like he could miss. As the buzzer sounded. Duke went on to retain their trophy. America could almost have loved him for this. Pure genius. And some did. He was a bit of a heartthrob apparently, and his brilliant play often drew the kind of squeals more associated with a boyband. But mainly he was hated.

In the documentary, naysayers lined up to throw shade at this win: *"C'mon, Laettner? C'mon Duke? It's horrible to watch them win. I HATE them."*

College basketball was at its peak as a soap opera. The documentary captures the theatre beautifully, it was exhilarating. Stories and sport can be a mightily effective combination. The thing about the documentary, and Laettner, and the story, and sport, is the hidden depths. It's *never* black and white, is it? Much as we'd like our heroes and villains in the requisite packaging. A quiet little sequence later in the documentary was poignant, when Laettner collected an award on stage. There he stood at the podium, standing 211 centimetres tall but not like the swaggering dude on the court. Not like the arrogant villain. He looked like a little boy lost. And pulled out a crumpled piece of paper. And tried to pay a tribute to his coach Mike Krzyzewski, known throughout America as 'Coach K'. Coach K has the face of a lawyer who'd work for free to get a good mother custody of her child in a 'made-for-TV' afternoon movie. Small, mop of black hair, kind face, blazer and tie. Like a father figure to his team, especially Laettner. 30 years later, Mike K was still the coach there. They can hate Duke, but they can't hate him. And Laettner himself is now a seemingly laid-back family man, hugely respected. Mike never had a son. When he spoke about Laettner, he spoke with fondness, respect and pride. With softness. In complete contrast to an armchair pundit ranting about him. The young player was like a son to him. And Laettner, look I'm going to say it, seems to *love* Mike. His voice cracked a little as he tried to thank him, like when you look inside the dalek and there's something vulnerable, human.

I sat on the Houston hotel bed entranced. I'd long since realised my work on sport had to aspire to this level of emotion, but I felt almost stricken. I felt like weeping basketball-size tears, though that may have been part jetlag. And I was hooked. The story got me into basketball. And by the way, if you watch *'Once Brothers'* about two NBA basketball players from the Balkans split by war - bring gas and air. It will destroy you. Possibly the best sports documentary of all time. So now I was engaged. And it was only a month until the 2017 March Madness. It took this one March Madness for it to become my favourite sporting event. Though perhaps this shouldn't be fully surprising, for someone who loves the unpredictable knockout format of FA Cup football. I filled in my first 'bracket' which is essentially a prediction game, played extensively across America, and adds to the fun of watching as the teams get knocked out. 64 teams down to 32 in quick time. 16 games per day overlap in a feast of basketball and *'buzzer beaters'* (game winning shots just as time runs out), and by the end of the first few days only the *'Sweet 16'* remain. That's their phrase, not mine! This becomes the *'Elite Eight'* and by the end of the second 'long weekend' only the *'Final Four'* remain. Winners of the two semi-finals are into the final. But winning isn't the only prize. This is *the* shop window for the young college talent. March Madness positions the best players in the *NBA draft*, where they are selected for fame and fortune, in most cases a better life for those who've come from next to nothing. In truth, this is the reality show journey aspect. It can be wonderful, it can be a little over-egged, and in some cases uncomfortable. Why weren't college stars paid properly from a sport that generates hundreds of millions? And what about those young hopefuls who don't make it to the NBA?

March Madness can conjure up some magic. And never better than the 2018 tournament, when America and I fell in love with Sister Jean. Who? Oh, you know, Sister Jean, chaplain coach of Loyola Ramblers, 98-years-old at the time! Loyola were outsiders from Chicago. A modest college in basketball terms who had achieved great things by reaching the *NCAA Championships*, the official name of the March Madness tournament. They brought some talent, and heart, and team spirit, and best of all they brought Sister Jean.

I love the colour in sport and Loyola fans illuminated their games with ecstatic celebrations, waving their maroon and gold scarves. They won a sequence of games with the last shot, the 'buzzer beater', which added to the drama and feeling of incredulity that they were into the last 32 teams standing. The Loyola fans were 'living the dream'. While the fans celebrated, the TV cameras intruded on the huddle, college hoopsters, tall, some still spotty, exhausted and listening intently to an elderly woman in a wheelchair. Somebody on commentary mentioned she is their team chaplain and like a mascot. But hang on what's she saying? Listen more closely and you can hear the word *"rebounding"*, a technical basketball term. She's helping to coach them! Goodness me, who IS this woman? How old is she? Yep, she's Sister Jean and she's 98. And the more she speaks the more it's clear she knows her hoops. There is a prayer too. What a team, what a college, what a woman! I'm all in!

The same thing happens in the next game, another dramatic win and more prayers from Sister Jean. And more advice. By now, we *know* who she is. The TV networks are starting to become excited; this is Christmas and thanksgiving in one. A 98-year-old chaplain-coach? Best story ever.

Does Hollywood know? Jeez what a movie. What a woman. Emoji heart eyes. By the time Loyola Chicago Ramblers were beaten in the 'Final Four' on the last weekend of the tournament, Sister Jean was famous, and their 'Cinderella' run to the final, with basketballs not pumpkins, had won many hearts, including mine.

Barack Obama had 'foreseen' some of their success in his bracket, showing loyalty to Loyola, a team from the Chicago area. It was a wonderfully 'Obama' thing that his predictions turned out to be better than the anointed experts. To my knowledge on this occasion Trump didn't claim Obama's bracket was fake, and that his own bracket was more accurate, featuring 64 perfect predictions. Cinderella didn't get to the ball the following year, Loyola didn't qualify. But Murray State University from Kentucky did, thank goodness. Because that meant I was introduced to my new favourite sportsman. The man who reintroduced me to the joy of watching an individual player in action. I say a man, but he was actually a boy. His name? Ja Morant.

So excited was I about Ja Morant that he started to feature in around half of my conversations about sport. It was getting out of hand. A friend saw me talking to a colleague and said to me: "I bet you were talking about Ja Morant." I was. It was borderline embarrassing, but I figured I had to spread the word, share the joy! This kid was everything sport should be. When he played in the 2019 March Madness for Murray State, Ja Morant was 19 years old. The commentators highlighted him as a good prospect and said he could be heading for the NBA. It wasn't hard to see why. When Murray State played, I was pulled in by the magic immediately. We get used to being sold mediocrity as something special. People watch sport for the sake of watching it, because they are used to it, attached to it. For routine, for escape. But how often as a neutral, do we leap off the sofa and click our fingers together like we're back in the school playground. Or sit and whoop. Smile. Cheer. If you fancy some of that and you're not a basketball fan I suggest you 'do a Google' on Ja Morant!

Morant walked on to court like Ali. And when he got the ball, it was sport from the soul. He moves like liquid. Bruce Lee would approve: "*Be Water*," he famously once said. But just as important is the spirit with which he plays, the inhibition. It's how he'd play with friends. Here is no fear. None. Do you do *your* job without fear? All the time? He does. He has unwavering belief. The successful baskets rained in as he glided across the sport, but the moment that sealed the deal had me punching the air across the other side of the Atlantic.

Morant bounced the ball and weighed up options as Murray State attacked. 191 centimetres tall, and wiry, but fluid in movement, hair loose and bouncing in time with that movement. Suddenly he lowered the ball and used his left hand in a flipper motion, like a pinball lever. There was no warning, this wasn't from a coaching manual, it was pure instinct and sporting intelligence because the ball went under, not over, and left the opposing five players standing like mannequins. Nothing was gonna stop Murray State now. The ball, passed under the radar, reached a teammate positioned under the basket. He scored. Each replay made it look more like a piece of genius. The kid can play. Sometimes when I see an over-coached footballer turn back and do what they've been ordered to do, rather than play with freedom, I think of how they'd benefit from the free spirit of Ja Morant. Pure talent and instinct. Sport could do with far more of this.

Morant aside, Murray State were not a strong team, and were knocked out on the first weekend of March Madness. But Morant made his mark. Because he was the second pick in the entire NBA draft, and would have been first if Zion Williamson wasn't around, who had been coveted by NBA teams for months. The system means the second 'worst' team gets to pick second, and Morant was quickly on his way to Memphis to play for the Grizzlies.

There was excitement at Morant's 'rookie' season, but expectations were also being managed. This was a raw talent, slim as a rake, up against experienced, physically imposing players, some of them already legends. Morant didn't care. From the first moment he played like it was a game in the park. It was infectiously thrilling to watch, almost cheeky. In his first few weeks as a professional basketball player he was doing extraordinary things. He was truly fearless, bordering on reckless, and almost shocking to watch. When he drives for the basket, there seems to be nothing distracting him from scoring. The moment that encapsulated his entry to NBA was once seen, never forgotten. Morant had the basket in his sights and no concerns about who might be in his way. That included five-time All Star player Kevin

Love of the Cleveland Cavaliers, over two metres tall and weighing 114kg.

Love had the experience and presence to stand tall, so there was no way past. But Morant had other ideas. And tried to jump over his head. An astonishing approach. And what made it so memorable is how close he came. There are jaw dropping pictures of Morant leaping like a superhero, his legs close to evading Love's head but clipping him, while every sinew of his right arm is stretched taut, ball in hand, attempting to dunk. He didn't score, but the incident made a big stir in the NBA. Love was as gobsmacked as the rest of us but was gracious in his reaction and said if the Morant had successfully 'dunked the ball' he'd have removed his jersey and left the court in respect!

After facing Morant for the first time, formidable NBA player James Harden, then with the Houston Rockets, said *"He's a beast man. He has no nerves at all."* With the balance of Morant, it's not surprising he is prepared to walk the tightrope between confidence and arrogance, and those around him might need to make sure he doesn't fall off. He accepts he is vocal. It's not always a good thing, but his verve should be cherished. I'm grateful he reminded me what it's like to play sport with freedom. Not with one eye on the coach's bench and the other on social media.

Late in 2020, Ja Morant was awarded NBA 'Rookie of the Year", a prestigious honour. Previous winners include LeBron James. And Michael Jordan. Over the space of two years, I'd come to appreciate how America does sport. I'd been a long-time fan of the Arizona Cardinals in NFL, who have a new, innovative, fast young quarterback with plenty of flair and talent, Kyler Murray. I'd also started to appreciate baseball, so much that I entered a 'fantasy team' in these two sports. But basketball has become my favourite sport to watch. It's like being a kid. This is a good thing. I'd never have dreamt that hoops would appeal more to me than football and cricket. But recently it has. The social conscience within the NBA, prominent throughout players and coaches, has been important. They are getting it right. And the structure works. But mainly it's the sport. Proper sport! Unrestrained, unrefined, raw. The backstories gripped me, now the action does too. LeBron James is showing his personality every time he steps on court. So is James Harden, and Michael Jordan. And now Ja Morant.

Sister Jean and Ja Morant helped me reawaken my love of sport, and I actually felt gratitude. It was a relief. And then the world stopped.

Chapter 27: THE FINAL BELL

"What a mistake, and it has cost them the match. What a tragedy."

Football fans are accustomed to hearing exaggerated and dramatic descriptions of events on the pitch and normalising it. Matches are described as battles in the language of war, goals are often "sensational", mistakes and defeats seen as "devastating". Perspective. Real tragedy is what happened at the King Power Stadium on October 27, 2018.

Claude Puel was managing Leicester, and the drama on the pitch had finally subsided. Leicester won some, they lost some. The season could even be described as mundane, and the club sat in the middle of the table. There was no realistic ambition of returning to the pinnacle of the Premier League but at least they weren't overly worrying about relegation. Because that's what people at clubs like Leicester City FC traditionally worry about.

On a chilly evening in late autumn, a few early fireworks were heard, and patches of smoke hung in the air. In the stadium, Leicester played a match against West Ham. With a minute left in the match, the visiting team were leading 1-0. Wilfred Ndidi scored for Leicester, and that familiar crescendo erupted around the stadium. They didn't win, but this was a pleasing end to the game. The fans were able to go home with something. There were smiles in the car park, in the streets, across the city, at the late 'rescue act' from Ndidi.

An hour after the match, a helicopter took off from the pitch. On board was Chairman Vichai Srivaddhanaprabha, two members of his staff, Nusara Suknamai and Kaveporn Punpare, pilot Eric Swaffer and passenger Roza Lechowicz. As they left the stadium, a malfunction sent the helicopter into an uncontrollable spin. The unusual sounds in the sky had grabbed the attention of the Leicester fans and staff that had yet to leave the ground. Suddenly the helicopter fell, as described by one witness, "like a stone to the floor", landing in a part of the car park that was mercifully empty, but bursting into flames. The following day, it was confirmed that all five on board had been killed in the crash and subsequent fire.

The people of Leicester returned to their homes, their places of worship, in their thousands again. This time, there was no match to watch, no win to celebrate. No Leicester shirt to buy, no friends to meet. No flags waved, no smiles. The sharpest and cruellest of contrasts to the scene two-and-a-half years earlier. The world was watching again, and this time it was witnessing their grief. Some sobbed, others stood with heads bowed. A common theme was "thank you" to the man they called *Khun Vichai*, for helping them to dream.

A year later, I stood in another football club car park, an empty one, and saw another football stadium that was the scene of sadness and loss. It was the home of Bury Football Club. Early in the 20th century they won the FA Cup twice, a team that were one of the best teams in the north-west and feared throughout England. Bury were regularly beating the big Manchester clubs from ten miles away.

In the summer of 2019, Bury Football Club were kicked out of the English Football League. Mismanagement can have such consequences in the lower divisions, where clubs desperately try to keep up, and find they are writing cheques they can't cash. But there wasn't enough to help Bury. Higher up in football, they didn't seem to care about the fate of this 134-year-old club. When I arrived in Bury, it was clear what the people of the town were experiencing. There wasn't just upset about the demise of their football club, but *grief*.

In return, I opened up to the Bury fans I spoke to. You must be prepared to give a part of yourself. My estranged father was dying. I'd been told he was about to pass and by now the wounds were so deep, so much damage had taken place, so much toxic masculinity, that we were irreconcilably estranged. I could only support the situation and those others affected. After many years of giving everything I could, there was no hope of reconciliation. The water was too choppy. I refused to drown. In Bury, I was unplugged, my wires were exposed. I was feeling it partly for them, and partly for myself. "It's only football." Not if your life is interwoven with a club. Not if your family is part of the history.

Joy Hart's father played for Bury and been a manager, coach and physio for them too. For over 40 years, the club had been part of her life, had been the pride of the town. Not just an easy catchphrase. It was literally the pride of Bury. So bereft was she by the club having been culled and the ground lying empty, that she handcuffed herself to the front of the club in protest. I arranged to meet her as part of our film, to try and take their story to a worldwide audience. I couldn't believe how little attention the story was getting in England. Fact is, they just aren't big and glamorous enough. Not part of the tip of the pyramid. Nowhere close.

When I saw Joy, I hugged her. It was the kind of hug you give someone at a funeral. This wasn't a time for handshakes. We're still in touch. I see the people of Bury with the same affection of those in Stranraer and Pontypool. The way they opened up to us. It was moving and real. Why would you expect these people to open up to you and then rush off to the next story and forget them? It was my assignment, but it's their *life*. Her voice cracking with emotion she said: "You have to be a football fan to understand what we're mourning. If they are thinking of us, they understand the death that we feel."

A Bury fan in his thirties, James Bentley, took me across the deserted car park at the front of the stadium to a turnstile in the corner. He had come to this 'Gigg Lane' ground with his father. His grandfather had taken James's father here. And he always used this entrance to the ground. Number 23. Out of a plastic bag, James pulled his original 'Member's Pass'. On the pass he is a young boy. A father and son who could share experiences together. It gave me a wry smile too. This, it's not just football.

James misses the people he stood near, sat near, for years. Strangers become friends, sometimes close friends. Or even if they don't, there's something comforting about knowing they are there. The same routines, the same frustrations. And the collective joy at a goal, a win. A place for the community to come together.

The ground stood empty, but the flame still burned. Fans plotted a *phoenix club,* new representatives of Bury who could join the league pyramid at the bottom. Amongst the tiny parts of the pyramid, but every single stone counts. A former journalist named Keith Maddock and his small team fought to ensure the community didn't lose Bury FC's unseen work. Such as football for children of all backgrounds. And a weekly group for dementia sufferers and their families, using Bury FC memorabilia. In that room, at that ground, amongst the people of Bury, is the soul of football, of sport. Of life and death and all that goes in between.

It's a shared experience. You make sense of it together. A community. Belonging. In my thirties, in the year my precious twin girls were born, I watched Liverpool play in the FA Cup Final. Their comeback was sudden, unlikely and exciting. When a goal to save the game was scored by the captain, that defiant intense hero of the fans, Steven Gerrard, I launched myself down some steps. So did a much older man. Slightly shaken and embarrassed, we made our way back to the original point. He gave me a little smile. You don't have to be related by blood to be related by red.

In Leicester within a decade, a barely imaginable sequence of events had unfolded, and still not enough time has passed to fully understand. How did the team actually stay in the Premier League at a time King Richard's magic appeared to sweep across the city? How did the team manage to sustain nine months of improbable results and do something unfathomable in the world's richest, most important football league? How did they sack the heroic manager? And how could something so bitterly, gut-wrenchingly tragic take place, to kill the chairman and four other people.

Whether you like football or not, put yourself in the shoes of a Leicester fan. When does this stop becoming about football and start to become your identity? When does a Jamie Vardy goal stop being a match winner, and start to dictate your happiness, your mood? How do you make sense of what took place at a single football club. The frustration, concern, resignation, relief, uplift, excitement, belief, euphoria, disappointment. The loss. The life.

Chapter 28: EMPTY

A chill wind blew through Leicester. The market fell silent, save for the sound of crows in the distance. Do you remember how it used to sound? Do you remember the stallholder's cry? *Tomatoes, apples, bananas. Wallets, pens, coasters.* Normality for sale. An elderly lady with a bag on wheels hears her name. Human interaction. It is the only time she'll hear her name today. She interacts. Smiles. There is life here. The school fell silent, save for the sound of the empty tin can rattling and bouncing across concrete in fits and starts. Do you remember how it used to sound? Do you remember the school bell? *Rucksacks, apples, hassled parents. Books, pens, knowledge.* Education for all. The boy hears the teacher call his name. Respite. It is the only time he will feel safe today. He interacts. Smiles. There is life here.

The stadium fell silent, save for the sound of the distant siren.

Do you remember how it sounded? Do you remember the roar? *Scarves, hot dogs, the green, green grass. Tickets, tackles, togetherness.* A cathedral for all. The 30,000 hear the sound of the whistle. Collective joy. It is the only time they will feel alive this week. Smiles. There is life here.

The chill wind blew through the car park of the King Power Stadium where the helicopter fell, through the car park under which he was buried hundreds of years before. The chill wind blew through the streets, and the diverse population were consumed with tension and fear. There was loneliness and despair. Anxiety and pain. A reassessment of what is and isn't important. The real frontline. Put your hands together. What is important? What are we clinging on to and what needs to change? Survival mode is a destructive place, recklessness too. Play safe, hang in there until the better days come, but try to be positive. They will come.

The tension hangs thick in the air with the sirens and endures, prolongs, torments. The head bowed at the gravestone. The eyes behind the mask.

Artificial life. The boy holds the console and recreates. The pixelated player and pixelated ball. Out of a television screen, a man watches nostalgia, orange shirts, the famous 'losers of the 70s'. Cruyff. One-nil. Find a way to cope. Hold your nerve. Find it.

Can you trust what you see, what you hear from the podium in the street of power? A thin line rises on a graph, a peak of despair, the tip of the pyramid. Can you trust what you see, what you hear, from the man, the woman, the leader, who puts their career before common sense? Career before carer. Have your own filter, conduct your own eyesight test.

In Leicester, in your town, in your country, on your planet, red lines rose on the graphs charting the pandemic. In response, heroes have never gone about their work so quietly.

*

My job is to report on heroes of sport. But I have a perspective on what an actual *hero is. And it's you people at this hospital. I hope you are all proud of yourselves because you certainly should be. You are an inspiration to many of us. It was the hospital I was born in many decades ago, and today it is a place in which you can take great pride. My Dad was grateful for the care you gave him. He thought you were all wonderful and so do I.*

Thank you all so much,

Lee Wellings, October 14, 2019.

He passed away a few months later, just before the pandemic. Psychological wounds don't always heal. Sometimes, it is 'Nil by Mouth'.

Before his diagnosis, the sun had shone through the hospital window. I reached into my holdall and pulled out a transistor radio. The dial was set to the station that would broadcast the cricket. The soothing backdrop of summer, and it was *The Ashes*. The right kind of drama. A theatre for a sporting miracle, a flame-haired gladiator at one end with an unlikely, bespectacled sidekick. For once, I know he listened. Through the whistling, crackling and reception, the clarity and humour, the description of the green grass and the pigeons, the men in white and the thwack of the bat on ball, the applause of the crowd. Seek it, find it, for it shall soothe you. In some circumstances it's not too late.

Sometimes, in the most desperate of circumstances, people come together. Sometimes you give everything you've got to build bridges, to save someone, yet it's not enough. But you tried, Lee, you *tried*.

Chapter 29: CHANGE

When the planet is gripped by an unprecedented, terrifying crisis, when millions are dying, when life has been turned upside down, when you are locked in, locked down, when it's all too close to home, why should anybody care about sport?

Did it, does it, really have a role to play? Is it important? Hundreds of millions of people gave us an answer. Yes. They were desperate for the return of their team, their sport. For the first time in our lives, we were bereft of the uplift, the routines, the rollercoaster, the togetherness. The sporting calendar provides routine, comfort, identity. Many of us bookmark our lives with the flow of sporting action, the support of our teams, the excitement and debate that sport can provide. It is not just possible, but commonplace, that your team winning lifts your mood. But it is more than that. As a child, the routines of sport, the certainties of the fixture list, gave me stability. We craved stability. What we collectively suffered from was a form of grief.

Now we all knew how those Bury FC fans had felt. What I saw there wasn't a glib, misguided overestimation of what sport meant to their lives. It *was* life. And they knew exactly what they had taken away from them. The people wanted sport back, and so did governments. Sport can be the softest of targets for politicians looking to make moral points, and then suddenly they see its importance. The public wanted sport back, and many governments gave it back to them quickly. Sport managed to return in 'bubbles', unseen workers going to extraordinary lengths to stage safe sport. In cricket, in football. In basketball, in baseball. In Leicester, in LA. In your town.

It was as if somebody had switched sport off and on again. But when this happens with our computers, it's often an attempt to fix problems. What you can't afford is for the problems to still be there. But there has been no cleaning up of sport, no deletion of problems. In the desperation to get the screen back, the files remain corrupted. The opportunity was lost. Sport could have been improved. We could have looked to the future. Who will host major sports events? Who will be able to afford to do this, and will their intentions be good? Will they protect the workers in fierce temperatures? Will they be held to account? Will the process be fair? The new normal is to select a host without a bidding process. What will lie behind the reason to install a host *unchallenged*? Politics and money?

Financial equality in football, in sport, will remain elusive. The gap between rich and poor will not be closing any time soon. Small clubs will continue to go out of business. A food chain rather than a healthy ecosystem. In many cases there will be greed, and management whose interests lie in what they can get, rather than what they can give back to fans. There is nothing wrong with making money from sport, but it shouldn't be at the expense of opportunity, fairness and history. Remember where a football club came from, and who it represents. Respect the past while you build for the future.

Short-termism haunts sport. Such as football clubs who sack their manager in a trigger-happy fashion, and powerful clubs who still spend more than they can afford. Far more. The debts will eventually catch up with them. Soon. Lessons have not been learned. The sound of the bell ignored. The pandemic changed lives. But did it change sport? Has it been returned to the fans?

A line that was trotted out repeatedly, that lost any real meaning, was *'football is nothing without fans'*. What sport in a 'pandemic bubble' showed indisputably, was that football *is* nothing without fans. And this can be applied to most sports. We took what we were given, beggars can't be choosers, but this was soulless, plastic football, plastic sport.

Where there are fans, there is life.

Elite football, such as the Premier League, carried on as best it could, but it was like watching glorified training games. There was relief at the resumption of action, and routine, and a small spike of interest in the novelty value in the sound. From the fake crowd noise pumped in by television sound engineers doing a sterling job, or a manager loudly admonishing his team. The novelty quickly disappeared. The football was hollow.

What didn't help matters was the bizarre officiating of football matches, though the debate it causes keeps many radio stations and websites in business. The Video Assistant Referee (VAR) was taking an age to reach decisions, and these were often *still* incorrect. In an empty stadium, an apparent goal was 'celebrated', then checked for a few minutes, then declared 'no goal', then debated again, and again, and all to a backdrop of eerie unsatisfying silence, or fake noise.

'Pandemic football' was nobody's fault. But VAR compounded the problem. The art of football was replaced by geometry, mathematics. What even is this? It's not football as I want it or need it. I barely recognised it. I felt a complete disconnection from pandemic football. And yet we continued to be sold this 'product' as a glittering prize. Some honesty would have been welcome. The men in shiny shoes raised their voices, and hyped it up, and growled, and spun, and marketed. The modern way is to repeatedly make a claim until it's believed by you and others. To an extent they are 'just doing their jobs'. But we deserve better, don't we?

The soul disappeared from stadiums. If they dared face the truth, some of the men running football, running sport, would be frightened about how much sports needs fans. They've been rumbled. Bobby Robson was right. Football, sport, is about the people whose lives are entwined with their clubs. There was a scramble during the pandemic, a desperation, to reinstate sport and fulfil television contracts. Sport was desperate for the return of fans to 'balance the books', rather than an incontrovertible realisation that the sports and clubs they run actually belong to fans, whoever happens to have bought them in the name of 'soft power', or as a business venture. Lower down the food chain, many football clubs were anxious for fans to return to give them a better chance of survival, and to pay their staff.

*

Fans make a club, make an event, make a sport. It is 1977. Anfield, Liverpool. A quarter-final match in the European Cup. Liverpool FC, champions of England, versus AS Saint-Etienne, champions of France. Liverpool in glowing, vibrant red. Saint-Etienne in their distinctive, appealing green. Time is running out. If Liverpool don't score again they are out of the competition, having still never won this trophy. A substitute with red hair, David Fairclough, had developed a reputation for decisive goals and become known as '*Supersub*'. But his most important intervention was on this spring evening in his home stadium. Suddenly Fairclough broke clear of the green defenders and approached the goal. Behind the goal, thousands of Liverpool fans with red scarves clenched in anticipation. The famous 'Kop' stand, trying to suck the ball into the net. Fairclough scored. It was one of the most significant goals in English football history. It started something extraordinary, a run of six consecutive years that English teams were European Champions, via three different clubs.

What never leaves the mind is what happened to the crowd after Fairclough's goal. The noise is like thunder, the fans ripple like red waves. There is that spontaneous and magical wave of utter euphoria. It instantly makes goosebumps. It feels seismic and moving and beautiful. Goal. Fans. Life. Now imagine that same scene in a stadium without fans. Fairclough races to the goal. He finds the way to poke the ball past the goalkeeper and win the game. We hear the ball nestle in the net. There are echoey cheers from his teammates and the staff on the Liverpool bench. A signal from the referee, it's a legitimate goal. A Saint-Etienne player howls with frustration. There are smiles and relief from the men in the red shirts. And behind that goal, there is nothing. Silence. Emptiness. No life. A goal is a goal, a win a win, a trophy a trophy. A goal still meant something in the pandemic, still lifted lives, still gave us focus and routine. Something to look forward to. But it was filler. A temporary fix. It wasn't the real thing. The real thing requires fans. The absence of fans was not the fault of those who run football, quite the opposite. But the dearth of atmosphere was a warning bell. And then suddenly, came *proof* that 'they' want to take football away from us.

While writing this book I was warning about 'land grabs' and greed at the expense of fairness and common sense. And before the ink was dry, in April 2021, the biggest clubs in England, Italy and Spain suddenly announced a new tournament, a 'European Super League', that they would run themselves and have the say on which 20 clubs would participate. There couldn't have been a more transparent example of what I was wary of in sport. Because European football, and its long, glorious history of opportunity for all, was about to disappear overnight. Strong criticism and concern from fans were not surprising, but the level of condemnation was remarkable, and generated up a vital energy. Football supporters were collectively vehement that their clubs would *not* be taken from them, to play in a tournament they didn't want. The backlash was genuinely effective and helped stopped the plans. 'Fan Power' made a difference, but there was also the swift and stark response of the existing leagues and governing bodies, promising the toughest of punishments.

Such as immediate expulsion from their current competitions.

The 'ESL' was in a corner immediately. Most of the clubs involved opted for unprecedented levels of contrition towards their fans. Others tried to fight on, using legal avenues, but were left exposed, with reputations in tatters. The clubs will more than likely be forgiven, one week is a long time in football, let alone months. But this was an extraordinary, historic and telling few days. If it sometimes feels the world revolves around football, the ESL 'scandal' shifted the ball from the axis. There was a wonderful realisation that fans have more power than they realised. Much more.

Cricket has also suffered from money and politics overly dictating the schedule. The 'big three' nations - India, England and Australia – have been far too dominant in the executive rooms. Other traditional cricket playing nations, including the West Indies, South Africa and New Zealand, have sometimes not had the respect and status they deserve, which has been demoralising. There has also been an uneasy level of influence and saturation from the Indian Premier League, which started as popular fun, but which risks being over-inflated. While the appetite is there from consumers, they will push this appetite to the limits.

Less is more. Try and think of cricket's three forms in food terms. 'One-day' matches are a starter, 'Test' cricket is a sumptuous nutritious meal, and 'Twenty20' is a tasty dessert. Cricket's bosses have feasted on T20, the dessert, and ruined the appetite for the other parts of the meal. There should be room for all formats, but money is the driving force, not player welfare. I can only remember one or two T20 matches, they are so disposable. Whereas Test cricket enhances lives and provides unforgettable stories. It fills you up in a healthy way.

English cricket is trying to reach out to a new audience, and should be supported for trying, via a revolutionary tournament named 'The Hundred' because it's only 100 balls for each team. Colourful, bold and inclusive – it's everything we would want. And basketball should be doing this. But they still haven't been able to with the 'old guard' having too much broadcasting involvement and then trying to 'get down with the kids'. 'Embarrassing Dad' syndrome. I hope they succeed and create the basketball equivalent of 'The Hundred'. It's right to try.

Some cricket matches need to be removed though. Did the 'pandemic pause' actually lead to a rethink of the packed world cricket calendar, and ways of removing some of the demands on players? Did other sports take time to examine whether their schedule and approaches are working? There can be no complacency, the problems are still there, just covered up. Can we trust in the people who organise sport? And those taking part? Cheating, doping will continue to be a problem. It hasn't gone anywhere. The sophistication of the cheats, or rather the chemists and criminals in the shadows, will elude the anti-dopers. And the good guys will rely on intelligence to stand a chance. The cheats will, sadly, still be getting away with it and leave us to choose which victories, which medals, we *believe* in.

Black faces will still be used occasionally in sports broadcasting by back-coverers, tactically and strategically. Rather than fair systems, rather than the weeding out of discrimination, rather than inclusivity that leads to Black executives in the boardroom, rather than the nurturing of disadvantaged young talent. Some management will hope the spotlight has moved away, the storm has passed, and they will return to apathy. Do not allow them. The gender pay gap still won't close quickly enough. Female broadcasters will still be abused online and judged on their appearance, while male correspondents can slouch like lounge lizards if they are deemed to have the right personality and 'gravitas'. Action on misogyny should have been taken many years earlier, it should not take horrific events for society to address issues and behaviour that affects so many lives every day. I hope that women don't suffer disproportionately as sport tries to recover from the financial effects of the pandemic. I fear the effect of bad habits from governing bodies and clubs will affect decision making, from the subconscious to the very conscious. If a 'male sport' brings in more revenue than a 'female sport', it will remain the first, second and third priority for some administrators. And the progress, the momentum made over recent years by women's sport will suffer an unequal amount of damage.

All sport, all society, all of us have suffered from the pandemic. But some more than others. And why should one gender suffer because their development was suppressed years ago. Don't make the same mistakes. This is the time to *change* for the better, not regress. Sport reflects society. The pandemic was all-consuming, so the gravest of issues was forced into the background, at a crucial moment. The climate emergency. Sport was just starting to wake up to its environmental responsibilities, some of them existential. But slowly. The time for action isn't next week, or next year, it's now.

In the midst of the pandemic a trailblazer named Claire Poole held a virtual global summit bringing together some of the leading thinkers, movers and conscience-shakers in environmental sport. It's a relatively new subject, but one pressing enough for the United Nations to take action and press for sports to be signatories to their action plan. The first step, as with other major problems is acknowledging the problem. But then it's important to *act*.

Problems for some individual sports can be obvious to the naked eye. Such as Formula One. Transporting cars and crews and parts across the globe for a travelling circus and then roaring around a track is something we can all see isn't sustainable. As shown in the pandemic with their help with ventilators, people in the sport are problem-solvers, and are trying to make the sport fit for purpose in the future. Mechanically they are starting to succeed, but travel is going to remain a contentious issue.

But other issues are less blatant. Should footballers really be traversing the globe playing matches? We can all understand a World Cup. And we all love a holiday. But carbon footprints have to be seriously considered by those in charge. We have all seen through those summer football tours to the other side of the world in recent years that when sport becomes more about marketing than, well, *sport*, it's rarely tasteful. If the footballers of Burnley in the Premier League can reportedly decide to 'pool' their transport to and from training for the sake of the environment, should other teams fly across the globe for a 'marketing match' to sell a few shirts? They shouldn't, but they will.

The sport of golf is one which is now signed up to the UN action group and is recognising the problem – I've spoken to complexes who are trying to delicately balance course design with the surrounding ecosystem and the vast amounts of water used to keep courses maintained. But some courses face an existential threat sooner than most. 'Links' golf, on the coast, is a special part of the sport. Those coastlines are under threat. They'll be fine today, and tomorrow. But they are "*putting*" on borrowed time. The landscape of those courses is literally changing. Sport has to, too. It needs to address the future now. And start to think about Plan B.

In some parts of the planet, in the near future, the temperatures will be too hot for outdoor sport. Some would argue that time is here now. The issue would have received more sustained prominence in 2020, when the devastating effects of the bushfire crisis across Australia reached the Grand Slam tennis event in Melbourne in January. In 2021, with sport still using pandemic bubbles, we saw some players struggling with the heat. Indoor sport is going to increase in importance, and that time is coming soon. The emergency for sport, but more importantly for the planet, is here.

We currently live in a world where the *temperament* of the world's most famous environmental campaigner becomes talked about more than her vital messages. Because she is a teenage girl, and too many middle-aged men think they know best. Greta Thunberg is educating many of us. But some choose not to listen. The climate emergency simply isn't near the top of sport's priorities. it's currently a *choice* to engage. Urgent proactivity is needed. Like a pandemic, it can't be ignored.

While the sun burns fiercer, serious issues cast a shadow over sport. And aren't about to disappear. A unique opportunity has been lost to address them. States who abuse human rights will still be buying football clubs and sports events unchallenged. In fact, invited to do so. Disreputable 'businessmen' are buying clubs unchallenged. In fact, invited to do so. Fans will continue to be enablers, and 'turn a blind eye', because their club wins a football match, and attack those who question this online. Technology will still ruin as many matches as it improves. Ticket prices will still be too high. Games will still be played to suit television audiences thousands of miles away, and not the teams' own supporters. Broadcasters will still overhype their 'products'. Women's teams will still not be paid what they deserve. Ethnic faces will still be kept out of boardrooms. Big clubs will still demand more, get more. Small clubs *will* die. True equality doesn't exist, but please never remove our opportunity. The chance to dream.

If football, if sport, if society couldn't change for the better when the world shut down, it will never change. But ultimately, these games belong to us. We have more power, more say, than we realise. We need to use it.

Chapter 30: HOME

And I thank you, for bringing me here,
For showing me home,
For singing these tears
Finally I've found that I belong here

'Home' by Martin Lee Gore

Through the bedroom door and into the hallway, the sound of a guitar, the opening strains of *Smells Like Teen Spirit*, softly. Down the staircase, the sound of a piano, *I Can't Help Falling In Love With You*, gently. Inside the front door to the house, there is boy with tousled hair wearing a scarf. It is yellow and green, and a woman with long dark hair is fastening his coat and smiling. They hug.

"It's time to go girls, where's *my* hug?!" The music stops. A teenage girl appears from the room by the door and we hug. A second teenage girl bounds down the stairs and we hug. They are beautiful inside and out, like their mother. Individuals, not 'identical' - that was the medical term 14 years before. I remember them standing as little girls, holding hands outside the red door in red coats. They blossom, they flourish, they forge their own paths and will continue to make people feel better about themselves. They will fill us with pride, and they will fly. "*Love you Daddy.*"

In the car, the boy talks. About Thor. About consoles. About chocolate. About music. And I listen. He plays with a '*Rubik's Cube*'.

"Did you know it was named after the Hungarian man that invented it?"
"*Yes Dad, you told me that last week. We've been learning about Neil Armstrong in school and I wanted to write about his brothers Stretch Armstrong and Louis Armstrong.*" I laugh and look in the mirror, and he is smiling.

We walk towards the neat, new, tidy little stadium. There is a yellow and green sign. It says *Horsham Football Club, founded 1881*. Up the forested path the people walk and smile. They wear yellow and green. Two guys talk about who's in the team. An elderly man with a stick stops to gather himself for the final push to the turnstile. Families, Family.

"I've heard a rumour you're in the team today," I say to the steward. *"They could do worse,"* he says, accepting the coin from the boy's hand and handing him a programme. *"Enjoy the game young man."*

The sun shines over the South Downs as the teams run out. The yellow and greens against the blues. The noise rises, and the Horsham fans sing. The small block in the pyramid, but what happens if you put all the blocks together. To the left, Horsham's *'Lardy Army'* group of fans have laid out their flags, and they glisten in the sun. *'Pride of Sussex'* says one. Another proclaims Horsham FC *Champions of Europe.* And there is a reason. In the eighth level of English football, before they were promoted to the seventh, the teams crossed the English Channel to play Guernsey FC, part of the English league. And won. European glory. Unbeaten.

The fans start singing. *"We all follow the yellow and the green"* precedes a range of 1970s disco classics. Then a 'tender' moment: *"Why do birds suddenly appear, every time you are near, just like me, you want to be, HFC!"* Then mock aggressive voices for the next song: *"No surrender, no surrender, no surrender to the low-fat spreads."* It eventually descends into laughter. I smile. My mind drifts up, up, and out of the stadium, like the Olympic film above London, life on a tape, snapshots of sport, of life. Starting with two Horsham matches that were good for the soul.

One in Lancing, on the Sussex coast. At a railway crossing on the way the barriers are up, the crossing is clear, and there is a man on the track. He is wearing a yellow all-in-one-suit. And holding up a giant flag. On the flag is Elvis. Wearing a Horsham FC shirt. *I Can't Help Falling In Love With You.* The clouds gather and the rain falls. And it's unforgiving. We are soaked through to our marrow. Cold, wet shoes squelching, a chill in the bones. And the ball hits the net. The yellow and greens are promoted. Going up in the world. And the opportunity to rise further.

The other eastwards across Sussex, to the *'The Dripping Pan'* football ground, home of Lewes FC. The time we saw Horsham FC winning in the

August heat. In the most charismatic, aesthetically pleasing and distinctive of football stadiums, also set in the south of England's stunning South Downs.

My friend and fellow fan Mark and I had stood on a bank that runs along one side of the ground. The 'yellow and greens' score a goal and we charged down the hill like schoolboys, scarf around wrist, celebrating with the players. The sound of the *Lardy Army* drifted across the downs. Packs of lard were assembled on the wall in front of the fans stood on the terrace. Assembled like building blocks. In less 'prestigious days' for Horsham FC, the star player had gone viral for scoring a goal, running to these fans and downing one of their pints of beer. I think of another game at Lewes. The women's team are in action. They happen to be paid equally to the men's team. I say 'happen', but it required integrity and a vision from the club's owners. Building something good often starts with a single stone. The times they are a changing. Just not quickly enough. Lewes FC Women score. A small girl punches the air. The players and the girl connect.

Up, up and away. Over to Lord's, the home of cricket. England's women are winning the World Cup against India. A young girl is watching and smiling. Heroes. The stands are packed. Behind the stumps in giant gloves is Sarah Taylor, whose cricket skills illuminated her home ground in Sussex, and far beyond. There is a sound, her yell of delight at winning another game with her quick hands. What a craftswoman Sarah Taylor is. How quickly those hands move. Do you believe in magic? And her batting. Looking back at her career it's inescapable to think of gender. Excusable in this case. At one point in Australia, she made history by playing against men. Then she started to coach men. What's most important is her lightning-fast hands, a lightning-fast brain and that she is a World Cup Winner. I hope the day will come that a sportswoman isn't compared to sportsmen. Sarah stepped away from playing international cricket when anxiety took over. A familiar story in cricket. As long as she knows how much we appreciate her. Please tell me she *knows.*

Up, up to east London, the Olympic Stadium has become home to West Ham United. Politics, you know how it is. Look down at the old stadium, *The Boleyn Ground,* so many memories if you first watched them as a small girl in the 1950s. In the 21st century, 87-year-old fan Audrey is wheeled into the stadium, and the green of the pitch has the same effect, the bubbles rise, the bubbles we want to see. A different time. There are fans, there is noise. She thinks of Bobby Moore, the West Ham and England captain who played with the panache of Vegas crooner. Never a hair out of place, always in his time. Peerless. Another World Cup winner. Not that English fans ever mention it. West Ham score. "*YES!*" shout Audrey and her daughter Angela. The crowd is roaring. You can move a home, but a football club remains a family.

Up in Bury, the original ground stayed empty but there was life. Fan power should never be underestimated. And so, a new club joined the bottom of the pyramid. But they found a ground to play in, and the fans came. Smiles. Nearly like old times. They score. James is there. He punches the air. It's not the same, but you know what? It means something. And there are new chapters to be written, whether here or at the old ground. *What is a football club anyway? Who does it actually belong to?*

In Stranraer they score. Frank leaps from the coach's bench and urges his players to stay calm. Keep finding it. In Pontypool, Graham watches a bearded young player leap and push the egg-shaped ball into the turf. It's a try. What a score! In Leicester, 2021, a football team lift a trophy, as champions of their division. And into the top division of football in England. Higher than they have been ever before. Their name? *Leicester City Women Football Club.* At Wembley Stadium, 2021, Leicester City's men's team play in the FA Cup final for the fifth time in the club's history. For the first time, they *win.* The heavens are open. The rain lashes against the green turf. The pandemic means many empty seats, but the euphoria cannot be doused. The late chairman's son looks up. In the stadium a giant banner, commemorating, celebrating his father Khun Vichai, and there is a message to us all: "*Our dreams can come true if we have the courage to pursue them.*"

Wembley Stadium, 2021, the power of empathetic, grown-up, caring leadership was shown to England and the world. Gareth Southgate, once mocked for missing a crucial penalty, now a leader to admire. It is more than redemption. Leadership this thoughtful doesn't come by chance, he is a special one. Nice guys can win. With or without a bell. Make your employees feel better about themselves. A culture.

England reached its first European Championship final, ever. A squad of players, diverse, socially responsible and without fear, created history.

They fell short. But the journey they took England fans on was important. It wasn't *just* sport. A pundit who understands that sport and society can't be disconnected is the eloquent, honest, and humane former Manchester United and England player Gary Neville. He said of his former teammate: "*Gareth Southgate is everything a leader should be: respectful, humble and tells the truth.*"

Flop or success. Hero or villain. Black or white? It rarely is. A sporting kaleidoscope, the backdrop, the rhythm of a life, the mixtape, the highlights, the peaks and troughs. Life through sport. A tapestry, a work in progress. All life is interwoven – like the 2012 Olympic film racing along the Thames, representing the ecosystem, the history, the future. We just need to stop and try and makes sense of it. Only the lucky few might manage to do so.

As I sit in Sussex, I turn my thoughts to America. Rise and shine. Ja Morant leaps and flies and smashes the ball into the basket. In Chicago, Loyola score. Sister Jean watches her boys play. She is 101 years old now. Basketball fans, America, we all fall in love with her and the story again. While she ponders the team's formation on the court.

Anyone still bothering to boo Tom Brady as he launches another pass?! 43 years-old and he signs a *new* contract. Borderline phenomenal. What do they call the special ones these days? Goats. Greatest of all time. It's 2019 and Tiger Woods, wearing red punches the air. That's on any 'mixtape' isn't it? He can't really have come back and done that, can he?

Serena guides the ball across court and makes history. This is what champions do. The special ones. Making their own luck. Federer unzips his tracksuit top. Still going. Up against Rafa again. The goats are feeding. The special ones. Messi dribbles and scores. Let us cherish them. For them, nothing's impossible.

The chequered flag waves. Seven-times. The king of the track Lewis Hamilton. I remember the day I sent a man named Dessie to interview Lewis the kid. The kid looked and talked like a champion. But did anyone expect him to be this good? He did. His Dad did. *Believe*.

*

The day of the World Cup final in 2014, around 8am. I walked along a street beside Copacabana beach in Brazil. Two figures approached me. One was a man, the other a boy. They both wore yellow. And their shirts were identical in size. For the man it was in place. For the boy, it was like a tent. Or a sheet. A giant yellow shirt. Like father, like son. I gently asked if I could take a picture on my phone. The man smiles. At the moment I was about to take the picture they looked at each other and smiled.

After we parted I stood. I stepped into the shade and looked at the photo. At their gaze. I had been away for weeks. My girls back in England were only seven years-old at the time, my son was just two. My family were on the other side of the world, and here in an empty Rio street I stood. I felt this overwhelming sense of loneliness. An ache deep in my gut. But we fight on don't we. We hold our nerve. Because better times will come. I looked at the photo again. And I smiled for what they had. And for what *I* have.

Horsham FC score. We fill with joy, and I ruffle his hair. His chips survive the excitement and I pinch one. *"You missed the biggest one Dad."*
"Hang on a minute, you need to put the chips down a second." I hug him.
"I love you."

In Gloucestershire a kind, proud lady, in her early seventies, who gave everything for her son and daughter, is polishing a mantelpiece. There's a young boy with dark hair in an old photograph. He is wearing a red football shirt. She smiles and picks the photo up to kiss it.

In Rome a kind, proud lady, in her late nineties, is drinking coffee and glances up at her mantelpiece. There's a young boy with dark hair in a black and white photograph, holding a football. She smiles. The boy would one day produce a miracle and spread joy far and wide. Next to his picture, there is a tiny bell.

Dilly Ding, Dilly Dong.

INDEX (REFERENCE BY CHAPTER)

FRANCIS, George (24)
FROST, David (16)
FUCHS, Christian (7,15)

GARFUNKEL, Simon (6)
GASCOIGNE, Paul 'Gazza' (14)
GERRARD, Steven (27)
GHIGGIA, Alcides (6)
GRAF, Steffi (5)
GRAY, Demarai (7)
GRONDONA, Julio (13)
GUARDIOLA, Pep (6,24)
GUINNESS, Alec (13)

HAMILTON, Lewis (5)
HARDEN, James (26)
HARRIS, Rob (13)
HART, Joy (26)
HAYATOU, Issa (13)
HAYTER, Reg (3,4,10)
HAZARD, Eden (19)
HEARN, Barry (4)
HEMINGWAY, Ernest (4)
HER MAJESTY THE QUEEN (20)
HIGGINS, Alex (4)
HIGGINS, Lauren (4)
HILLS, Adam (20)
HOLDING, Michael (12,21,22)
HOLLIOAKE, Adam (10)
HOLLIOAKE, Ben (10)
HOMES, Larry (24)
HOUDINI, Harry (15)
HOWE, Darcus (13)
HUTH, Robert (7, 15)

JAMES, LeBron (21,26)
JEFFREYS, Ben (25)
JOHN, Elton (11,14)
JOHNSON, Dr Samuel (3)
JORDAN, Michael (5,17)

KAGAWA, Shinji (7)
KAEPERNICK, Colin (21)
KANTE, N'Golo (7,23)
KEATON, Buster (3)
KEEGAN, Kevin (12)
KEFLEZIGHI, Meb (6)
KIMMAGE, Paul (10)
KING, Andy (7, 19)
KING, Billie Jean (14)
KING, Don (5)
KING HENRY VIII (4)
KING RICHARD III (1,7,19,23)
KLAASEN, Jelle (4)
KLOPP, Jürgen (10,16,24)
KRUL, Tim (18)
KRZYZEWSKI, Mike (26)

LADY GAGA (26)
LAETTNER, Christian (26)
LAWRENCE, Stephen (21)
LECHOWICZ, Roza (27)
LE TISSIER, Matthew (18)
LEE, Bruce (26)
LINEKER, Gary (19)
LOVE, Joanne (16,25)
LOVE, Kevin (26)
LUTHER KING, Martin (21)

MADDOCK, Keith (27)
MAHREZ, Riyad (7,15,23)
MARADONA, Diego (13,22)
MARSHALL, Stewart (25)
MATTHEW, Catriona (18)
MAYWEATHER JUNIOR, Floyd (24)
McENROE, John (16)
McGREGOR, Conor (24)
McKEOWN, Frank (25)
MESSI, Lionel (16,17)
MICHELANGELO (12)
MICHELS, Rinus (6)
MITCHELL, David (8)

MOBY (19)
MONROE, Marilyn (3)
MOORE, Brian (12)
MORANT, Ja (26)
MORE, Thomas (19)
MORGAN, Wes (7,19)
MOTSON, John (12,14)
MOURINHO, Jose (8,9,15,24)
MUHAMMAD ALI (17,21,24)
MURRAY, Kyler (26)

NADAL, Rafael (5)
NAVRATILOVA, Martina (16)
NDIDI, Wilfried (27)
NEESKENS, Johan (6)
NEVILLE, Gary (30)
NICKLIN, Frank (3)
NIXON, Richard (16)
NOVELLO, Ivor (15)
NUREYEV, Rudolf (2)

OBAMA, Barack (26)
OBAYIUWANA, Osasu (19)
OLSSON, Jan (6)
OSAKA, Naomi (16,21)
OVETT, Steve (5)

PANENKA, Antonin (18)
PARTRIDGE, Alan (12)
PATEL, Akhilesh (25)
PAVAROTTI Luciano (14)
PEARSON, Nigel (7)
PERRY, Katy (25
PETTERSEN, Suzann (18)
PLATINI, Michel (13)
POOLE, Claire (29)
POULTER, Ian (18)
PRICE, Graham (25)
PROFESSOR GREEN (12)
PUEL, Claude (23)
PUNPARE, Kaveporn (27)

QUEEN ELIZABETH THE QUEEN MOTHER (19)

RABBATTS, Heather (21)
RADFORD, Ronnie (14)
RAMOS, Carlos (16)
RAMOS, Sergio (22)
RAINFORD-BRENT, Ebony (21)
RANIERI, Claudio (7,11,15,16,19,23)
RAPINOE, Megan (16)
RASHFORD, Marcus (17)
REARDON, Ray (4)
REEVES & MORTIMER (13)
REGO, Emanuel (6)
REID, Eric (21)
REILLY, Rose (16)
RIGGS, Bobby (16)
ROBINS, Mark (23)
ROBSON, Bobby (4, 9)
ROGGE, Jacques (20)
RONALDO, Cristiano (13)
ROPER, Eleanor (16)
ROSENBERG, Larry (18)
ROSSI, Paolo (6,11)
ROUTLEDGE, Kevin (20)
RUMSEY, Fred (24)
RUMSEY, Matt (24)
RUTHERFORD, Greg (20)

SALAH, Mo (22)
SANCHEZ FLORES, Quique (11,23)
SARRIS, Giorgos (7)
SELES, Monica (5)
SCHLUPP, Jeffrey (7)
SCHMEICHEL, Kasper (7)
SCHMEICHEL, Peter (7)
SCHUMACHER, Michael (5)
SHAKESPEARE, Craig (23)
SHAKESPEARE, William (5,19)
SHEEN, Michael (9)
SIMPSON, Danny (7)
SISTER JEAN (26)
SMITH, Steve (22)
SOCRATES (6)
SOULSBY, Peter (19)

SOUTHGATE, Gareth (17,18,30)
SRIVADDHANAPRABHA, Aiyawatt (23,30)
SRIVADDHANAPRABHA, Vichai ('*KHUN VICHAI*') (7,27,30)
SPIELBERG, Steven (12)
STERLING, Raheem (17)
STIRLING, Andy (25)
STRINGER, Ian (19)
SUKER, Davor (18,20)
SUKNAMAI, Nusara (27)
SWAFFER, Eric (27)

TAYLOR, Breonna (21)
TAYLOR, Dennis (4)
TAYLOR, Graham (11,14)
TAYLOR, Jack (6)
TAYLOR, Phil (4
TAYLOR, Sarah (30)
TEMPLE, Shirley (2)
THOMPSON, Nancy 'Cannonball' (16)
THUNBERG, Greta (29)
TIMBERLAKE, Aminu (26)
TRAVOLTA, John (4)
TRUMP, Donald (26)
TYSON, Mike (1,5)

ULLOA, Leonardo (7,19)

Van GAAL, Louis (18)
Van NISTELROOY, Ruud (15)
VARDY, Jamie (7,11,15,17,19,23)
VILLA, Ricky (14)

WALSH, David (12)
WADDELL, Sid (12)
WAGNER, Richard (12)
WALKER, Murray (12)
WAREING, Marcus (17)
WATTANA, James (4)
WERBENIUK, Bill (4)
WENGER, Arsene (8,24)
WHEELER, Patrick (21)
WIDDICOMBE, Josh (20)
WILLIAMS, Serena (5, 16)
WILLIAMS, Venus (16)
WILLIAMSON, Zion (26)
WHITE, Jimmy (4)
WOODS, Tiger (5)

ZANARDI, Alex (20)
ZICO (6)